Tartan Temptress

Tartan Temptress

The Story of One Woman and her Dark Side

Felicity Forbes

This is a work of fiction. Names, characters, places, and incidents either are the product of the author's imagination or are used fictitiously. Any resemblance to actual persons, living or dead, events, or locales is entirely coincidental.

Copyright © 2023 by FELICITY FORBES

All rights reserved. No part of this publication may be reproduced, stored in a retrieval system, or transmitted, in any form, or by any means (electronic, mechanical, photocopying, recording or otherwise) without written permission of the copyright owner. Except for the use of quotations in a book review.

978-1-80541-370-7 (paperback)
978-1-80541-371-4 (eBook)

1. How it all Began

HAVE YOU EVER WOKEN UP one day and felt like your world has just ended? This happened to me. Prior to that I would have said I was a well-balanced, educated, gorgeous-on-a-good-day (going by the reactions of men) young woman. I come from a normal, everyday family and grew up in a happy environment where I never wanted for anything. Don't get me wrong, I didn't have everything, but who does? I always worked, even whilst I studied at school; I've never been afraid of hard work.

My group of friends had been the same since starting school at the age of five; I guess that is what happens when you grow up in a small town and only have one school. There are six of us that always hang out together, but I would say that I am closest to Emma and Lucas. We grew up together as our mums were also best friends, so I guess from before we could even walk, we had already spent so much time together. I had always thought that the six of us had a bond so close that we enjoyed the same things and knew each other so well, but by my late teens it soon became apparent that my circle of friends was only interested in three things: drink, drugs, and sex.

I remained close to Emma and Lucas, despite our differing interests. I was very into exercise, I wanted to look after my body and mind, so drink and drugs left me cold; I didn't like the feeling of not being in control. My first drinking experience was horrendous; it ended up in a hospital stay. If someone dares you at a party to drink a pint of whisky, vodka, and very little juice, say NO! As for drugs, I am not into them either. I'd seen my friends on various things over the years and they looked disgusting, swinging their jaw from side to side while not having the faintest idea where they were. Once I was watching them rolling about the ground pretending, they were swimming on grass, which was enough to put me off drugs for life. Much to the irritation of my friends, who spent most of every weekend either drunk or wasted on drugs or a combination of both. The third activity however, I had a healthy interest in...

By this point in my life the sexual encounters I had had were, for the best part, disappointing; they were either outdoors where you were freezing cold and always ended up covered in mud and leaves or frustrating, drunken fumbling at a party. Mostly it was uncomfortable sex in a car or sex so boring I could have fallen asleep. I even had some same-sex encounters to see if it would make things more appealing and be able to satisfy me, but, as much as I enjoyed myself, I still felt something was missing. I tried being in several long-term relationships, which gave me regular sex, but none satisfied my needs enough to keep me interested in only them, apart from one, Arthur.

Arthur was amazing in bed; his dick was on the large side, but sex was very enjoyable, he gave me jelly legs every single time we were naked together. We had been friends for years then dated for a long time and even after our time together had come to an end, we seemed to always end up in bed together. The sex was always great, the problem was his head. We were very well suited, having the same high sex drive, but regardless of how much he made me laugh, how brilliant the daily orgasms were, it was too much to constantly deal with his tantrums, so the best sex of my life eventually had to be forgone.

By my early twenties I had a few failed relationships under my belt but hadn't given up on finding a man who could make me laugh, was intelligent enough to hold a reasonable conversation and, most importantly, could match my sex drive. I was never short of attention: I have always been physically active; I work out regularly, run and love the outdoors. My body is toned, I have pert B cup breasts with the most sensitive nipples, my tummy is flat, my ass peach-perfect, my legs are slim and toned. All told, it's a rather attractive size 10 package finished off with a long mane of hair, eyes that can seduce someone from even the quickest glance and a smile that lights up a room...

So, attention was never a problem, but finding the right man was. By my mid-twenties, I had been seeing a lad for several months; it had started well, but, before long, the sexual side started to deteriorate. He was younger than me and would orgasm way before I was even close to climaxing, leaving me very frustrated most of the time, but that wasn't the reason it all came to a head one evening, though it hadn't been good for a while. Like every weekend he had been drinking heavily, and on this occasion when he got home, I was not there. I had gone to have drinks with my best friends, Emma, and Lucas, and, well, what can I say? We ended up back at Emma's house having a full-blown party. Time ran away from us and the next thing I knew my phone was buzzing away in my pocket. I looked around to try to see a clock; I didn't need to look at my phone, I knew the only person that would be calling me at this hour.

I ran to the door, but Emma caught my arm just as I was leaving. 'You can't go,' she said, pulling me back inside. 'I'm not letting you leave, not after last weekend.'

I knew that she was only looking out for me, and I wish to this very day that I had listened to her, but I didn't. I thought I knew best; I thought the situation would get a lot worse if I just ignored him.

Emma stood there, scowling at me, shaking her head from side to side and muttering, 'No.'

After a lengthy discussion, we finally agreed that if I went home, I had to call her to say I was OK and if I did not call her in ten minutes to say I was, then she was going to come round to check on me.

I got my coat and started walking home; my thick tights weren't enough to stop my legs freezing. It was bitter cold, the idea of wearing a dress in the middle of a Scottish winter was now somewhat stupid. I was regretting wearing my favourite boots as well as I was slipping on the road with it being so frosty underfoot. Emma and I lived less than five minutes away from each other, so it did not take long to get there. I was dreading going home; Keith did not like it if I went out and I knew he was going to be mad at me.

I got to the door, and, as I lifted my hand to put the key in, I saw how much it was shaking. I took a deep breath and pushed it open. Silence. I went down the hall to my bedroom. Just as I was about to take my coat off, Keith came flying through the door. Slam!

'Where have you been? Do you know the time? Why weren't you at home?' All these questions but he gave me no time to answer any of them.

He threw me against the wall. The talking turned to shouting then screaming, then it quickly escalated and turned to physical violence. Again. Just as it always did, everything happened so quickly. I managed to move past him and tried to run out of the bedroom to the front door, but he grabbed my arm and threw me to the ground.

'Tell me where you have been?' I tried to scramble away, but he held me tight, kneeling beside me. I was now pinned to the floor by my throat, his thumb and fingers were digging into my skin he had me held so tight. I shut my eyes, but it didn't make a difference; I was just as scared.

His breath stank of whisky; every time he screamed in my face, he was spraying saliva all over me, 'Tell me where the fuck you have been?'

'I've been at Emma's, I haven't done anything wrong, please stop, please stop this!' I tried so hard to get away, but I wasn't able to move much; he had his knee pushing down on my arm. Then I remembered that my phone was in my back pocket, so I managed to squeeze my free hand down to get my phone out of my pocket, and, just as I was trying to unlock it, he noticed and grabbed it from me, smashing it as he threw it down the hall. I was really frightened, but somehow, I managed to find the strength to push him off me and scrabbled towards the bathroom. Again, he managed to grab me, this time by the ankle, and as he pulled me back my face smashed against the floor. I could feel my nose burst open; there was blood everywhere. I kicked out, catching his chest with my other foot and was just able to wriggle away. I snatched up the house phone and ran to the bathroom. I managed to lock the door behind me, fingers trembling so badly I could hardly do the lock. I knew the door wouldn't keep him out for long.

Thud. Thud. 'Open this door before I break it down.'

'No, Keith, please just leave me alone. I'm calling the police.' I punched in 999, shaking so hard I almost dropped the phone. 'Please help me, I need the police. My boyfriend has gone crazy again and I'm locked in the bathroom.'

'OK, so first tell me your address please?'

I was sat with my back pushed up against the door with my legs hard against the side of my bath; between sobs I was able to give the operator my address.

'Are you away from him now? Can he get to you?'

'I've locked myself in the bathroom, but I don't know how long I can hold the door. I'm really frightened, how long will it take for them to get here?'

'Don't worry, the police are on their way. They should be with you in under five minutes, but please stay on the phone till they arrive.'

Crash. Every time he kicked the door it pushed me forwards. I was shaking and struggling for breath. It felt like hours, but it was only minutes later that the police arrived at my door. I heard someone knock, but I knew Keith wasn't going to answer the door, so I got up, opened the window, and screamed as loud as I could. 'Come in, please help, I'm in the bathroom!'

I heard the front door open; I couldn't see – and I certainly wasn't going to open the door – there was a lot of commotion, and I could hear two male voices and Keith's. I wasn't able to hear what was being said, but I told the operator that the police had arrived, so I was able to get off the phone.

I heard someone shout, 'Are you safe? Do you need urgent medical attention?'

'I think I'm OK.'

'Please stay where you are, ma'am, we have more officers on the way. Do not move until you are asked to open the door.'

The two officers that came in first went to deal with Keith. I collapsed into the empty bath. When

Felicity Forbes

I looked down at my shaking hands, they were covered in blood. Blood was everywhere. My heart was racing, and I couldn't seem to catch my breath. One. Two. I narrowed my focus on one breath at a time. *In. Out. Breathe. Just breathe. That's all you have to do.* Then I heard Emma. 'I'm here.'

I was so relieved to hear her voice. I instantly got up and opened the door; Emma was standing there with two police officers. She gasped, but almost immediately enveloped me in a warm, reassuring hug.

Emma explained that I had just come from hers and that she had told me not to come home because she knew this would happen. Emma was now crying just as much as I was, great big gasping sobs. She felt so guilty that I had talked her into letting me come home.

As I tried explaining what had happened, a police officer came out from the bedroom and said that they were off to the police station with Keith and that I had to go there too because Keith had told the officers that I attacked him when I got home. I could tell the police knew that it was bullshit, but they explained that they needed to take what he said seriously so they had to take me to the police station to be interviewed. I was absolutely mortified. I had never been in a police station before in my life. The officers told me that I should get changed into other clothes as they needed what I was wearing for evidence. Also, I was to move to the living room while the officers took Keith out the house.

After Keith had left, I was accompanied into my room by the female officer. As soon as I got to the door of my bedroom, I froze. There was blood all over the floor, all my bedding was missing – bar the bottom sheet – and there were pictures missing. I turned to the female officer. 'What happened?'

'Everything that is missing would have had blood on it, so we have to take it for evidence.' She replied.

I sat on the end of my bed, quivering, resting my head in my hands. Then I just wept, I couldn't control it. I wanted to curl up and be alone but knew I couldn't and that I had a long night ahead of me. The two officers that were with me were so lovely; they explained that as I was to be taken in for questioning, they had to take me to the city station as our small town no longer had full staffing levels. They even said to wear cosy clothes as it wasn't the warmest place. I walked over to my wardrobe to get out some comfier clothes and, at that point, caught a glimpse of myself in the mirror. I was in shock; I looked horrific. I had to just look away. I pulled out clothes I knew would keep me warm and put on a few layers, picked up my hat, and off we went out to the police van. The drive there was dreadful; it was so uncomfortable in the back of the van, but I guess it is intended for criminals, so it is not going to be luxury.

When we arrived at the police station, we went into a large hallway with seats along both walls, then walked up to the main reception desk where I was told to hand over all my belongings. I reluctantly placed all my things on the counter, then the huge, scary man behind the desk said, 'The hat as well.'

I hesitated, then said, 'Can I please keep it as it is my favourite hat because I knitted it myself.'

There was a long silence, then the gentleman leaned towards me and said, 'No, lass, I need that hat. I will take good care of it though.'

I must have looked puzzled as he went on to explain: 'I can't let you keep it as you could undo the wool and use it to hurt yourself.'

I burst into tears. Again. I was being treated like I was the one who had done something wrong, and I hadn't.

After I was signed in, I was told that as it was a Friday night it was busy and there was a list of people to be seen before me, so they were taking me to a cell until someone was able to talk to me. I couldn't believe it; *I was* going to be locked up. I was being locked up for calling the police to ask for help. They were treating me like I was the criminal, but I wasn't the one who had done anything wrong.

The officer led me up a corridor. It was horrid; people were shouting and swearing, and the place stank of urine and vomit. It certainly was not where I thought my Friday night was going to end up. We stopped at a door halfway along the corridor and as they opened it, they said, 'Here we are, this is your room for the evening.'

I reluctantly looked in through the door, not knowing what to expect. It was clean-ish, not to my standards but I am OCD. There was a single bed with a plastic-covered mattress and a sheet that certainly wasn't Egyptian cotton, but, nonetheless, it was somewhere for me to lie down. The room was that small that I could have touched the bed, toilet and sink all at the same time. I paced up and down the length of the bed for some time. I was restless; I wanted this over with, I wanted to go home. That said, after a few hours of waiting, the events of the evening caught up with me and my eyelids grew heavy. I lay down on the most uncomfortable mattress and, surprisingly, managed to drift off to sleep.

I woke hours later to the smell of toast, then lots of shouting. I kept my eyes closed, but knew I had to open them eventually. I just wanted it to have been a nightmare and for none of this to have happened. I ached all over; I felt absolutely broken. I slowly opened my eyes and sat up. I rested my back against the wall and moved my feet in towards my bum and my knees close to my body, my arms wrapped round the front of my legs. Then I just sat staring at the wall, hugging myself.

I couldn't think. I felt numb, mostly I felt ashamed. This was the first time I had called the police, but I had to this time; I couldn't keep this going any longer. I was completely exhausted from constantly worrying when Keith would explode next. I was so disappointed that all of this had happened again; I had stupidly believed Keith when he told me that he wouldn't hurt me anymore. Now I didn't trust him, nor did I want to be with him. Having this time to dwell on things made me see that the pattern of his behaviour was getting more frequent; looking back over the last month the violence was getting to be too regular an occurrence. My bruises weren't even getting enough time to heal between the beatings.

I longed to go home, I didn't understand why I was still there, I thought they would have had time to see me by now. I certainly didn't think that I would still have been in there at 8am on a Saturday. Just then there was a tap on my door.

'Good morning, my dear, would you like some tea and toast?'

I couldn't see who was at the other side of the door, but they were very pleasant. I didn't feel like eating, but the smell of toast was too good to resist. 'Yes please, can I have milk and one sugar please.'

My mouth started to water at the thought of hot thick sliced brown bread, lightly toasted and smothered in Lurpak topped off with a thin layer of my gran's homemade strawberry jam. My mouth stopped watering as soon as I was handed two bits of cold white toast wrapped in a serviette. Still, a good cup of tea would sort me out. Now, tea can be made in so many ways. I am a tea bag squeezer, much to the disgust of my friends who seem to prefer hot milk! Just as I was wondering what condition my cuppa would be in, I was handed a plastic cup that was only slightly warm, and it looked like one teabag had made a whole bloody pot. I was disappointed, but I guess I wasn't overly surprised – after all, I was in jail!

Eventually, my name was called. I got up off the bed; I couldn't wait to get out of there. I was desperate to get home. I concluded that the best thing to do was to not let Keith back into my house. At all! He wasn't living with me as such, but he was certainly at mine more often than not; over several months more and more of his belongings had seemed to accumulate there, so I needed to remove all his things and change the locks before he was let out. I was escorted from my cell along the corridor through to another area. When I entered the room there were two police officers sat staring at me. They asked me to take a seat, then went on to read me my rights. I had no idea what was going on and it was all very scary. I was under the impression that I just had to talk to people; I didn't realise I was to be interrogated.

The policeman explained that I was on video so that they were able to refer back to what I said later if needed. At that point I started crying; my eyes streamed for some time before I was able to talk to them. After my interview I was taken to a room with two female officers and told to go behind the curtain and undress so that I could be photographed for evidence.

I sat behind the thin curtain in only my pants and bra, feeling very vulnerable. But also, angry. So angry. I was the victim! I'd called them for help, and I was being treated like this! I reluctantly pulled back the curtain to step out onto a white cross on the floor. It was then that the officers could see my body; they were able to tell which marks, cuts and bruises were from last night as they were very fresh and still a bright red. They were also able to tell the bruises from last weekend as they were a deep blue and purple now, and they could tell the ones from the time before that too as they had gone a horrid yellowish-brown. Their attitude changed from that point and, finally, I felt like I was being treated with compassion.

I would say that this was the lowest point in my life. I had to stand there, almost naked, holding rulers next to every mark on my body explaining when I got it and how he had given me it. This took far longer than the questioning, but they had to photograph every mark on me for evidence. After they were finished, I went back behind the curtain and the tears streamed down my face once again. I was really struggling to hold my shit together. I kept having to take a deep breath in through my nose, then exhale out my mouth. I guess this was the first time I had really spoken about it. I'd mentioned it to Emma, but only this week.

Normally Emma and I go to the gym together, but I couldn't go last week, and she kept asking and asking so I had to tell her. After I told her she made me show her and all week she had been trying to get me to leave him, but it wasn't as simple as that. I had tried so many times before, but he would start to say that he couldn't go on and that he would hurt himself. Once I found him on the bed with a huge kitchen knife and had to get Lucas to come in to help me get it from him, so, for me, his threat of him doing something was very real and I didn't want that to be on my conscience.

Once I was dressed again, I pulled back the curtain and was startled to see more people in the room. They were all staring at me. I couldn't make eye contact; I felt so ashamed and worthless. I just wanted to hide. One of the women stepped forward and asked me to follow her. I was taken to an office this time, which I was glad about; I didn't want another third degree. Then two men came in. They started off with an apology as to why I had been kept waiting so long. Then they went over their reasons for me being brought in, which I did understand. After all, they needed to know the whole story, but I guess my body being in the colourful condition it was meant that they were able to verify that I was telling the truth and that I was the one that had been abused.

They talked to me about next steps and what would happen to Keith and also the support that they were offering me. I just wanted to go home by this point. When I asked how long it would be, they said that they were just organising for someone to take me home. I was so looking forward to going home and also relieved to know that Keith was being kept in until his court appearance on the Monday. When it was finally time to go, I was escorted to the desk, so I was able to get my belongings, and we headed home.

I hadn't spoken to anyone as I didn't have a phone. I longed for Emma to be able to give me a cuddle and tell me it was all going to be OK, so I asked if I was able to be dropped off at her end of the street rather than mine. I sat alone in the back seat of the police car, blankly gazing out the window, occasionally bumping my head against the glass, with the miles of narrow, twisty country roads. As we got to the edge of town, I noticed my hand was bleeding where I had been picking at it so much. I felt like I couldn't move; like I had been hit with a massive weight and it was pushing me down. I hid my hair in my hat and pulled my hood up in the hopes no one would be able to recognise me in the back of the police car.

The town itself is picturesque, but, like every town, it falls into areas: Upper-class people occupies the west, but that is possibly since houses can sell for just shy of three quarters of a million pounds; they all have huge gardens and private drives. I grew up in the north; it's more your middle-class / family-friendly type, houses are for the most part detached with private gardens. Now, however, I live on the south side of town. It's similar to the east; more of an up-and-coming area so houses are more reasonably priced. We call it the young side of town as it's more affordable for people to be able to purchase these houses if you're new to the property market. The street we lived on was a mix of semi-detached cottages, blocks of flats and terrace houses.

As we passed my little semi-detached cottage at the end, I looked the other way. I didn't want to think about my house just now, all I wanted was to see Emma. Emma lived in a terrace house two houses in from the other end. We pulled up outside her house and I got out quickly. I thanked the driver for the lift, then went running to Emma's front door. I banged on the door, worried that she was going to be out. I didn't want anyone to see me looking like this, I just wanted to hide away until I was better. Thankfully, the door opened immediately and, as soon as we saw each other, we burst out crying at the same time. We sat drinking tea and hugging on the sofa for some time. I was sore all over and was trying my hardest to stop crying, but I just felt so sad. When I had finally stopped crying and had calmed down a bit, Emma said that she would come to my house to help me tidy it as she was locked out when I was taken away by the police. I was so glad she was coming with me; I certainly wasn't looking forward to seeing the mess from last night. Emma said she was going to call Lucas and we would all go together so that I had someone to sit with while she tidied up.

Knowing Lucas is like having my very own bodyguard; he is huge, not fat at all but very muscular, can be extremely friendly, having said that he is also extremely protective of us and is always there to look after us both so without hesitation he came to pick us up as I did not feel like walking down the street. I assumed all my neighbours would have been woken by the commotion last night so I was glad that my friends were with me; I couldn't face having to talk to anyone today.

I was dreading going into my house, I knew it was going to be a mess, but I wanted it all cleaned up and his things out as soon as possible.

As I walked up to the door, I started getting flashbacks from last night; I instantly started shaking like a leaf.

Emma told me to wait with Lucas while she went in first, so I handed her my key's. She came back out after about five minutes, 'I think it's best if you guys go for a drive and I'll tidy up. It's bad in there so maybe best you don't see.'

I knew that she was looking out for me, but it was my home, so I said, 'Thank you, but I'll come in. You guys are with me, so I'll be OK.'

Emma's furrowed brows said it all, but I needed closure. Lucas barged past us both, 'I'll decide who goes in once I've been in.' Then he slammed the door behind him.

I stood staring at the ground; I couldn't think straight, and I just wished all this were a bad dream and that none of it had happened. Lucas opened the door and stood there, tears forming in the corner of his eyes, then he moved towards me and put his arms round me.

Nothing was said for a few moments, then he said, 'If you want to go in, do. But promise me you know that we are so sorry for letting you come home last night.'

'It wasn't anyone's fault apart from mine,' I said. Then I walked past them both and opened the door.

As I stepped into the hall, I let out a gasp and the tears flowed down my face once again. They were right: it was a mess. There was blood over everything, the police had taken what was left of my phone but there were still tiny pieces all over the floor, the wall in the hall had a huge dent in it where he had thrown my phone and the handle on the bathroom was hanging off from when Keith was trying to get to me. There were several bloody handprints smeared down the walls and my beautiful woollen rug was completely ruined. After a few deep breaths I went through to the bedroom; it wasn't as bad as the hall, but a lot of things were missing. I could feel my breathing get faster, my hands were sweaty, and I needed to get out of there so off I went through to the living room. Emma was right again; it was too much for me. Thankfully, the living room was blood-free apart from a blanket on the sofa from when I was sat getting questioned, so off it came and into the wash. I lay on the sofa trying to find something funny on the telly while my friends tidied as best as they could. Even watching "The Big Bang" wasn't able to make me smile.

A funny smell woke me; what I thought was the smell of paint. I couldn't hear anything, which was odd as Emma is never quiet, so I went to go and see what was going on. Just as I opened the door to the hall, the smell of fresh paint became overpowering. I couldn't believe it. All the blood was gone, and they had painted my hall and my bedroom. I walked over to the front door and there was a note propped up against my key stand, it said:

Don't touch the walls, they are wet. Back soon, just dropping Keith's things off at his parents' house.

I nearly smiled. I was so relieved that Keith's things had gone and that I didn't have to see his parents. I was so lucky to have friends like them.

The next few days were hard, but Lucas and Emma took time off work to stay with me. They knew my confidence was shattered; I had gone from being a sociable, bubbly young woman to being so scared I could not even leave my house. I struggled to eat and sleep. How had my life changed so much?

My friends stayed with me for the best part of a week, it was like they took shifts to look after me. I didn't go out; I didn't want to be seen until the bruises on my face had gone. I felt embarrassed. The bruising had now turned a dark blue and covered most of my face and under my chin. All down my side was bruised and there was a bruised footprint on my upper arm. My friends kept me busy and desperately tried to cheer me up; we watched countless Disney films, drank wine, even had a few games of charades, which is my favourite, but even that didn't work. I was broken inside.

This carried on for some time until, one day, I woke up and felt different. I'm still not sure what happened, but I just realised that none of it was my fault, that I shouldn't be embarrassed; I wasn't broken. I was naive, however, for not spotting the warning signs of his controlling behaviour sooner.

The next morning, I woke up, got up, got dressed and went to work. For the first time in so long, I didn't cry; it felt like the tears had run dry and I finally had a smile on my face again. Of sorts, anyway.

I'd concluded that, for the most part, men were selfish, boring bastards unworthy of my trust and respect; I did not want another relationship for the foreseeable future.

Months passed before my need for sex came back. As I didn't want to date, I would go out to the pub, meet someone, and take them home for a one-night stand. I didn't want any emotional attachment; if they were cute and I needed an orgasm, I used them for sex then chucked them out of my house when we were finished. None of them spent the night; I didn't feel comfortable having a man sleep next to me. This went on for a while. Then, as I wasn't much of a drinker, I decided to join a dating site. It was so easy to meet men for sex; it was almost like flicking through a menu. You'd look at photos and say yes or no if you wanted to speak to them or not. When I saw a man, I liked the look of, it didn't take long to get a meeting organised. Usually by the end of the day we would have arranged where we would meet.

As I was from a small town where the population is around 6 to 7,000 people, I put my search to cover an area of twenty-five miles so it would include the city of Aberdeen. Aberdeen is the biggest city on the east coast of Scotland. It's also known as 'The Granite City' and has around 200,000 people. Most of the guys I met were from the city, so we would meet halfway and either do doggy style bent over the bonnet of the car or go for a walk and have sex in the woods. If it was raining, then it was usually in the car. I didn't want men in my house that I'd met online, I didn't feel safe in a private, confined space with them.

Online dating was convenient for me, but it also became boring. It was also somewhat disappointing as there were far more idiots on it than men that could satisfy me. It was then that I came up with an idea.

2. My First Thought was 'No'

EVERYONE HAS OUTRAGEOUS IDEAS AT some point in their life, but people rarely act on them. Peter Medawar once said, 'The human mind treats a new idea the same way the body treats a strange protein; it rejects it.' Which I feel is apt for the majority of people in the world. When most people have an outrageous idea, they are sensible and listen to the little voice in the back of their heads telling them to stop, that it's not a good idea. I, however, have a darkness inside of me, the voice in the back of my mind is a little devil; it never says stop.

It was as I lay awake one evening that my mind drifted off to the outrageous idea once more. Again, it started with me thinking, as always, about sex and the only man that had truly been able to satisfy me, Arthur. Even the first time we slept together was memorable; Arthur made me feel things I had never experienced before. He was older than me by a few years and he was far more advanced in the bedroom than anyone I had been with before. To this day I can still picture it like it were yesterday. I had known Arthur for many years before we became sexually involved. The first time we slept together was a bit of a scandal. Arthur was best friends with a boyfriend I had been dating for just shy of a year; his name was Thomas. Like most of my relationships, it became boring, Thomas and I never had that spark. Arthur and I, however, seemed to have this electric energy; harmless flirting soon became something far more sinister. Thomas worked away from home often, but, oblivious to the chemistry between Arthur and I, Thomas asked Arthur to check on me as he was to be away for weeks on this occasion.

Arthur and I had been texting for a little over a week, but neither of us seemed to have the courage to say how we felt. Unable to sleep for pondering over Arthur, I decided to get up. I shivered as I pulled back my thick, warm duvet, then moved to the end of the bed and slid my feet into my slipper boots. I wrapped my dressing gown tight around me, tying the rope in a bow at the front. Off I went downstairs to the kitchen; tea and cake was just what I needed.

Just as I put the kettle on, my phone beeped; it was Arthur: *Are you OK? It's late and I was driving home and noticed your lights on?*

I was unsure what to reply; I wanted to tell him to come round and rip my clothes off and fuck me on the table, but I didn't have the courage to write that, so I replied, *Thank-you for checking on me. I am fine, I would be much better if I had cream to put on this cake I made today though.*

As I was pouring my tea, I started to huff and puff; what a stupid reply. I couldn't help but shake my head; what was I thinking?

I sat sipping on my tea, still angry at myself, then the doorbell went. Clatter. I dropped my cup on the table, startled from the bell. I certainly wasn't dressed enough to be entertaining; after all, I only had a thin silk nighty on under my dressing gown.

Ring, ring. The door went again; this time I decided to go and look through the spy hole, I had to go up on my tip toes so I could see. 'Fuck!' I leapt back from the door, my heart racing, I couldn't believe my eyes. It was Arthur.

I ran to the bathroom and patted my bed head hair down as best as I could, undid the rope holding my dressing gown around me, pulled my nightgown down tight over my breasts and then quickly had a swig of mouthwash and headed back to the front door. Just as I started to turn the key, I realised that I hadn't spat the mouthwash out; I had no choice but to shut my eyes and swallow!

I greeted Arthur with a face that must have looked like I was sucking lemons, Yuk. I tried to shake the shivers from having to swallow such rancid stuff. But Arthur was no fool and his first words to me were, 'What the heck is wrong with you?'

I smiled and shook my head. 'Nothing at all, just got a cold shiver.'

Arthur was standing with one of his hands behind his back, 'Shut your eyes and hold out your hand,' he said, almost laughing.

I reluctantly closed my eyes and put out my hand. I stood, rigid, slightly nervous but more puzzled as to what it could be.

'Keep still now, you don't want to make a mess!' Then he placed something onto my hand. 'No peeking, you have to guess!'

My hand instantly went cold, and I started laughing. 'I know what it is, you have brought me cream.' I opened my eyes to find a small carton of cream resting on my palm. I looked up at him and smiled.

'Well, do I get some cake since I brought cream?'

'Oh yes, you can get anything you like.'

We never made it to the kitchen for our cake, it was straight to the bedroom. Towards the end, the condom broke. His dick was so big, to be honest, he really should have had an extra-large size on, but I was on the contraceptive pill, so I wasn't worried. We finished and said our goodbyes, but he seemed slightly subdued. I asked him if he was OK a couple of times and he said he was fine, so off he went home...

The next day I went round to Arthur's house to tell him that I had broken up with Thomas as I couldn't keep seeing him after what happened, and I thought it was best to find out if it was a one-off or if Arthur felt the same as me. As he opened the door to me, he had his phone glued to his ear. He was always a bit jittery, but he seemed extra anxious on this occasion. Arthur nodded towards the living room and then went to sit on the stair, his leg bouncing had seriously gotten out of control; it was like he had tremors he was shaking so much, not only that, but he was sweating profusely. I could tell how anxious he was from a glance, and it was starting to make me nervous. I sat down in the living room to wait until he'd finished his call.

Eventually, he let out a huge sigh of relief followed by, 'That's brilliant. Honestly, that's brilliant. Thank you so much, you've made my day.'

By now I was itching with curiosity, but, of course, I had to wait to see if he was going to tell me what was going on.

When he came into the living room, he was the opposite to how I'd seen him just a few minutes earlier. He was now grinning from ear to ear and the annoying leg bouncing had stopped, but he was still rather sweaty.

I moved forward, to the edge of the sofa, eager to know what was going on.

Arthur said, with a huge smile on his face, 'It's nothing to worry about. It's all fine. I'm so relieved.'

I asked him what was going on, but he just laughed. That is typical Arthur though: Arthur does what Arthur wants. He's brilliant in bed, but he did my head in. If he didn't want to discuss something or answer a question, he would just ignore it; his behaviour was somewhat childish most of the time!

Later that day, Arthur suggested we go out for dinner to discuss what happened, but also to celebrate. I was still unsure what we were to celebrate, but I was eager to find out. After a lovely meal and possibly too much wine, we headed for home. Just as the door closed behind us, he blurted out, 'The results were negative, no need to panic.'

Of course, I started to panic. Why is it as soon as someone says don't panic, you straightaway start to panic?

'The reason I was acting so strange is that I have been petrified about something. The last time I had sex before you was with a prostitute while on holiday. I got tested when I came home but hadn't received the results yet. So, when the condom broke with us, I was a bit freaked out.'

I was in shock. 'What the fuck?' I kept saying, over and over again.

Finally, I managed to say something else: 'So you had sex with a prostitute, this is what you're telling me?'

'Yes, but we're fine. I haven't got anything.' Arthur said.

I was in shock; I thought it was disgusting. I am not sure why I thought that; I guess it's the stigma around it. People hear the word prostitute, and they cringe; mostly the first thing that comes to mind is that it's disgusting or dirty. I'd only every gained knowledge on this from being in the red-light district in Amsterdam.

After my initial explosion, I calmed down enough to talk to Arthur about it. Arthur told me that he and most of his friends did it a lot. I was shocked. I had always thought that if someone was having to pay for sex, that they were either old or really ugly. Arthur opened my eyes to the fact that a lot of normal men have, at some point, paid for some sort of sexual encounter. Arthur went on to give me his opinion of the different sorts of paid-for sexual services.

'Prostitutes: Work for people, usually on the streets or in brothels. Usually paid less with a higher turnover. When the word prostitution is used, you tend to think of girls doing it like this to fund a drug habit or have been forced into it. Which is one reason the profession gets such a bad rep.

Escorts: Pre-arranged meeting, usually at hotels. They are more your in-between girls; they can sometimes have pimps or madams that control who they see, or they can work for an agency. They can be used for more social events like dinner parties or as a companion; sex is not always a given.

Call girls: Most that I have met work for themselves. All meetings are pre-arranged, services usually provided at the client's home or a hotel but also as in-calls at the call girls apartment. Relatively expensive because of the low client turnover. Quite often students who are paying for their degree.'

After that conversation with Arthur our relationship carried on for some time; I wasn't bothered by his naughty little secret of paying for sex. Our relationship broke down eventually due to other issues, mainly his constant tantrums. Even after many years that conversation has always stuck with me; to me, being an escort or call girl seemed a dream job. Have orgasms and get paid. So, the prospect of me becoming a call girl was far to appealing to just let it pass by.

It would alleviate all my issues – or so I thought! I don't like sex, I love it; I am addicted to it! Emma had once said to me, 'One day, you are going to stand in a room full of people and happily say, "I am Miss Felicity Forbes, and I am a sex addict."' It made me laugh; it was true I just wanted regular sex without having to talk to men too much.

Felicity Forbes

Over the following days I immersed myself in researching what being a call girl entails. And to be honest, I was getting rather turned on just fantasising about it. From the first time I became sexually aroused, I loved the feeling of getting wet pants and tingling nipples. It makes me feel alive. I remember watching *Dangerous Liaisons* when I was about eleven with my friend on a sleepover. We found it on a tape and, well, that opened my eyes to things; it was the first time that I was sexually aroused. My first sexual encounter was when I was fourteen. We had gone on a family holiday to Lanzarote, or Lanzagrotty as it is called now. Not only was it my first time abroad, but it was also the first time my sister and I really got on and the first time I was fingered. So, overall, it was a holiday to remember.

My mother, father, older sister, and I all went away for a week. My parents had rented a villa; the villa was lovely and the weather ridiculously hot. The first few days we had to do family things which was pretty boring. I think by day four our parents were fed up with us, so they said that we could go and do our own thing during the day if we checked in with them at different intervals throughout the day. My sister is called Jessica and she is four years older than me. We tolerated each other; sometimes we loved each other and other times we fought a lot. I think it's normal to be like that with siblings. Jessica was not best pleased that she had to look after me; she made that noticeably clear by telling me I was just going to be 'a cock block for her.' The first day we were allowed out alone we just walked around, and she seemed to stay about four steps in front of me the whole time, obviously trying to make it look like we weren't together. The second day we seemed to get on a bit better, but it was because I spotted a guy from across the road. He was stunning, so sexy. He had his shirt off and his body was incredible; I nudged Jessica and pointed him out. She immediately stopped walking and just seemed to gaze at him from over the road. I tapped her on the back of the head and then walked on, grabbing her arm as I passed her.

'Stop that, you idiot! He might have seen us,' Jessica said to me. She scowled, then she said, 'So you like boys, do you? I always thought you were going to grow up to be a lesbian from the way you dressed.'

I was used to her speaking to me like that, but that time it hurt my feelings. I stopped walking along the road and looked down at what I had on. I guess she was right in a way; I looked like a boy going to a football match. I was wearing an oversized t-shirt and baggy shorts that passed my knees, high-top trainers and a baseball cap that seemed to never leave my head. I didn't feel like going anywhere else. Jessica knew that what she said had hurt my feelings, so she came up with a plan.

Jessica was going to give me a makeover and we were to start by losing the baseball cap I always wore and letting my beautiful long hair out of the high ponytail I always put it in. Then we were to get me new clothes. I was slightly worried; I did not like the way Jessica dressed. She seemed to wear things that made her look like a cheap tart most of the time. Still, I needed her help.

Jessica grabbed my hand and pulled me along the street till she found a little clothes shop; she picked out short shorts for me and then a top that stopped below what little breasts I had. I screwed my face up; I didn't like what she had picked. I liked my baggy shorts and oversized t-shirt, they were comfortable. Still, I could see her point. So, I humoured her and went to try them on. As I pulled back the curtain she gasped.

'Wow! I'm in shock; you look so pretty when you dress like a girl.'

I rolled my eyes. I felt stupid, but I did like how it made her smile, so we bought the clothes and Jessica put my old ones in her bag.

We had only walked about two hundred metres and we had guys whistling at us and saying hello as they walked past. Jessica had a huge smile on her face; she was so happy. She moved closer to me and linked her arm into mine and we kept walking towards the beach. I was in shock. Jessica had never been this close to me before, well, not in the last ten years anyway, it was nice that we were getting on. When we got back to the villa our mother was standing in the doorway with her hands on her hips, shaking her head that much that it would not have surprised me if it wobbled off her shoulders. Jessica and I looked at each other, we both knew we were going to get into trouble for the clothes I was wearing. Jessica got into trouble the most as she was the one in charge, I was just told to go to the room. That night Jessica said we were going to wait till our parents were asleep and sneak out of our room to see what the nightlife was like. I felt like this was a really bad idea, but I had never had my big sister want to do anything with me before, so I said yes. Jessica pulled out a dress for me to wear, put make-up on me and then made me wear one of her bras. She stuffed socks inside as she said my lack of boobs would mean we wouldn't get into a pub.

Jessica wrote a note and left it in our room; after all, we didn't want our parents freaking out if they saw we were gone. We snuck out and made a run for it, well, as much of a run for it as I could considering it was the first time, I had worn high heels. When we got to the main street, we walked past a few places. Jessica said that she wanted to find somewhere that wasn't too busy so we could sit down, as I looked like Bambi walking in her high heels. I was nervous and kept looking around, but Jessica told me to relax and that it was fine. She ordered us piña coladas. The first two were delicious, by the third I'd started to feel a bit lightheaded and by the fifth I was dancing in my heels as if I had been in them for years.

By the third pub we had quite the following of young men and we didn't need to pay for anything. We had everything bought for us; it was brilliant. I had my first shot from a girl who was basically naked, and then I turned round to wrap my arms round a guy and proceeded to shove my tongue down his throat. I didn't know his name, I didn't know where he was from, all I knew was that his body made my pants wet and I seemed to have this abundance of confidence from the alcohol; I didn't care and just went for it. Jessica tapped me on the shoulder and when I turned round, she grabbed my hand and pulled me out of the pub to the street.

'Why did you do that? I was having fun, what's wrong?'

She replied, 'I'll show you. Come here, look, I found two brothers.'

They were called Craig and Phil. Phil was the one closer to my age, but would have been around sixteen, I think. He looked amazing; he was tall and thin, had very curly dark, short hair, and his eyes were hazel. I guessed he was sporty due to the clothes he was wearing. Craig looked a lot older than Jessica; he had stubble and not just bum fluff. He was a slightly bigger build than Phil, but that was probably due to him being more mature.

Craig went to go and get some beers for us to have down on the beach. Jessica and Craig went on ahead and I was a few meters behind them walking barefoot, holding hands with Phil. We went to sit down and, straightaway, started kissing. The kiss turned into a snog, then it led to him having a feel of my boobs. This made me paranoid as I knew they were just sock's; I moved my hands down his side and found a huge bulge in his shorts. I took his cock in my hands; I remember thinking it was larger than I imagined them to be and ridiculously hard. Just as I was trying to work out what was the best way to do this, he rolled me over onto my back. He slid his hands up my dress and cupped his hand over my pelvic bone, then spread his hand out and pushed a finger inside me. I took a deep breath; I wasn't expecting that. Phil moved back and asked if it was OK. I told him yes and said to carry on. I lay on my back listening to the sound of the water and looking up at the stars as I was fingered by a complete stranger. He started to get faster and faster, and the feeling got even more intense; I kept grabbing the sand, not knowing what I was meant to do with my hands. Phil was going in and out with his finger really fast, then he would keep it in as far as he could, then he went round and round. It was very enjoyable, and I would say I was stimulated! I think if we had carried on then I would have had my first orgasm, but Jessica ruined it by running over and shouting, 'Come on! Let's go, hurry!'.

I was startled and could tell something was wrong, I quickly moved away from Phil desperately trying to push my dress down before Jessica came within sight. I jumped up. Jessica grabbed my hand, and we started running, holding our shoes in our free hands. When we got to the street it was far quieter than before; it was littered in plastic cups and beer cans. The people that were walking were rather drunk and falling over. Jessica and I stopped running.

'What's wrong?'

'It's nearly five and we have to get back in before Mum wakes up.'

I couldn't believe the time. We walked briskly back to the villa and managed to sneak into our rooms without being caught.

The following day, our parents wanted us to go on a bus tour with them, sightseeing. I certainly didn't want to do that; I wasn't hungover, just slightly under the weather. Mainly lack of sleep. Jessica said to our parents that she was happy to watch me and for them to go and enjoy themselves. So, Jessica and I lay by the pool and chatted about last night and that's the day that the bond I share with my sister began.

Felicity Forbes

After that encounter I was curious as to what sex was like, but I didn't jump into it. I had a few more fingering episodes, but none that were very exciting. I nearly got as far as sex at one point, but it didn't feel right, so I waited till I was sixteen. I'm not going to lie, it wasn't special or glamorous; it was in the back of a car – a Peugeot 205 to be exact – it was cramped and extremely uncomfortable, but it was with a guy I had been going out with and I felt comfortable enough with him to go all the way. I did have an orgasm, but it wasn't as exciting as I thought it was going to be or like they are shown in the movies, but I think it was due to the awkward positions we had to go in while in the car. Still, the feeling of intense pleasure I got when I started to orgasm made me instantly hooked. The feeling was intense, but, to date, had never lasted long enough and I knew better, much better, was out there.

To me, sex is more than just an immense pleasure; it acts as stress relief as well. I have had sexual encounters in the strangest of places to try to get the kicks I crave. Once I was out walking with a boyfriend I had at the time, Ross, and we had taken his spaniel for a walk through the woods. We came across a fallen tree and, as I walked over to it, I said, 'Look, it's the perfect height' As I wiggled my bum at him, then went to lean over it.

He walked up behind me, pulled my trousers and pants down and said, 'Get on your knees and make me harder.'

So, I sucked his cock until it was rock-hard, then I turned and leaned over the tree. As soon as he pushed his cock into me, we were going at it like rabbits, but I wasn't able to open my legs enough as my trousers were down at my ankles, so he said, 'Take one leg out of your trousers so I can be deeper inside you.'

Once I had pulled my leg out of my trousers and pants, we were back to it straightaway. It felt amazing; I love having sex outdoors. Just as I was building up for an orgasm, I spotted a Great Dane walking towards me. I got a huge fright – especially as we had a spaniel – there must have been someone close for the dog to be beside us.

I panicked 'Ross, look there is a dog, get out of me' all while pointing at the dog; the dog was coming closer.

He pulled out and moved back. 'Hurry up, the dog is coming closer!'

Easy for him to say; he just had trousers pulled down past his ass, but I had a full leg out. I was frantically hopping around trying to get my trousers back on. Just as I thought I was almost there; I fell and that's when I saw the man standing staring at us.

'Ross, help me!' He quickly helped me yank my trousers back on, pulled me up and we ran as fast as we could to get back to the car. Even to this day when I pass the entrance to the woods, I have a little giggle to myself.

Another time I was caught bonny was when we were on our way back from a night out in Glasgow. We were getting the train back to Aberdeen. There was a group of about sixteen of us that had been away since early afternoon and we were all friends so that's what makes it OK. I was horny and I pulled one of the guys into the toilet on the train. We had stripped our clothes off; he was in his socks, and I had a bra on. I was bent over, and we were going at it for about five minutes, then somehow the door opened, and everyone saw us at it.

I always seemed to be caught or spoken about. I think it was due to the fact that I was going through men like they were disposable razors, but I didn't see the point in going back for a third shot if the second was no use. I mean, everyone can have a bad day so you can't judge on the first occasion – I would always give someone the benefit of the doubt – but if the second time still didn't satisfy me then they were discarded and replaced.

I would like to say at this point: if a man is sexually active and sleeps with lots of woman, he is lauded by his peers as a real 'lad.' Conversely, if a woman does the same, she is classed as a 'slag'. Ha-ha. It's a joke, one of those perennially unfunny ones. Alas, living in a smallish town, where everyone finds out everything, I decided not to push my luck being a female 'lad', so the more I thought about being a call girl, the more it appealed to me. I would get sex when I wanted without being emotionally attached to someone or having to go on stupid dinner dates when all I really wanted was to be naked. It would also be completely discreet and people round town wouldn't be able to keep tabs on who I took home as I would be meeting them away from my town.

I had thought about it long enough; I had secretly harboured thoughts about it for some time, but I kept those thoughts suppressed over the years whilst in relationships. Now it was different; I was single and I neither trust nor want a man in my life. This was my time!

After about five solid days Googling, I concluded that the safest and smartest way to start my adventure was to join an agency. There are pros and cons to this route. An agency would arrange the bookings, so you cannot vet the client yourself, and they take a percentage of your earnings. However, on the plus side, they know where you are, and have people on call should the booking go bad, and obviously I would learn from more seasoned call girls. My only concern was: what if it was sleazy with horrible perverts? I wanted something upmarket with high-class clientele... Anyway, I was now ready to become a call girl and, yes, I had decided to join an agency to kickstart my new venture.

Finding an agency to work for in Scotland proved harder than I thought, but that's due to the fact that it only has seven cities. The capital, which is Edinburgh, Aberdeen (which is where I am closest too) Inverness, which is on the opposite coast from Aberdeen altogether, then there are Perth and Dundee which are rather small, and further south Stirling and Glasgow. I eventually found Craigslist and Back Page, the naughty equivalent of Gumtree! I found ads for three agencies and emailed all three.

As I lay in bed that evening, I could not sleep for the thoughts running through my head. What had I done? What if anyone I knew found out? What if someone murders me? I could not sleep at all. I had used my own email address and kept thinking, what if someone recognises it as mine? After tossing and turning in my bed for a little over an hour, I got up to make myself a cup of tea and watched the telly until I managed to drift off to sleep on the sofa.

The following morning, I woke to find not one, but all three agencies had emailed me back. To be honest, all I thought now was, I have not had satisfying sex in weeks, so why not give it a go. So, I replied to all three. One of the agencies stood out from the rest; it was run by a woman who had worked high end in London, and it seemed the most elegant and upmarket to me. Within ten minutes I received a reply asking if I was free to meet in Glasgow that coming weekend. It was now Wednesday, and I said yes without hesitation. I was going to do this. If I said the next three days dragged, I would be lying; they were like three Christmas Eves when you are a child...

Felicity Forbes

My life had been pretty boring of late, Keith drama aside. I'd had the same job for years, which I hated. It was just a way of paying my bills; to be honest, I only carried on going because the girl I worked with was so much fun. I'd stopped going to the pub to pick up guys after I'd joined the dating app, but, because there was no chase, it wasn't very exciting. I enjoyed the boxing class I had started. I'd thought that it would be beneficial to be able to look after myself in the future; I wasn't going to let another prick like Keith ever get the better of me again – also I thought it would be useful especially with this new adventure on the horizon.

Saturday loomed large and I was so nervous my hands were trembling; I didn't have a clue what I should be wearing, and I didn't know how my friends would react, so I had decided to keep this new adventure to myself for the time being. I just kept flicking through my clothes in the wardrobe, occasionally stopping at something and looking at it for a while before moving on. I eventually decided on a pair of black high-waisted trousers, a white fitted blouse, dark-grey cashmere cardigan and my favourite ankle boots from Dune. The boots were the ultimate: so comfortable, but also very high. I finished off the look with a bright scarf. I thought it was better that I look classy than something that had fallen out of a New Look store. I decided on minimal make-up and wore my hair up in a high ponytail. I checked through my bag, then I was ready to go.

The little town I live in is a very close-knit community, so I certainly was not going to try and do this where I lived. Living in a small town like mine is horrendous; you can't do a thing without everyone talking about it. Even though I am a few hours from Glasgow, I thought it was better to try my new adventure there as I knew it wouldn't get back to anyone I knew, so I took the train and off I went.

We had arranged to meet at a Costa in the city which I thought was a rather strange place to meet, given what we were about to be discussing. I arrived early, ordered my favourite; a large cappuccino with caramel syrup and sat as far away from everyone as I possibly could. As I sipped my coffee, I couldn't help but laugh. Never in my life did I think I would be interviewed to become a call girl, and I certainly wouldn't have thought it would be in a coffee shop of all places.

To be honest, I didn't know what I thought I would be doing in life. I still hadn't used my business degree and I worked in a dead-end job. I always wanted to travel; to see the best views in the world. My father was a joiner and owned his own business, my mother was a vet and golden girl Jessica was training to be a doctor, so I dread to think how disappointed they would be in me for attending this interview.

The longer I sat there on my own, the more my mind went into overdrive and a million thoughts flew round my head. Then the nerves crept in. What will they ask me? What do I say? Am I wearing the right clothes? What if she knew me? After about twenty minutes of mental torture, a well-dressed woman accompanied by a man walked straight towards me, drawn by the bright-orange scarf I told them I would be wearing.

When they got closer to me, I let out a sigh of relief, I didn't know them. Phew! I was worried about that. They introduced themselves:

'Hi, Jane, lovely to meet you, I'm Olivia but please call me Nikki and this is Colin. Thank you for meeting with us today.'

My hands were still trembling and, for once, I did not know what to say. Anyone who knows me would be rather surprised by this...!

Eventually I managed to blurt out: 'Hello, Nikki. Hi, Colin, lovely to meet you both.' I secretly hoped they didn't want to shake my sweaty hand. Thankfully, they didn't and just sat down. Colin went off to get more coffee while Nikki and I got to know each other a bit more.

As time went on it got much easier; they were extremely relaxed and that helped settle my nerves. Then the more significant questions arose.

'Why did you apply for this job?' Nikki asked.

Without much thought, I answered, 'To be honest, I have a high sex drive and I'm fed up with dating. My last relationship ended so badly that I have lost trust in men.'

Nikki and Colin were both nodding their heads, but completely silent. I paused for a moment. 'I guess I have thought about doing this several times over the years but somehow never plucked up the courage to enquire about it. This time is different; I don't want to be plain Jane anymore; I want to have fun!'

Soon we were in free-flow mode, talking openly about sex in a Costa in Glasgow!

After around thirty minutes I felt completely relaxed, listening to Nikki talking about her time working as a call girl.

Then Nikki said, 'I'll give you a bit of background on how we came to set up our agency. I came to the UK to work and travel, but I soon became annoyed at working all the hours under the sun in a bar for £7.50 an hour, so I decided to try escorting. The agency I went with was in London and was very elegant. I learned so much, but the agency charged £500 an hour to clients, and I only got £350 of that money. I did have so much fun, and it gave me the free time to travel. I met Colin in one of the bars I worked in, but, as he was from Edinburgh we decided to come to Scotland and start our own agency. Basically, I felt that I would be able to do what they did in London. We only take twenty-five percent of your takings for arranging the bookings for you. We have 24/7 support and assistance available from Colin and his friends, should it be needed, but I want to reassure you that I have done this for eighteen months now and have never needed help or back-up.'

I was amazed when she told me she earned up to £500 per hour to basically date. And when she said that she'd only had one bad experience, that seemed very low odds indeed.

As I had only replied to their advert *'looking for open-minded girls that want to stop giving it away for free'*, I hadn't seen what their website was like so, when they showed me, I was amazed. It looked brilliant; it was classy like I wanted, not sleazy in the slightest. After more than an hour of chatting, Nikki asked me if I would like to get my pictures done. So off we went to her apartment. We hadn't gone too far up the street before we got to these massive glass doors; her apartment was in a huge building. There was even a guard on the door; we walked past him to the end of the corridor to the lift, her apartment was on level five. I started to get a bit nervous in the lift; after all, they were complete strangers. When we got to her apartment, I was speechless. It was beautiful, they clearly weren't short of money. Nikki showed me through to the room that she used for taking pictures and Colin went to get me a glass of wine. Their apartment was so lovely, the side wall was glass, and you could see for miles over the city. The bed was massive and there were matching bedside

Felicity Forbes

tables on either side with a huge bunch of flowers on one, and a chair in the corner of the room. Fast forward a bottle of wine and I was parading about her apartment with nothing but my underwear on. I felt great, I felt sexy, I felt alive, and, at that moment, Felicity was born.

Nikki said she would select the best pictures and edit them to capture the finest parts of my body, whilst not revealing my identity of course. Once she had finished, she would send them to me to get my approval before posting them on her site.

It all happened so fast. One week I was thinking about it and the next I was going to be on a website. The next morning the photos were there, waiting in my inbox for me when I woke up. I was nervous and excited, but, when I opened them, I was totally blown away. I looked amazing. Nikki had captured the absolute best parts of my body and portrayed them in such a way that they were classy, intriguing, and, best of all, managed to conceal my identity. I emailed my acceptance back immediately. The worst bit was now over. Wasn't it?

3. Homework and Training

I GUESS LIKE ALL JOBS, THE key to career success is fully understanding every single aspect of what your job requires. I have tried various career paths, starting with seasonal work whilst at school – usually this was picking strawberries at my parents' friends' farm – then I waitressed at a local restaurant, moving on to work in clothes shops while completing my business degree. I have always been professional, confident, independent, and invariably work my way up to a higher position, so I know I'm a natural leader.

Every new venture has its own unique challenges, and one must learn those or be prepared to deal with them as they arise. Nikki had asked if I was able to go down to her apartment one night through the week so that we could complete my first homework exercise. This was to revise all the unique acronyms associated with being a call girl, and once I understood what those entailed, I was to tell Nikki what

I was comfortable doing so that she could add it to my page on the website. I had already said to Nikki that I do not do anal, which Nikki assured me was completely fine as it was not something that she would do either, but I thought that was the only thing I would preclude.

It was a Wednesday evening, and I was boarding the train to Glasgow once again. I was slightly more prepared than last time; I had to use my large Michael Kors bag so that I was able to take a notebook and few pens with me. I was really looking forward to it, I wasn't nervous at all. I was to meet Nikki at her apartment, and we were going to go through my homework together. When I got to Nikki's she had cheese and biscuits, crisps and carrot sticks with hummus laid out for us, and of course wine waiting. We had a catch-up over the first couple of glasses of wine, then we got right down to my homework. I got the site up that Nikki requested I went on and when the screen loaded, the first words that came out were 'Holy shit!'

Nikki started laughing at me. I honestly thought I was rather clued up on the sex scene as I have always loved it and had done it countless times, so I thought it would be straightforward with little if nothing to learn. More fool me! Most people will be aware of the more frequently used acronyms, 69, BJ etc. The list left me speechless...

AR – Anal Rimming
ATM – Ass to Mouth.
BB – Bareback (no condom)
BBBJTC – Bare Back Blowjob to Completion
BBBJWF – Bare Back Blowjob with Facial
BCD – Behind Closed Doors
BDSM – Bondage, Domination, Submission and Masochism
BLS – Ball Licking and Sucking
CIM – Come in Mouth.
COF – Come on Face.
DAP – Double Anal Penetration
DDF – Drug and Disease Free
DDP – Double Digit Penetration
DFK – Deep French Kissing
DT – Deep Throat
FBSM – Full Body Sensual Massage
FFM – Two Females and one Male
FHRITP – Fuck Her Right in The Pussy.
FJ – Foot Job
FS – Full Service

GFE – Girlfriend Experience
GND – Girl Next Door
GS – Golden Shower
GSM – G-Spot Massage
HJ – Hand Job
HME – Honeymoon Experience
LFK – Light Face Kissing
OWO – Oral Without Condom
PSE – Porn Star Experience
RCA – Reverse Cowgirl Anal
RPG – Role Playing Games
SOF – Shit on Floor
TUMA – Tongue up my Ass
WF – Wild Fuck

The list seemed never-ending. I sat in shock, staring at the screen, then Nikki started randomly shouting them out and I was to tell her what they meant. We seemed to do this for hours and lots of wine was consumed, far too much for me to be able to remember things. As we were now drunk, I said that it would be best for me to head off home as I had work in the morning. The train ride back gave me time to take stock of what we had gone over during the evening, and I was left wondering if this was really for me. All

I could see were things I certainly wouldn't be participating in, that's for sure! I was starting to think I had made a mistake. When I got home, I made myself a cup of tea and settled down for the night. I needed to zone out and take stock of what I had just learned. Surprisingly, rather than sit in shock, I sat chuckling away at myself about how my life had taken this turn. Three months ago, I wasn't even feeling up to leaving my house, and now I am on adventures in Glasgow. And I had homework! It was certainly a positive distraction having this to focus my energy on this rather than dwell on what could have been with Keith. I didn't miss him; I was glad to be free from him. In fact, since I had decided to undertake this journey, he hadn't crossed my mind at all.

The following morning, I woke to the noise of my alarm, head thumping from all the wine I had consumed. I certainly wasn't in the mood for work, so I lay in bed with my eyes still closed, groping for my phone so that I was able to snooze my alarm. The third time my phone went off I knew I had to move, so I reluctantly started to push my covers off to get ready. I was like a zombie walking to the shower. I stood in the shower with my head resting against the wall. I managed to get dressed and call a cab; my car was still at the train station as I wasn't able to drive it home last night. I got into work to be greeted by Milly standing with her arms folded and her lips pressed tightly together with a frown on her face. To be fair, I was thirty minutes late but, in my defence, customers never came in wanting anything till around an hour into my shift, so I always disputed having to start so early. By lunchtime, my hangover was full force; I was collapsed at a table unable to hold my head up. I never normally turned up to work in this condition. I mean, yes, hungover, but I was way past that today.

Why is it that the simplest of things like: What do you want for lunch? Can turn into the most monstrous of tasks when you're ill from alcohol. Unable to decide on food, I spent my break half asleep lay on a bench, occasionally checking my phone. Nikki had messaged asking me to meet with her this weekend to pass on tips about what to do, what to say and how to act. I thought this was nice of her as she knew I was a complete novice, and I was glad she was taking the time to help me.

My Monday to Friday was so boring, I was looking forward to meeting Nikki again, although I wasn't enjoying the aftermath of our drinking. I was definitely ready for my new adventure; I was excited for this new phase in my life. I had let myself go a bit with Keith and the last time I was properly dressed up with my hair done was on the night it all ended with him. Fortunately, it wasn't long before Saturday was upon me and, once again, I was on my way to Glasgow. I made my way to Nikki's apartment and, just as I got to the doors, Nikki was walking along the hallway towards me, she looked fabulous. Her fashion was amazing; she was extremely attractive. I certainly had a bit of a girl crush on her. She had a tight-fitting light-pink blouse tucked into a high-waisted skirt that stopped just above the knee and exceedingly high leather boots, topped off with a beautiful cashmere jacket that must have cost a fortune as it was almost down to her ankles. Nikki had suggested we try a hotel in the city as she had heard from a client that the food was amazing. I did love decent food, far better than pub grub, so off we went.

When we arrived, I was shocked at how fancy it was; Nikki was certainly leading a completely different life to me if this was the kind of places, she has lunch in. We managed to get a table further away from everyone else, which made it a bit more private. The place was busy, but it wasn't loud, so we were able to speak freely without having to shout. As I sat with my notepad on the table, pen in hand, listening intently to her every word, taking notes, I felt like I was at school again. I have always been very professional and want to do absolutely everything to the best of my ability, so taking notes was the only way I was going to remember everything she was telling me.

Nikki started retelling some of her encounters, and already they sounded far better than any of my recent hook-ups. She moved on to the safety aspect of the job, and I knew this was the most important part.

Nikki explained: 'So the way we work things is I get a call from a prospective client, and he stipulates which girl he would like to join him for the arranged time/evening. Then I ask the client what they would like to happen within the time. I call you to see if you are happy with meeting the client and discuss what they are looking for in the time you spend together. If that's all OK, then the booking goes ahead.'

Nikki finished by asking, 'Does everything sound OK so far?'

'Yes of course!' I replied.

Nikki went on to say, 'I have made rules that have to be followed. It's important that everyone in the agency abides by these rules for one another's safety. Don't worry, you'll remember them as they are simple: the client advises where the meeting is to take place. Once booked, this venue cannot be changed. This is to ensure the safety of the girls, so that help can be there very quickly if the situation takes a turn for the worst.'

I must have looked worried as Nikki paused for a moment, then said, 'Don't worry, this never happens!'...

Before I was able to say anything, Nikki carried on telling me about the next step. '...payment: an envelope is placed in the room; you pick it up and excuse yourself to the rest room to check the agreed fee is there. Once that is done and you are comfortable enough with the client, you have to text me within fifteen minutes of arriving to say that everything is in order and you're OK. If that text is not sent, I send Colin and his friends to pick you up ASAP.'

It was all so much to take in, but I felt at ease knowing that there is a safety plan in place and back-up if need be. Nikki carried on telling me 'The next step was to set an alarm on your phone for the agreed booking time, less five minutes, this would give you time to dress and compose yourself prior to leaving. Oh, and ALWAYS to have your phone with you and wear a watch so you can keep an eye on time discreetly!'

Nikki then covered what to take with you when you were working: make-up, toothbrush, toothpaste, mouthwash, mints, underwear, and flat shoes. And, of course, the real essentials: condoms (all shapes and sizes), lube and wet wipes. It was now beginning to feel like hooker boot camp!

'Why flat shoes?' I'd asked.

'Two reasons. One, you might have to run away.' I must have looked worried because she quickly reassured me, 'I've never had cause to do this.' Then she added, 'If the venue of your booking is a hotel, a girl in flat shoes looks far less suspicious than a girl wearing four-inch heels.'

I laughed but agreed with her. Four-inch heels on anyone would draw attention, especially if it was during the day and I was dressed to the nines…

The next topic was what to do on your booking. Nikki explained that most clients are looking for a

GFE, Girl Friend Experience. This was basically that they would like to chat about their day, ask about yours and pretend it was normal, everyday behaviour. She added that I should never ask questions, always listen, so in effect it was more of an acting scenario than anything else. Most importantly, never count money in front of a client. They want to forget very quickly that they are paying for your time. Her final words of wisdom were always to remember the following – this was the unwritten code for becoming a successful call girl:

Confidence
Respect
Elegance
Enjoyment
Professionalism
Secrecy

CREEPS concluded our chat; she told me that was as much as she could pass on, the rest was now up to me. When I boarded the train to go home, my mind was racing. But to be honest, it was excitement. I wasn't scared or even that nervous. I know to some this may appear mad, but you know what, I was really looking forward to starting my new job. Everything was in place, all I needed now was the first call...

4. The First Call

WE ALL HAVE THIS PERFECT picture in our minds of how things are supposed to be and that's why we end up disappointed. All I know is it had been five days since I met Nikki and, truth be told, I was feeling rather disappointed that I had not had a booking yet. I had just finished work and was in the process of driving home when my phone buzzed with a text from Nikki:

Hey, I've just had a call. Are you free tonight? I hope so, he sounds lovely.

I drove into my driveway before I responded: *Yes, of course.* I then stared at the windscreen, waiting for her to reply. I didn't have to wait long.

How long will it take you to get to the south side of Edinburgh?

Shit, I am at least three hours from Edinburgh as I would hit rush-hour traffic, and I'm still in my work clothes. I quickly replied: *possibly Four hours, but I'll try and be quicker than that!*

I ran into my house and jumped in the shower. I think it was the fastest shave and shower I have ever had. Just as I stepped out of the shower, my phone flashed. It was Nikki. The client had picked someone else as they could not wait four hours. To say I was disappointed was a huge understatement. Nikki said that due to my location, she would try to put me forward for advance bookings, so the travel time would not be an issue. I was gutted; all dressed up and with nowhere to go, it was Plan B, a few drinks with my friends. I had just finished my third drink when Nikki messaged again:

Hey, little lady, a client called wanting an hour at 10pm, I have said you can do this, hope that's OK?

Damn, I was on my fourth drink now, so I was over the limit for driving. I sheepishly replied: *I am really sorry, but I can't now as I'd had a few beers to settle my disappointment at losing that client and I can no longer drive to the train station.*

Nikki was less than impressed and I guess I would have felt the same too. I was so annoyed with myself; I left my friends in the pub and went home. I felt awful and just wanted to be alone. Once home I realised that if I was going to be serious about this, then I had to make changes in other aspects of my life, no more going for a beer from this point onwards. I sat at home, alone, watching TV. I felt so bad; I had told Nikki I was available, and I messed up. From that night on, if I say I'm available, I will be.

Friday morning and off to work I went. The first thing I did was text Nikki and apologise again. I told her it was the first and last time it would ever happen. My work had now become a tedious boring chore, the drive there and back was boring, different day same shit, I longed for some excitement in my life. I stopped for lunch and straight away checked my phone, hoping that Nikki was ok with me about last night. Nikki had messaged me back saying not to worry about last night and asked me to call her. I was nervous, incredibly nervous, and all I could think was, have I fucked this up before it had even begun?

I grabbed a coffee and went out to call her, heart pounding and head spinning. It rang for what seemed like an eternity. Eventually she answered. We chatted for a bit, then she dropped the bombshell. I had a booking for tonight! Nikki said my booking was with another girl and was for three hours... She then asked what my limitations were whilst working with another girl. I said to Nikki that I was comfortable working with a girl as I have had previous encounters with the same sex. I went back in to finish my shift. I really just wanted to go home and start getting ready, but I couldn't just leave halfway through my shift and it's not like I could have said I wasn't well as I went back into work with a massive smile on my face and everyone wondered what I was up to, as my mood had changed so dramatically. After all, I was singing and dancing at work and that was something I never did! By my next break Nikki had sent through all the booking details.

I was to be in Glasgow for 8pm. This would give me time to meet the other girl before our hour taxi ride to Edinburgh for a booking that started at 10pm. I finished work at 3pm and drove home; I was still on a high, singing and smiling. I got home and started to get ready. When I got out the shower the nerves started kicking in, thoughts racing round my head: *Another girl? The last time I was with a girl was years ago!* The next thought was, *what if she wasn't nice?* I quickly changed my mind about that after looking at her on the website: she was called Emilia and wasn't from the UK. She looked about the same size as me, but with much bigger boobs. Mind you, that wasn't hard as mine are on the small side, but they are perfectly shaped, like upturned champagne glasses.

Nikki wanted us in matching outfits, so I pulled open my wardrobe doors and started to flick through all the dresses I had hanging up. How was I to know what was the right thing to wear? I pulled out a black dress that was knee-length and a body-con red dress that stopped just below my ass. This was my first job, so I wasn't sure of what to wear or what Emilia had for us to be matching. I filled a huge holdall to the brim; best to have too much than not enough.

Once I was packed, I started to put on normal clothes; after all, I was to be driving for hours! Then I did a final check of my things. I was nervous and fumbling around, panicking that I had forgotten something. When I got in the car, I took a deep breath. I was so nervous and excited at the same time; I didn't know what to expect.

After a long drive on roads that I hadn't ventured on before I eventually arrived at Emilia's flat and sent her a text to say I was there. My heart was about bursting out of my chest! As I opened the door of my car the first thing that hit me was the polluted city air, the stench tickled my nose. Thankfully, it wasn't raining. I walked round from the car park to the main street. It was so busy, but it was a Friday. The buildings were incredibly old and had huge bay windows, I eventually found the entrance, and no sooner had I pressed the buzzer, a voice told me to come up just as I heard the door unlocking. The two flights of stairs were not what I was used to; dark grey and graffitied. The banister was broken off and the stairwell stank of urine. My step got faster the further I went up the stairs –just as I was about five steps from the top, the door opened and out popped Emilia.

'Hello. Wow, you look great. I'm so excited to work with you!'

My first impression was that she seemed lovely, her accent instantly made me smile. She could clearly tell I was nervous as she went on to say, 'Come in, come in. Don't be scared. I will be with you, and we will have so much fun.'

I just smiled and walked in. To be honest, I was now completely petrified. Emilia showed me through the flat, so I knew where everything was, when I got to the living room I was blown away, the huge bay windows were beautiful, the seating in them was almost as large as a two-seater sofa. The rest of her flat certainly wasn't what I was used to; you could hardly see the floor, there were cups, plates, and clothes everywhere.

'I'll go and get you a drink, you need one after the drive.' She went to the kitchen and returned with a glass of orange juice.

I thanked her and took a large mouthful, then nearly choked; it was full of vodka. 'I can't drink, I'm driving.'

'No, drink and stay. Nikki said I was to babysit you, so have a few drinks to relax. We're getting a taxi tonight anyway. Then you stay here once we're finished; you can't drive all the way home in the middle of the night. And we'll be late back tonight, probably two or three.'

I wasn't sure about this – I had only just met her and it seemed a bit weird to me.

Seeing the uncertain look on my face, Emilia added, 'Nikki said I have to look after you and I can't look after you if you go home, so you stay, and we drink.'

I replied, 'OK, but Nikki told me rule one is not to drink around clients.'

Emilia said, 'Fuck that, it's boring listening to Nikki all the time.'

I was now a bit concerned as drinking when seeing clients was on Nikki's NOT to-do list! There wasn't much on Nikki's NOT to-do list but being drunk with a client was one of them.

1. Don't get drunk around clients (it's not professional and, more importantly, it's not safe).
2. Don't make the first move (clients pay for your time so let them spend it as they wish).
3. Don't forget to send the text within fifteen minutes (or you will have a gentleman come to the door).
4. Don't change the location of the booking (we need to know where you are at all times for safety).
5. Don't count money in front of the client (they want to forget the fact they are paying you).
6. Don't stay longer than the agreed time (without speaking to Nikki).
7. Don't have unprotected sex (it's dangerous).
8. Don't give a client your number or your real name (this could be dangerous).

They all seemed very sensible apart from, possibly, rule number eight, which I felt was more in place so that we didn't organise to see the client ourselves rather than going through Nikki, so she was able to take twenty-five per cent of our money.

Emilia and I had a while to go before our booking, so I agreed to have another drink, but I still had reservations about it. Emilia started telling me about the clients she had seen so far; I think this was to calm me down. I was glad to be doing my first job with her, or so I thought. Emilia said to go next door to unpack in the spare room. I was hoping that it would be in a better condition than the living room and I guess it was, there was a bed that was clutter-free, but the rest of the room was covered with boxes stacked right up to the celling. You can imagine how I felt by this with being OCD. With my type of OCD, I seem to obsess over cleaning and organising, but also verge on the repetitive side as well. My house is always gleaming; I can't leave the house if I have dirty dishes and when I do leave the house, I switch everything off, then check and double-check.

As Nikki wanted us in matching outfits, I laid out everything I had brought down with me, and Emilia looked through them to see if she had something similar.

'We have remarkably similar taste,' she said. Emilia suggested I choose, so I gestured at a little red dress that was tight-fitting, so it showed off my curves. It stopped halfway down my thighs and had delicate shoulder straps.

Emilia nodded and left the room. She came back holding a red dress that was very similar to mine, but with slightly thicker straps.

She held it up and said, 'See, told you, they're nearly the same.'

We started getting dressed and it felt like we were getting ready for a normal night out; we decided on black high heels, did our nails, curled our hair, and had a few more drinks. By this point my nerves had all but disappeared.

Emilia explained 'So, we're going to an apartment in the centre of Edinburgh and it's two guys; I guess that's why they want two girls.'

It all seemed quite straightforward, and, with a few drinks fortifying in me now, I was ready to go.

We sat on the window seat gazing at the road below while flicking our ash out the window. I didn't like smoking in doors, I guess being able to sit at the window made it slightly better. Just as we had finished our cigarette our taxi beeped its horn, 'quick, quickly it's time to go' Emilia said.

Coat on, bags in hand and off we went, down to the waiting taxi. Emilia was very relaxed, but I think she was rather drunk by this point. I had a few drinks in me by this stage, but I'd stopped; I wanted to make sure I knew exactly what was going on. I thought Emilia was being a bit unprofessional, but Nikki had said that she was her best girl, so it wasn't my place to say anything. Maybe she thought it was safe to get drunk as I was with her. I had drunk enough that I was now at the happy stage with no nerves at all.

I didn't know Edinburgh at all. I had been to the shops on a weekend before, but it wasn't really a place I went often so I didn't have the faintest idea where we were going or what it was going to be like. The taxi pulled over and we paid our fare. It was freezing cold in our tiny dresses, so we walked round the corner to find a sheltered bit. We still had fifteen minutes before our booking started, so we decided to have a quick cigarette then popped a few mints, quickly pulled out our makeup bags and put on more lipstick. Once organised, we headed round to the apartment.

It was more like a hotel than a block of apartments; it had a very grand entrance with huge revolving doors. I took a deep breath in and out; *no going back now, this was really happening!* When we got on the other side of the doors, the heat hit us. I was so glad to be back in the warm, I hated Scottish winters. However, I didn't dwell on the cold for long, the hallway was spectacular, the artwork was beautiful. Down the hallway before the lifts sat a security guard at a desk.

When we started to pass the security guard, he moved towards us, 'Good Evening, ladies, who are you off to see?'

I froze with an attack of nerves. My heart started racing, my hands sweating, and my breathing got faster. I couldn't speak.

Fortunately, Emilia was there, and she took over: 'Good evening, Sir, how are you? We are off to see our friends in apartment twenty-eight for some drinks.'

She was so calm, like what we were doing was normal, she didn't even flinch.

'Yes, not a problem, just wait a moment while I ring up to double-check.'

We waited for a moment, but I can tell you it seemed like forever!

'Yes, that's fine, head up to floor four please.'

We got to the doors of the lift and Emilia noticed I was panicking. She grabbed my hand, pulled me into the lift, then said, 'It's OK to be freaking out. I was so nervous on my first job that I actually didn't go in and ran away.'

I'm not sure what response she thought I would give her after telling me that, but it made me giggle.

Emilia reassured me further by saying, 'If you don't feel comfortable at any time, we can just leave. Remember, I'm here so don't worry.'

'Thanks, Emilia.' I gave her a quick hug and we stepped out of the lift. Then she dragged me along the corridor, telling me to chill and that I would end up having a wonderful time.

What the heck, you only live once, I thought to myself. As we walked up to the door, we set the timer on our phones for the agreed time, less five minutes of course.

We rang the buzzer and a guy in his late twenties answered. 'Good evening, Wow, you are both so beautiful, I'm Mathew'. Instantly I started blushing – Mathew was gorgeous.

'Hi, Mathew, I'm Emilia and this is Felicity.' We stepped into the apartment and Mathew took our coats.

'Can I give you lovely ladies a tour, so you don't get lost?'

'Yes please,' Emilia replied.

We walked through to the living room and there was another guy sat on the sofa; he looked absolutely smashed.

Mathew said, 'This is Liam, don't worry about him. He's had too much to drink.'

Mathew took us through to the kitchen, where there was another guy. He was introduced as James; he seemed rather quiet. I froze, my pulse spiked, I was concerned that there were three and not two guys and only two of us, but when I looked at Liam again, I felt a little better. He didn't look like he could even move!

Mathew said, 'Now, what would you beautiful ladies like to drink?'

As he went over to a bar area, Emilia said, 'White wine please. Thank you.'

He didn't wait for me to answer, just poured two glasses, and brought them over to us. Once we had our glasses in hand, Mathew showed us around the apartment; it was open-plan and extremely modern. All very neutral, but colour added through artwork; the best I'd ever seen. In the kitchen everything was Smeg. There were three bedrooms, en-suites with two of the bedrooms and a main bathroom, a games room and then the huge open-plan living kitchen area with a well-stocked bar area.

I was blown away, not just by the apartment, but by the fact that they were young, attractive men. I excused myself and went to the toilet, so I was able to send Nikki a text to say we were there and fine. The bathroom was just as spectacular as the rest of the house, with a roll-top bath and candelabra positioned in the corner; I could just imagine myself soaking in here with a lovely glass of red. When I opened the door, I saw two piles of money on the table in the hall: £450 for myself and £450 for Emilia. It seemed silly to take mine and leave Emilia's, so I placed both piles of money into my bag. All was going to plan so far.

I returned to the living room and sat down next to Emilia, then whispered that I had her money and mine. We sat around drinking and talking and, to be truthful, it felt just like a normal party. Emilia was far more touchy-feely than me; she kept touching Mathew's leg. I kept in mind what Nikki had said, to not make the first move, so I was far more reserved. I looked at the guys and kept wondering: *why did they need to pay for us?* Liam, who was still sat on the sofa, had not said two words. He was in his forties, well dressed and not the worst-looking guy I had seen. Mathew was in his late twenties, tall, dark, and handsome. He was very funny but slightly too loud. James was in his thirties, good-looking and obviously spent a lot of time in the gym. I just did not get it; they all seemed normal, good-looking guys; what was their need for call girls?

Well over an hour had passed and all we had done was talk, laugh, and drink. The drink flowed freely; however, I kept pouring mine out when I went to the kitchen to top the rest of their drinks up. I wanted to stay in control. Emilia was totally wasted, but I guess she felt happy and safe enough to let herself go. I went to freshen up in the bathroom, and as I was doing my make-up, I stood wondering what the hell was going on. Don't get me wrong, I was enjoying getting paid to party, but in my head, I thought it was going to be one giant gangbang or something similar. Not that I was wanting all five of us to get naked and go at it together, I just thought that something more would have happened by now. Once I'd sorted my make-up, I left the bathroom.

Mathew was waiting for me in the hall. He took me by the hand and led me to his room. Before the door had even closed, he had me pushed up against the wall, kissing my neck. I could feel his hand running up my thigh; this was enough to get me wet, and, before I knew it, our clothes were on the floor, and we were in bed! I was really enjoying myself. It was such a surreal feeling I was getting off with a guy that I would have picked up from a pub, and I was getting paid for it... He then jumped up from the bed and said, 'Do you want any flake?'

I was a bit confused, so I said, 'No thanks.' I was trying to understand what he meant. Then I watched him pick up his jeans from the floor and take out a bag of white powder, pour an amount on the bedside table and sniff it up his nose with a fifty-pound note. The penny dropped; they were all smashed on drugs. I was less impressed with Mathew now. He jumped back on the bed beside me, and we started kissing again. Then the door opened and in came Emilia.

'Why am I missing out on all the fun?' She closed the door behind her, took her dress off and got into bed with us.

I looked at her, shocked. Now, don't get me wrong, I found Emilia attractive, but I was confused that she would want to join in when she wasn't being asked. Saying that I was also relieved that I wasn't alone. She didn't waste any time at all; her tongue was in my mouth, and we seemed to get lost in the moment. I find that females are better than men at most things in the bedroom, kissing being one but also oral. In my previous experiences of experimenting with women, I found that they were able to make me orgasm far quicker than men. It wasn't long before Emilia's hand was sliding down my face, stopping at my breasts for a moment, then moving down my body to my hip, then reaching round to squeeze my bum. I was really enjoying myself and I had completely forgotten about Mathew being there. It wasn't long before Emilia was running the tips of her fingers over my clit; nowI was really getting turned on. All of a sudden Mathew got involved. I'll be honest; I was slightly annoyed, but obviously wasn't able to voice my opinion. After all, it was Mathew that was paying for our time. The three of us were rolling around naked on his bed for quite some time. Mathew was fumbling around with himself for much of the time but still unable to get a hard penis; he professed he had 'been on it since lunch'. I assumed he meant drink and drugs...

'Please excuse me, I have to go to the bathroom.' I said as I walked to the door, I grabbed my shoes, bag, and dress, so I was able to go to the kitchen after I had been to the bathroom.

I went to the bathroom, shut the door, and locked it. I didn't need the toilet; I just wanted a few moments to myself. I pulled on my dress then slipped my shoes back on, took a few deep breaths, then sorted my make up. Once I had composed myself, I walked through to the living room and went to sit next to James who was also high, as I noticed he kept sniffing and wiping his nose.

Soon Emilia emerged from the bedroom; a lot more sober than when she went in. They were all on it. We only had twenty minutes left on our timer, so I needed to call a cab. I didn't have any numbers saved as this was so far away from where I lived. Just as I was asking for a number, Liam came round and jumped up off the sofa.

He introduced himself and I said, 'Sorry we haven't had time to catch up, but it is time for us to go.'

Liam quickly replied, 'Name your price.'

I was shocked and laughed as I thought he was joking.

His smile dropped and he said again, 'Name your price.'

Emilia blurted out, 'Two hundred each for another hour and I'll have to check with the agency that it's OK for us to stay.'

Without any hesitation at all, Liam pulled out his wallet and put four hundred pounds on the table. I could not believe it; I was completely gobsmacked. Another hour on the timer and I sat back on the sofa. Liam got up, went to the kitchen, and returned with a bottle of Dom Pérignon. He popped the cork and started to pour us all a glass. I was now completely blown away; I had an extra £650 in my bag; I had sat drinking for hours with three semi-normal guys and one really crazy bird...

Liam was actually really nice, and I was rather disappointed that he had been out of it previously. Soon our time was up again, and Emilia and I gathered our things ready to leave. Then Mathew appeared, putting down more money on the table. He said, 'You need to stay for another hour and you two (Emilia and I) should play together.'

Before I could say a word, Emilia was kissing me. I felt slightly drunk by this stage, but I didn't feel especially vulnerable. The guys didn't seem the sort to be violent, so I didn't feel in any danger. Emilia took off all her clothes again, then proceeded to strip mine off too, until I lay naked on the floor. She then started to kiss my neck and slowly moved down my body without taking her tongue off me at all until her head was in between my legs. I shut my eyes as she started slowly licking my clit while also rubbing my pussy. I could hear her moan softly and I opened my eyes and looked down and watched as her head was buried between my legs, then I noticed she was being fingered by Liam. I was glad it was her on me and Liam on her. I closed my eyes again and completely zoned out from what was happening; to me it was just Emilia and me. Every time I opened my eyes, I'd quickly closed them; Mathew and James were standing over us, staring right at my face. Liam was not so bad; he was fully focused on Emilia, so it was fine. Emilia was really hitting the right areas with her tongue; she had clearly had several encounters with the same sex. I couldn't climax though as I was being watched and it certainly wasn't something I was used to, no matter how much I tried I just couldn't fully relax. Just as I was wondering why the timer hadn't gone, it went. We continued on for about another five minutes, then stopped.

Liam called his friend to come and get us and said he would be there in ten minutes, so we got dressed, got our things together, thanked the guys and left the apartment. Emilia was rather drunk, but I managed to get her in the lift, get her heels off and flats on, which made it easier for me to shift her around. Once outside we had a cigarette. While waiting outside I had a horrid thought. Should I have trusted a man I had just met to phone me a taxi; what did he mean by friend? Am I going to be in any danger? Is this a real taxi or just a man coming to pick us up? Unable to ask Emilia as she was falling about all over the place, I had no real option but to wait and see. Just as we'd finished our cigarette, a taxi appeared. We both climbed in, and I gave the driver her address and off we went. Emilia kept on trying to kiss me, but the moment had gone for me.

Thankfully, we returned home safely, and I was worrying over nothing. Once we arrived outside Emilia's flat, I realised I would be unable to get her up the stairs in her condition, so a trip to McDonalds was required to sober her up since it was just around the corner. The street was well lit; several people obviously had the same idea as us, as they too were making their way towards McDonalds. As we sat there eating a Big Mac, I burst out laughing, I could not believe the night we had just had. It was crazy, but it worked out fine and I had my first job under my belt. I mean normally on a night out I would spend nearly two hundred pounds, sometimes more, but tonight I got just as drunk, had just as much fun and I'd made heaps of money.

As soon as we got back to Emilia's, she went to her room and passed out straight away. I was shocked that she didn't want to shower after all that happened but was glad that I was able to go straight in and not wait till she was finished. The shower was not something I would normally have stepped in, but this was an emergency; I felt dirty and needed to wash. There were broken tiles everywhere and it was filthy, like it hadn't been cleaned in months. I felt like I should have been wearing flip-flops inside it, but it wasn't going to stop me from getting in, that's for sure.

I had the water on full while I slipped out of my dress; I was desperate to feel the water run over me. I stepped in with my eyes shut to not see or think about the dirtiness of it. I went straight under the water with it running over my head and down my hair. I was so happy to feel the water run over me. I quickly washed myself and felt less dirty than when I got in, but still like I needed to clean myself. I guess having two naked bodies on me was not something I was used to.

Still, each time I washed myself I got a little bit more of my smile back, to the point that by the fourth time I had covered myself in bubbles and washed it off, I was now laughing and could not stop. I couldn't get over the fact it was like any other weekend, only this time I had not spent money; I'd made it! I dried myself and went through to my room. I would have preferred to have been at home, but I was well over the drink-drive limit, and I valued my licence far too much to risk it. I did not feel sleepy at all; it must have been the adrenaline. I felt so confident, so at ease with myself. I had done it. And not only had I done it, but I also loved it! I had a strange feeling that this was just the beginning of my dual life.

5. Round Two

I COULD TELL IT WAS A beautiful day from the heat of the sun beating in through the windows. I hadn't even opened my eyes, but I was guessing it was late afternoon as we didn't get to bed till the very early hours of the morning. I knew I had been asleep for a while. If I'm honest I didn't want to open my eyes, but the noise of traffic on the streets below was too loud for me to sleep again and I was in desperate need of a coffee, so I reluctantly pushed my cover off and slowly started to open my eyes. I was right, I didn't want to open my eyes; it was like a bomb had gone off. I went through to the kitchen to find the kettle. I absolutely hate mornings until I have had my caffeine fix. It was nothing like my home; there was not a clean dish in the kitchen or a thing in the fridge. I went through to check on Emilia; she was lying there half of her body hanging out of the bed but was still sound asleep, so I decided to go and get dressed and to go to the shop. I am not one for eating out, but after seeing her kitchen there was no way I was eating there! I found a Costa and got bacon rolls and coffee's and went back to the flat. I got in and woke Emilia; she was not on the best of form, probably due to the amount of drink and drugs she had consumed the night before. We ate our breakfast, then sat watching the TV for a while. Just as I got organised and was about to leave, I got a text from Nikki:

Hey, how was your night? Did you have fun? The guys loved you, so well done. What are your plans tonight? I have a guy wanting to see you at 8pm, is that OK?

I burst out laughing; I could not believe it! I sat for a moment then replied: *I had a really enjoyable time last night; it was lots of fun. I was just away to leave but it is no problem to stay and see someone tonight at 2000.*

Nikki responded straight away: O*h, that is great. I will send you details through in a little bit.*

I told Emilia and she suggested I stay with her until my booking later that night. We now had a few hours to kill, so Emilia and I went for a power nap. When the timer went it was just gone 1600, so we decided to go for an early dinner and have a few cocktails to pass the time. I was no longer nervous or scared and I had found a reserve of confidence I never knew I had; I felt unstoppable. Emilia was feeling rather sorry for herself. No surprise there, to be honest. Had I taken what she had, I would still have been in bed!

By the time we returned to the flat we were now feeling last night catch up with us, so I set my alarm for just before 7pm and had another rest. When the alarm went it was all go, shower, hair, outfit, and make-up. I was going to a hotel in the centre of Glasgow, so Emilia ordered me a taxi whilst I did the final check to make sure I had everything I needed. The taxi arrived, and it was time to go. I felt fine, I was not nervous or scared. Nikki had sent me a text telling me it was a one-hour booking with a very wealthy Middle Eastern businessman who wanted the GFE. The taxi ride was only ten minutes, but by the time I got there my feelings had changed; I was so nervous my hands were shaking when I was trying to pay the driver. I think it was largely due to the fact that I was alone.

I gave myself a shake as I stepped out of the taxi. The hotel doors were lit up like a Christmas tree. There were staff at the reception, but I walked right past them to the lift. I now felt the same as last night; I was anxious, I had sweaty palms and I wasn't sure about this at all. As the lift approached the floor, flats off and heels on, I looked into my eyes in the mirror and told myself, *have fun you can do this,* so I did. I walked calmly out of the elevator to the room and knocked on the door.

The door opened, and I was greeted by two large men in suits. I instantly felt weak, almost queasy, and my heart sank. I was petrified, what was going on? Nikki hadn't mentioned anything about this. The two guys could see I was not comfortable, but before I could even step back and say I needed to check something with the agency, the suited men walked past me and let me in. When I walked into the room, or should I say suite – and a huge one at that – I was greeted by a gentleman sitting on one of the sofa's. He got up, introduced himself and apologised if his bodyguards had scared me. He offered to take my coat and then asked if I would join him in a glass of champagne. The room was one of the best I had ever seen; it was obviously the penthouse suite, and it was huge. It had a living area which had two large sofas in it with a massive coffee table between them and there was a separate dining area that had a table to sit six. The bedroom was the biggest I had ever seen; it had a super-king-sized bed in it with a table and two chairs and a velvet chaise longue in the corner. There were three flat-screen TVs around the suite and the bathroom was to die for; it had a freestanding bath with the taps in the middle so you could comfortably have two people in it.

While looking round I spotted a thick envelope on the side of the dresser, I excused myself and casually picked it up on the way to the bathroom. When I shut the door, I dropped my bag and stared into the mirror. I took large, deep breaths and calmed myself down a little. I knew it was the bodyguards that startled me. When I was calm enough, I checked the money and texted Nikki to say I was OK. I could not believe what was in the envelope; there was far too much, but I wasn't going to tell Nikki that. She hadn't mentioned what to do if you got too much money, so what she didn't know wouldn't hurt her.

As I returned to the room, I said, 'Thank you but this is too much.'

To which he replied, 'Nothing is too much for you.'

We sat drinking champagne, the finest champagne I may add. It was nice; he never let my glass empty and kept asking about me. I tried to answer with things that were true without giving anything away about my personal life. He was such a lovely gentleman, but there was no physical or sexual attraction at all. This was so different from last night; this is when I realised what Nikki meant about acting. He asked me to join him on the bed. As he made his way there, I quickly drank what was left in my glass whilst his back was to me. As soon as he saw my glass was empty, he got up and filled it again. To be honest I was glad of the champagne, and all I was thinking at this point was *fuck the no-drinking rule!*

We lay on the bed beside each other, and he started running his fingers through my hair, I didn't like it at all. This sent shivers down my spine, so I changed position and rolled over towards him, at which point he asked me take off my dress. I got up and slowly peeled my dress from my body, revealing very sexy red underwear. I climbed back on the bed, whilst managing a sneak look at my watch. Fortunately, only twenty minutes to go, this made me feel a little better. He bent over me and started kissing my foot, slowly working his way up my leg, always checking I was OK and comfortable with it (which I thought was lovely). He stood up and started to unbutton his shirt, then removed his trousers. I rolled over and had a drink of my champagne. He was a large man and obviously didn't look after himself; his breasts were the same size as mine, if not larger, and the amount of hair on his body was somewhat disturbing. I took a deep breath and tried my best to relax; I could see his erect penis in his pants, which was no larger than my index finger. He then asked me to touch my breasts while he went back to licking my foot. I was trying so hard to keep a smile on my face, but I was struggling. He started to suck on my toe, and I hated it. Luckily, it didn't take long before he had ejaculated in his pants. I could not believe it, I was shocked.

He stood for a moment, then said, 'Please excuse me.' As he went to the bathroom.

As soon as he was out of the room I drank more champagne, then waited till he got back from the bathroom. When he walked back into the room he said, 'Thank you, I am finished so you may leave.'

I was relieved. I felt really uncomfortable and just wanted to get out of there. I headed through to the bathroom to organise myself and get dressed.

When I opened the bathroom door he was standing there, holding my coat. I was startled but wanted to leave so I turned round for him to put it on me. By the time I had turned back he had opened the door to the apartment and the two bodyguards were stood there. They both smiled and one of them walked me to the lift. I had asked my taxi driver to pick me up in an hour, so I had enough time to have a smoke until he arrived.

My feelings were mixed, at best. It was nothing like last night; I wasn't smiling, I wasn't laughing, I just sat and gazed out the window all the way back to Emilia's. When the taxi pulled up at Emilia's I could not wait to get into the flat. I thanked the driver and paid the fair, then ran up the stairs to her door. When Emilia opened the door, she could tell instantly how I was feeling. I assume she must have had a similar experience before. She didn't ask questions or say anything, just gave me a hug and said she was away to put the shower on for me. I was glad that I was with Emilia, I didn't want to go home and sit by myself. I wasn't dreading going in the shower, even though it was disgusting. I felt disgusting, and I just needed to be clean.

I washed my hair and body repeatedly, each time I felt no cleaner than the last. I still did not feel like getting out, so I slowly slid down to sit in the bottom of the shower, I just needed to let the water run over me as I kept washing my feet. The door opened, and Emilia walked towards me then knelt down at the side of the shower. Neither of us had said a word. Then she handed me a towel followed by a lit joint.

She just looked at me and said, 'Smoke this, you are staying here tonight, and I will cheer you up'.

I could tell she knew how I was feeling. She said she was there if I wanted to talk, then she smiled and left. This was a completely different feeling from last night. I sat with the water running over my head mainly going down my front, I had lost count of the times I had washed my feet. I wasn't one for drugs and didn't like feeling of being high, but I thought: *what the hell?*

I started to smoke the joint. I have to say it helped after I got halfway down, each puff felt like it was calming me, and my memories from the evening were slowly fading away. I finished it, then got up feeling slightly lightheaded. I could not sit in the shower moping about all night, so I started to wash my hair and body once more. I was pretty wasted off the smoke, so it was time to get out, get dried off and put my PJ's on.

We sat and watched TV while eating a heap of chocolate. To be honest, I have no idea what we even watched; As I wasn't one for smoking weed, I was now pretty wasted, and I wasn't really in a talkative mood, so I guess that was fine considering we were now both stoned.

My eye lids heavy, my head confused, my mouth had gone to cotton; It had been many, many years since I had woken with a 'stone over'. It was still incredibly early, but I slowly peeled my eyes open, yawned a few times and wiped the sleep from my eyes. I couldn't get up, it was like my legs were too heavy, so I rolled side to side to get enough momentum up to roll me out of bed. Clatter, Bang! I made it. Granted, it was not graceful, but I was alone, so it didn't need to be. I organised my things and went to check on Emilia; she looked to be most uncomfortable, but she was sound asleep, so I left her a wee note to thank her and headed home. Once home I emptied my bag, put my clothes on a really long wash, hid the cash in my freezer and went for a shower. I loved my shower; it ran off the mains, so the pressure of the water feels amazing hitting against my skin. The shower didn't seem to work its magic on my mind this time, so I decided to go out for a run as that's always a good way for me to unwind. When I got home, I was feeling slightly better, but was still in no mood to be seeing anyone or having conversations, so it was phone off, curtains shut and TV time.

A week had passed since my last encounter. I had gone to my day job, but even that was a struggle. Nikki had been in touch several times, but I had already refused two jobs. The most recent experience had been so unpleasant that I wasn't sure if I was able to mentally cope with doing this job or not. The gentleman was lovely – both kind and considerate – but he was so overweight and a lot older than me, had more hair on his chest than a cat. He was certainly not someone that I would have taken home from an evening out, that's for sure. Oh, and yeah, he sucked my fucking toes! Two jobs in and I was already starting to doubt I was cut out for life as a call girl. Honestly, I felt rather disgusted at myself, I had never let someone lick my feet before, nor was it an enjoyable feeling. And, to top it off, it was with someone I had no physical or sexual attraction to. Now, don't get me wrong, I had gone home with guys before that weren't appealing on the eyes, but I had my beer goggles on and at least at some point they would have made me laugh, but that last encounter left me cold, nothing clicked whatsoever. I felt that I had let myself down. I knew that not everyone was going to be attractive, but I guess I overlooked it as Nikki had made out that it was always glamorous and always fun.

The whole week felt different to me; I got up and went to work, came home, went for a run, had tea, watched telly, and went to bed. I felt numb, almost robotic.

Nikki had messaged me again, asking how I was, but I could not even bring myself to reply. Was I a bad person? What was I? That is all that ran through my head. All I could think was that I let someone touch me that I didn't like. I felt a bit lost and alone, I could not talk to my friends about this, I couldn't tell them how I was feeling or seek advice. And now to get to sleep I found myself watching telly until I passed out.

Ten days had now passed since my round two experience and Nikki had sent me a huge message; she had obviously figured out how I felt, and her words were not only needed but also made me realise I wasn't alone, nor was I being silly, I was normal. She explained if I wasn't experiencing those emotions then I would be heartless. We chatted for some time on the phone, and I felt so much better. Nikki was right; I just needed to talk, not hide, and keep my thoughts to myself. I needed to see the funny side and she made me see that. That same night I slept right through with no issue at all; no bad thoughts or bad dreams, it was bliss.

I didn't just jump back into seeing people. I told Nikki that I needed a bit of time to get back to myself before I wanted to see someone. Day 13 since round two and I finally felt back to me, so I texted Nikki that morning and told her I was back and ready to go. By the time I had finished work at 3pm, she had replied with details of a booking. This time it was a young guy in Glasgow, and I was to go to his house. Nikki gave me his number and said for me to call him for a chat as she wanted to make sure that I was OK about seeing him. So, I called him on a withheld number to have a wee chat to see if he sounded OK. I was glad she suggested this, and I knew this was to reassure me after my last encounter. After the phone call I seemed to feel a bit better about it and I started to get ready. I hit traffic going into Glasgow, which was dreadful; I hate sitting waiting at the best of times, never mind when I have so much on my mind. My thoughts started running wild; *what if it is the same as last time? What if he is horrid? Should I just turn round and go home?* The traffic started moving at the right time; if I had sat there much longer, I would have turned and gone home.

I arrived at the address and found a multi-storey car park close by. OK, car parked, make-up sorted and off I went to find the house. I could not find it. I kept thinking, *Is this a sign to go home?* I called my client, and he told me to stay where I was, and he would come to me. I was glad I had my flat shoes on as I was waiting for some time, then I saw someone wave at me from across the street. It must be him? Then I thought, oh gosh, what if it's not him and it's someone who knows me and I'm away to be caught meeting a stranger! Once he was over the street, he introduced himself as Andrew. I asked where we were going, and he replied not far, just round the corner. We walked through an underpass towards multi-storey buildings. To me this was another world; I couldn't even begin to imagine what they must be like to live in; there were probably more people in those buildings than there is in the town I live in. We continued until we were beside two of the four towers, then Andrew turned around and announced that we could not go inside as his gran was home! Could we do it outside? All I could think was great, another shit booking. I laughed – we were in the middle of Glasgow! Andrew said there was a bit just around the corner. I walked with him; why not, he was young and good-looking, and I was already there, no harm in having a look, I thought.

When we got there, there was no one in sight, so I did the awkward bit – mentioned money – only to be told that he couldn't get the money until later as his gran was in. He suggested we do it anyway! Now I knew why Nikki had always said wear flat shoes; I was in an area away from where Nikki thought I would be, and the client had turned weird. Without another thought, I immediately turned around and ran. I ran as fast as I could, but Andrew was hot on my heels, shouting, 'We could do it in your car?'

I knew if I could outrun him to the underpass there were shops and people on the other side of the street and that I would be safe there. I ran so fast; my heart was racing, and my legs were in overdrive. Each stride I took I felt the burning of my heel and little toe, it was being rubbed raw from the patterned material on the cloth pumps I was wearing, I finally made it to where the street was full of people. Still trembling, trying to catch my breath, I realised everyone was staring at me, so I stopped running. I walked briskly to the car park, looking over my shoulder to check that Andrew wasn't following me.

The moment I got back to my car, I called Nikki. She could not believe it; she was mortified, and I could tell she was genuinely sorry. By the end of the call, we were both laughing. Just as we were saying our goodbyes, she told me she had not heard from Emilia in a couple of days, so I said I'd go home via her house to drop in some flowers to her as a thank you for looking after me.

Driving through Glasgow was a nightmare; it took forever. All the way there I had been trying to call Emilia on my hands-free in the car. I got no answer, and this was strange as she would always answer her phone; she was glued to it. I was now worried; it wasn't like her not to answer. I got to Emilia's, parked up and went straight to the door. I hadn't even bothered stopping to get the flowers, they seemed less important now. I pushed the button for her flat. No answer. I was now extremely worried, especially after I had seen the state that she got herself in on jobs. I kept trying to call her whilst ringing the flat buzzer, nothing. I then started pushing every buzzer on the front door in the hope someone would let me in. Finally, the door opened, and I sprinted up the two flights of stairs to find her front door open. I ran in shouting, 'Emilia! Emilia!' again and again. I checked every room, my heart now racing. I was so scared, *where could she be? Had she let someone into her flat as a booking?*

I sat on her sofa with my head in my hands. *What do I do now?* It was really strange that her door was open, and she wasn't here. I rang her phone again, but this time I could hear it ringing. I listened to where the ringing was coming from and leaped towards the window, pulling back the dark, dingy curtains and there she was, laid on the large bay windowsill. I started to shake her shoulders, shouting her name.

I had trained as a first aider many years ago and it all came back to me the instant, I saw her. I rolled her into the recovery position, still shouting her name. Nothing. I had no other choice but to call 999; once I got through, I explained the situation. I bent over Emilia to carry out CPR as I had been instructed to do until the paramedics arrived. And then, just like nothing had happened, Emilia opened her eyes and said in the calmest of voices, 'Hey, Felicity, how are you?'

'How am I? How am I? Seriously, I thought you were dead! What the hell?' I honestly thought she had overdosed and died.

I collapsed onto the floor. My heart was racing, my hands were trembling, and I couldn't talk. The feeling was unlike anything I had ever experienced. After a moment I realised I was still on a call to 999. I tried to cancel the ambulance, but they said that once they received a call like this they had to come and check. Just as I ended the call, the paramedics walked through the door. I did not know what felt worse: the fact that I felt I had wasted their time or the fact that one of the paramedics knew Emilia, and, by all accounts, her passing out and people thinking she was dead was normal.

I can tell you now; there is nothing normal about that to me. I texted Nikki to tell her Emilia was OK and that I would call her on the way home. I stayed with Emilia until she'd showered, and I'd gotten her to eat something; she looked to be in a better place.

Once I was satisfied that she was fine, I set off up the road. My thoughts were chasing one another wildly around my head. Emilia had a problem, a big problem. She had already confessed to me that she used Cocaine to see clients and that she took Valium to sleep at nights, but I felt she was far more dependent on drugs than she thought she was.

Once at home, I made myself a cup of tea to calm down. I called Nikki and explained the whole situation. She said she would go round and check on Emilia later and let me know how she was. I was so tired. I was used to my quiet little life and for the past three weeks I had had more ups and downs than I've had in my whole life. I dread to think what will happen next...

6. The Ugly Side of Drugs

PARTY TIME! THE WEEKEND WAS here. I hadn't taken any bookings this week as I was busy with overtime at work and hadn't been able to find the time. Nikki had asked me to go to Glasgow for the weekend to stay with her and Colin, as the girl that used to live with them had moved out, so they now had a spare room which they said I was more than welcome to use. Nikki said it would mean I was able to go to bookings in the city on short notice rather than having to just take advanced bookings and miss out on clients that couldn't wait for my travel time. So off I went to Glasgow. As usual I was running late, but when I am only plain Jane, I seemed to be late for most things.

Nikki called, I gave her an update and she told me to get a move on as all the girls were already there. That made me feel a bit strange; I didn't realise 'all the girls' were going to be at the apartment. I

Felicity Forbes

wasn't sure about meeting them; after all, I had met Emilia and you know how that went...!

I eventually got there and managed to find a parking spot, which isn't the easiest thing to do in Glasgow. I had a funny feeling about this, and usually I am right; at this point I should have gone home. When I arrived at the apartment it was obvious that everyone was drunk. I'm not keen on being around really drunk people after Keith. I dropped my bag in the room Nikki had said I was to stay in and made my way through to the living room.

Nikki and Colin were on one sofa, Emilia, and a guy (who was introduced as her boyfriend – I was in shock) were on another, and there was also a girl called Amy who I had never met before but had seen on the agency website. Amy was taller than me and very loud. She was orange with the amount of fake tan on her skin, and had fake everything: boobs, lips, even her nose had been done.

I did not take to her; you know when you look at someone and just know that you will not get on with them, well, that happened the moment I set eyes on her. Then there were Eve and Lacy on another sofa; they've been friends since school and have been doing this for about two years. They work mainly as a duo, they're around my age and seemed really nice. They had only recently joined the agency as they felt that they would be safer, and they had brought a lot of their own clients with them. They seemed very touchy-feely, so I wasn't sure if they were a couple or if they were just close.

Everyone seemed well on their way to being drunk. I had brought some pre-mixed cocktails as they are not strong, and I didn't want to get drunk with these people. Before long nearly everyone was smoking joints, doing lines of white powder, and drinking shots; they were all totally wasted. We had planned to go out later with flyers to try and recruit some new girls and hand out business cards, yes, business cards! I think we were the only agency that had them, but this is what made us different and classy. I soon figured out it was the Amy girl who had brought the drugs, and this made me like her even less. The lines they were doing, I was reliably informed, was MDMA.

For those of you who don't know, MDMA is a mix between a stimulant and a hallucinogenic, giving the user increased energy, enhanced pleasure, emotional warmth and distorting the senses of time. This could possibly be why everyone was stroking each other! I felt awkward, so I stopped drinking. I was in a room full of complete strangers who were completely wasted on something that held no appeal to me at all. Everyone in the room was already dressed to go out, so thankfully I had an excuse to leave the room to go and get ready. I pulled on a tight-fitting purple V-neck dress that went just past my knees; it was classy and seemed similar to what the other girls were wearing. I started sorting my makeup out in the bathroom, and the drinks that were brought to me went straight down the sink.

The noise from the living room was getting louder and louder, and it was mainly Amy. I listened as she recounted a story about how she had done water sports with a client. I did not have a clue what she meant and nor did Emilia's boyfriend (William), who was bold enough to ask.

'How can you not know?' Amy said, laughing. She then proceeded to explain that it was when you urinated on someone. I was so shocked I poked myself in the eye with my mascara.

William was clearly also in disbelief and asked, 'As in, piss on someone?'

Amy said, 'Yes', and continued laughing in a creepy cackle, adding, 'I had to do it in his mouth.'

At this point I gagged and felt the gorge rise; that was horrid, and not something I would ever contemplate at any price. It did not end there; there was worse to come. Nikki told Amy to tell us about the hard-sports client. I completely froze and a part of me went into shock at the thoughts running through my head. I gave myself a shake and thought, *surely not, no it can't be...*

Amy and Nikki were laughing for what seemed like an eternity before Amy announced, 'Yeah, I have one regular client.'

I thought regular; this means that whatever she is about to say has happened more than once and the hairs on the back of my neck stood up. I wasn't ready for whatever was going to come out of her mouth next...!

Amy then proceeded to say, 'My client, a guy in his forties, a real gentleman...' (Fuck knows why she thinks gentleman is a word to describe a complete weirdo). She carried on saying, '...who I see once a fortnight. Each time we meet we give each other oral, then he fucks me up the ass. Once he has finished, he lies in the bath, and I shit on his chest.'

I thought that was it but then she went on to say, 'Then we have a smoke while he lies there covered in my shit, and we finish by having sex in the shower!'

I was now gagging and could not believe what I had just heard. Obviously, that was two more things I needed to add to my never-do list...! I sat there in complete shock for about ten minutes. I could not even move; it was the most horrific thing I had ever heard. EVER...!

Nikki came through to tell me to hurry up, but when she saw me, she said 'Are you ok? You look like you have seen a ghost?'

'Yes, I'm ok I won't be long'.

I didn't want to tell her that I was sick in my mouth listening to them, so I sorted myself out and went through to the living room, Colin and Amy were having a heated discussion. I could tell that what he had heard really upset him; after all, his girlfriend is the one that talks to those creepy guys on the phone! Amy was now absolutely wasted and could hardly stand; however, she stood up, stumbled across the room, and slammed the door on the way out. The whole atmosphere had now changed, but then again, they were all wasted. Emilia handed me a drink and I excused myself and went out onto the balcony to have a smoke, at the same time discreetly ditching my drink. You could tell it was the weekend as the streets were full of people. Luckily, the weather was starting to break into spring, so it wasn't as cold this evening as it had been the last few weeks. When I went back in, Nikki was asking how Emilia and William had met, after all, we knew nothing about him. They'd both sat there all evening not saying much, just cuddled up together. Just as William started talking, an advert came on the TV about internet dating. Nikki, Colin, and I all started laughing and agreed it was a complete joke, then William quickly jumped in and told us not to laugh as that was how they had met!

Nikki, Colin, Lacy, Eve, and I looked round with shocked faces. Colin quickly said, 'What, you're joking?'

You could tell from his expression he was very anxious; the mood had changed in the room again, even Emilia looked worried. Before she could say a word, William jumped in and told us they had spoken on a dating site for a month, but with Emilia being so busy with work (work being a full-time call girl...!) they had only met last week. The five of us were shocked; they made out they had known each other for ages. Then William announced it had been love at first sight, and he thought her job was a turn- on!

Immediately, I thought hold the boat here. She's brought along a guy she hardly knows to meet and listen to us talk openly about work, and she doesn't even know who the hell he is. I was panicking, and I could tell that Colin was too. Colin immediately asked to speak with Nikki in the other room, I could feel a horrid tension in the air, and I did not like it one bit.

Nikki appeared to calm Colin down and, once again, we all congregated in the living room. Emilia then gave us all a shot of Apple Sourz; I knew I could not get away with pouring this one away. I felt so uncomfortable now; there had already been one argument which led to Amy storming out and I knew it wasn't finished there. Drunk people on a cocktail of drugs, now doing shots, I could not think of a worse combination. In hindsight, I should never have come, I should have turned the car round and gone home when I had a bad feeling about the evening.

Just as we finished the shots, I turned to see Eve and Lacy lining up more. As the next round went down, everyone seemed to be getting on a lot better; maybe it was because Amy had gone. Nikki was finishing the last of the flyers we were going to be handing out, and we all agreed we would leave in thirty minutes so we would be going out at midnight. The six of them were now completely and utterly hammered; by this point they had consumed four bottles of wine, two bottles of spirits and a few bags of MDMA, as well as a never-ending chain of joints. I'd lost count of the shots they'd had.

Nikki then decided that it would be a clever idea to watch a documentary about call girls that she had recorded during the week. It had been on for no longer than ten minutes before I could see Colin getting very agitated again. William then started asking questions about being a call girl and what it was like. I, for one, did not feel comfortable talking to him as he was a stranger, however Nikki, Eve, Lacy, and Emilia started chatting about it all freely. Colin was now getting more and more agitated; his legs were shaking, and I knew that he was even more uncomfortable than I was. I assumed that the paranoia from the drugs was making Colin worry about why William was taking such an interest in it all. I guess it was because he could get in so much trouble; after all, he was the boss of the agency. Nikki just organised the bookings, hired the girls and helped them.

Nikki had let me into the secret that Colin had tried to be a male escort before they met, but he wasn't able to perform and was more talk than action. I think it was Colin that had said to Nikki to try escorting in the first place.

Things started to get slightly more relaxed then William turned and asked Colin how he felt when Nikki was working and how he handled the fact that other men were 'ball deep inside his woman?'

I knew it wasn't going to end well. Colin leaped out of the chair like a jack-in-the-box, soaking us all with drink as he knocked over the table as he swung at William. Nikki jumped up into the middle of them, holding Colin back. Colin had snapped so quickly, but I knew it was coming. William was trying to go over and talk to him, but Colin was screaming at him: 'Get out before I fucking kill you!'

Eve and Lacy must have been really high as they were surprisingly calm and kept saying 'Every thing's cool, just relax'. They were almost laughing, like this was all a joke, but I could tell from Colin's eyes that none of this was a joke to him.

Nikki had Colin in the corner of the room, I screamed at Emilia and William to get out of the room, but they were so drunk they didn't understand. Thankfully, Eve and Lacy started to take this seriously and helped to get Emilia and William out of the living room. I just managed to close the door behind them, but, seconds later, Bang Bang on the door. Emilia and William smashed their fists against it and came back into the living room, closely followed by Eve and Lacy.

Colin's temper erupted and he started screaming at us all. He stormed into the kitchen and pulled a knife out of the drawer. It wasn't any old knife; it was a twelve-inch kitchen knife. Nikki dashed for the door dragging Emilia and William with her, Eve and Lacy were just behind them. Colin ran for the door too, but I managed to get in front of him and stood with my back against the door. I wasn't sure what I was thinking; I was now stuck in a flat with a guy I hardly knew freaking out on hard drugs and with a knife in his hand. I was relatively sober; I'd had my cocktail mix and a few shots, but that was it. I hadn't participated in the drugs like everyone else.

Colin kept trying to get out of the flat, saying, 'I'm going to kill them both!' meaning Emilia and

William. He ran out onto the balcony. I wasn't sure what he was thinking –*maybe he somehow thought he could climb down to get them?* I wasn't sure what my plan was, but I thought if I could get him to stop freaking out then he would calm down enough to put the knife away. I was on my own with someone I had met a handful of times, who was in a drug-fuelled rage and holding a massive knife. I knew he wasn't gunning for me, but I also knew that could change at any minute; after all, drugs and knives can be a deadly combination.

I kept trying to talk to him to calm him down. 'Colin, this is stupid, they aren't worth you getting into trouble. They're just silly people, they'll be miles away now so just put the knife down and we can go and find Nikki.'

He wasn't listening, he just kept trying to get past me. I'm not sure what came over me to think I was able to take him on. Colin was now pacing up and down the balcony, muttering under his breath. I felt that if he was going to attack me then he would have done it by now, but by no means did I feel safe. Each time he tried to pass me, I stood in front of him and said, 'No, you're too good a person to do this.' That was utter bollocks; he was an asshole, but I did feel he had serious psychological problems and that it wasn't just the drugs that was driving this erratic behaviour. This went on for some thirty minutes, but I can tell you it felt like a lot longer than that. Colin then pulled his phone from his pocket and started dialling. I hoped it was someone who would calm him down. Then I heard him say, 'You need to help me, I'm being held against my will by a woman I don't know, I'm trying to get out to kill someone.'

I wasn't sure who he called, but the person on the phone asked to talk to me and he passed me the phone. I couldn't fucking believe it; he had actually called the police on himself! I said, 'He's just really wasted and confused, don't listen to him.' I'm guessing in his messed-up head he thought they were going to tell me to move. The call handler asked me for the address, but I said, 'I'm sorry, I don't know the address.'

Then Colin came over, grabbed the phone, and told them. I was so worried about the police coming; the apartment was full of all sorts, including flyers offering sexual services.

Out of everything that had happened this was the first moment that I truly felt scared. The police were on their way, I couldn't believe it! I needed to get inside; the house looked like it was a brothel. I didn't get time to dwell on anything thing else, the door was bashed down and riot police with guns and shields filled the apartment. I was grabbed and pulled away from Colin while four officers managed to disarm him and got him to the ground. He kept screaming, 'No, you were meant to help me get them!'

He was clearly completely away with the fairies if he actually thought the police were going to help him leave the house with a knife. They kept Colin in a bedroom, and I was taken into the kitchen. I couldn't believe it; in the same year I'd had the police interview me twice.

Just when I thought things couldn't get any worse, I heard Emilia's voice. I couldn't believe it; she was being interviewed. I was in disbelief that she hadn't left the building; all while secretly hoping Nikki would be there as well, but I had a feeling she had made a run for it. I knew Emilia was only going to cause more trouble. I asked if I could go to my room to get my phone so I could call Olivia (Nikki) as she lived in the house with Colin, while in the room I quickly hid the condoms and business cards; I was worried the place looked like a brothel.

As I walked through the apartment Emilia saw me and started shouting 'Felicity, Felicity are you ok?', by this point I had told the officers my real name. So, I just shook my head and said 'who's that? I don't know a Felicity'.

I tried to catch what Emilia was saying, I couldn't believe what I was hearing: 'We were taking MDMA, and I don't know what happened... we are all really wasted...it was no one's fault...it was a staff night out and then people were arguing...he is my boss, they both are, Colin and Nikki. I don't want to get into trouble with him...can I go see him? Can you get Felicity, please tell me she is ok?'

I couldn't believe the things I had just heard Emilia say, she must have been hanging around in the corridor this whole time. I'm guessing everyone on MDMA had now reached the peak of the drugs full effect as Colin was in some state and hearing what Emilia was saying she too must have been just as wasted as Colin. It was concerning me that Emilia was telling the police that I was called Felicity and that we were at a staff party. I knew I had to be honest with the police as to who I was especially since they wanted to see ID. As much as I didn't want a record of this, I couldn't pretend to be someone else after all my ID plainly says my name is Jane.

Thankfully, as I was the only one clearly not on drugs, and also the only one who could give photo ID to reassure who I was the police seemed to listen to me. I heard them say that they were going to take Colin to the hospital first; it was obvious that he was on a cocktail of drugs and delusional. I guess it would be required for him to be deemed medically OK before being put into a cell. It was just as obvious that Emilia had a cocktail of drugs in her system too; she was told that if she didn't leave, she would be taken down the station as well, so off she went. Colin had said he didn't know who I was to the police, so they weren't letting me stay in the apartment. To make it worse, they weren't letting me take my bag of things either, they said that they weren't able to verify if they belonged to me and that Colin was adamant that we had never met before.

I was petrified; I was stuck in a city I don't really know, dressed to the nines, too far over the drink-drive limit to drive and no idea where I was going to stay. Thankfully, I had my wallet in my hand which had my car key in it, but my house keys were in my bag in the other room. Just as I was being escorted to the lift by the police officers, Nikki came out of the lift. I was so relieved. She immediately wrapped her arms round me. I was so thankful that she had come back; it was just at the right time. The police officer said, 'We can't let you stay here; you need to leave!'

Nikki turned and said to them, 'This is my apartment, and she is my friend. We'll be going back in.'

'You must be Olivia?'

She nodded, then grabbed me by the hand and led me to the door of the apartment, took out her key and let us in. Two officers followed and said they had to speak to her about what had happened. Olivia asked them to come into the apartment and they followed her thorough to the kitchen area. I had tidied up a bit when I was trying to stall the police while waiting on her to come back, so it wasn't a total mess. I went back to tidying up and Olivia went on to say, 'This happens all the time. Colin has a drug problem, and he gets undesirable people to come round and then this happens. I hate it, I'm terrified of him when he is like this. He's not nice to be around when this happens so I leave. I didn't go far; I was just across the street. I wanted to wait till Colin left before I came home as he frightens me when he's like that. I only know this woman.' She turned and pointed at me. 'The others that were here are nothing to do with me, they came round with him.'

Nikki then went on to say, 'How long will he be away for? Do I have enough time to move out? I can't keep doing this; every time he's left alone, he takes lots of drugs and brings strangers back to the apartment. If it wasn't for my friend being here it would have been even more frightening.'

I have to say, I liked Nikki's style. She hadn't said my name as such; perhaps as she didn't know if I had said my name or my work name to the police, and also, she had said the same as me – that she didn't know who the others were, so that at least made us look like we were telling the truth, having the same story. After nearly an hour the police left. I was glad Colin wasn't coming back tonight.

I told Nikki about what happened and also that I was scared as Emilia had told the police our working names rather than our real names and had told them that Nikki and Colin were her bosses. I didn't have a clue if the police had spoken to William, Eve and Lacy, but I was very unsettled with the night's events, considering the situation.

Nikki and I were sitting looking at each other in silence, shock and disbelief over the events that had unfolded over the course of the evening. All I wanted to do was go home and forget the whole thing as quickly as I could. But I knew I could not leave her alone. Nikki seemed surprising calm considering what had just happened. My beathing was finally slowing down and when I held my hand out it was no longer trembling.

'Are you ok?' I asked Nikki,

'Yes, this happens possibly once a month, he just takes too many drugs, he's nice when he's sober'.

I didn't believe that he was nice when he was sober, I have spent too much time around men like Colin, I saw right through him. We cleaned the flat up a bit more, drank tea and talked. I persuaded Nikki to take down her website for a bit. She didn't want to, and I understood she had put a lot of time, money, and effort into it, but after tonight's events I did not want to take any chances. Emilia had said all our working names and I didn't like the fact that the website showed pictures of us along with our working names. Also, Colin didn't appear to be very dependable, so who knows what he will say. Once the website was down, the flat straightened out, and all evidence relating to what we had been doing destroyed, we could relax slightly. We moved a mattress into the living room and set up camp in front of the TV. I was still petrified; and couldn't help but think, *what if all this got into the public domain?*

Given the night we'd had, neither of us could sleep, so we sat watching a movie and talked. It was the first time Nikki and I had spoken properly; it was nice to be able to get to know her. She told me she had taken a year out from her studies, that she was from Canada and that she was meant to stop seeing guys herself and just run the agency once it was established, but that she loved doing her job. So, she kept seeing clients and that angered Colin. She broke down into floods of tears and begged me to stay the whole weekend. To be honest, I just wanted to go home and forget the whole thing, but I couldn't leave her. After all, I knew what she felt like. I said I wasn't happy being in the flat in case Colin or anyone else returned, so I suggested my best friend came down. I hadn't told Lucas that I was a call girl, I was petrified too, I knew the lecture I was going to get from him, but I trusted him with my life, and it seemed the only option. I sat for an hour not knowing what to say, if I was doing the right thing, wondering if I should just leave, but looking at Nikki crying and shaking, I knew I couldn't leave her. I didn't even know her – I had met her a handful of times – but she was at rock bottom, and I felt bad for her, so knew I had to take her with me. Once I'd plucked up enough courage to text Lucas, I wrote:

Hey hun, how are you? Got a massive favour to ask, totally random I know, but can you please get a train to Glasgow and come and get me and my car. Long story will explain when I see you.

He replied straightaway saying yes, but that he would drive down. I told him I had my car here and was in no fit state to drive. I would perhaps have been under the legal limit by now, but I wasn't taking any chances and I was still shaking like a leaf. The thought of driving was not one I wanted to consider.

Nearly four hours later, he texted to say he was just getting off the train. He walked in, sat down and, straightaway, asked, 'How are you?'

I was so happy to see him, he always made me feel so safe. I smiled at him and then just burst into tears. Why is it when you feel like you are on the verge of a meltdown all it takes are those three little words to set you off: how are you? Nikki excused herself to give me space to explain to Lucas what was going on. I didn't know where to start, and, for the life of me, I could not stop crying. I told him about the events of last night; he was reassuring, but I could tell he was also confused.

He said, 'Yes, I get all of that, but why are you here? How do you know these people?'

I started crying again, smoking fag after fag, and after about ten minutes I confessed that I had become a call girl; about a month or so ago. He said he thought something like that was going on. I was now completely petrified; if he had an inkling, who else did?

He reassured me that he did not think anyone else would know, and he only thought this because in the last month I wasn't going out socially, wouldn't commit to any planned events, but the main reason for him was that my nails were now constantly painted, and I wore heaps of make-up which I never did before. I could not believe I had told someone my deepest, darkest secret. I felt sick to the stomach; not only had I admitted what I had become, but worst of all, he had already thought it!

Nikki came in and handed me a coffee. We agreed it would be safer at my home rather than Glasgow. Nikki wanted to come, and Lucas agreed this would be a good idea, so bags were packed and off we went to safety.

7. Two in the bed

TWO CALL GIRLS, ONE MAN and two beds. It was now Monday, and after two nights of Nikki and I staying in Lucas's spare room together, we were feeling better. I had called in sick to work; I didn't feel comfortable leaving someone I hardly knew in my friend's house alone. Lucas had gone to work early so Nikki and I had the place to ourselves and had a rather relaxing morning; we had a lovely breakfast and went on a long walk together to try to think of a plan.

The plan we came up with was to take Nikki back to Glasgow, but that soon turned into a nightmare. Just as we were showered, sorted and ready to go, Colin called saying that he was just out of court, and that he and Nikki were over. She was to get her belongings out of their flat that evening. This was a bit of a shock. Colin was very clearly distressed and to me appeared to have serious psychological problems which I assumed were most likely from years of drug abuse. Again, Nikki broke down. She did not know anyone in the UK or have anywhere to go. Nikki had confided in me that she had no money, so was unable to get a ticket home. Colin was pleasing on the eyes, however he was a bully, he always took any money from her, so it would make Nikki completely dependent on him. To me, having seen Colin and the way their relationship was, I felt that Colin had somehow talked Nikki into doing this so that he was able to fund his drug habit.

I knew what it was like to live with someone abusive and I wouldn't wish that on my worst enemy, so I told her I would take her down for her things and that she could stay with me until she felt better and had time to get herself together. *What else could I do?* I won't say that it was the most-thought-out decision I've ever made in my life.

Back to Glasgow we went. I asked Lucas to come home from work so he could come with us as Colin was a large male who was clearly incredibly angry and, in my opinion, not very mentally stable. We drove down in silence. It was hard to sustain a conversation; I was too busy wondering why I had just offered my spare room to a stranger for much of the journey. Lucas, Nikki, and I arrived at the flat in Glasgow. Colin and his mother were waiting outside the building; I was glad Lucas had come with us. I waited in the car with him; I'd had enough conflict to last me a lifetime. Nikki was in and out in a flash. Fortunately, we'd come in Lucas's jeep; it was filled to the brim. I could not understand how someone travelling had managed to accumulate so much stuff!

Nikki wasn't in a good way – her world had just fallen apart – and the drive home was just as quiet as the journey there. We arrived at my house, and I was scared, my head a mess. *What was I thinking? How was I going to explain this to my friends?* We unpacked the car and said our goodbyes to Lucas, then headed to the shop for basic supplies to see us through a few days. That night was strange. I was trying hard to come to terms with what had happened over the last three days of my life. I am the type of person who enjoys my own company; I am by nature an introvert. I'd burst the bubble of my quiet life at home and now have someone living with me. I live in a three-bedroom house, but one of the bedrooms was filled with boxes of stuff from redecorating and the bed was under a vast number of boxes with the mattress hard up against the wall. There were also two clothes horses covered in washing in it, so more a laundry than a bedroom. The other spare room was halfway through being made into a dressing room, so I only had one usable bedroom and one bed. It was late and we were shattered, so it was two in a bed again.

A loud noise woke me, followed by silence. I sat up looking around, I wasn't sure if I had heard something or if it was a dream. Either way I woke to find myself alone in bed. I instantly thought: *Amazing! It was just a dream. Phew!* I got up to go and shower, then heard Nikki shout through that breakfast was ready. Bugger, it was real after all. She really was living with me! When I walked through to the kitchen, I couldn't believe my eyes. The breakfast she'd prepared was five star and I didn't even remember getting enough things for her to make all of this. After a lush breakfast we went for a long walk so I could show her round the town that I lived in, as I was back to work the following day. Going round the town didn't take long; it wasn't very big, but we had all the essential shops and more. Nikki turned to me 'Oh wow look at the streets, it's like a fairy tale'.

I'm guessing Canada must not have cobbled streets.

I quickly realised that Nikki was both an amazing cook and a fitness freak like me; she loved going for walks and runs. We ate the same things and we liked most of the same things on TV. Phew. After showing her round the town and getting her settled in, we started to go through the spare room and got the boxes in the loft to uncover the bed. Once we had got the room looking respectable and made up the bed with Egyptian cotton sheets, I called it a night and went to bed as I was up early for work.

Wednesday came and it was back to reality. Off to work I went. The drive there was horrid, it was the first time I had been alone and had time to think. I was still coming to terms with what had happened and, to be honest, it was complete madness. Once at work all I got were questions as to why I had been off work and was everything OK? Everyone could see I wasn't myself. My first break came, and I texted Nikki to see how she was, secretly hoping that her and Colin had worked things out and that she would be leaving. The reality was quite the opposite: she said she was OK, but Colin wanted nothing to do with her. I couldn't even bring myself to reply; I

Felicity Forbes

was devastated. Work was slow that afternoon and that made things worse; *how long would she be there? What if my friends came around, what would I say? Or, worse still, what would she say? What if my parents came round?* I still could not believe all this had happened. The only things I could think of to do were to either get Nikki a B&B or book her a ticket home. I convinced myself to be strong, and to go home and discuss those options with her. I drove home, reciting what I was going to say. But when I got in, I was shocked to find my house gleaming and a delicious three-course healthy dinner waiting for me. After dinner we spent the night in face masks, did our nails and it was so lovely I could not bring myself to discuss the options of where she was to go. I was a huge softie; that was what had got me into this in the first place.

A week had passed since the incident, a week of me looking after her and, I'm going to be honest, I loved having Nikki stay. We had great fun, ate lovely food and she didn't annoy me one bit. In fact, I wasn't bothered about her staying with me anymore; we got on really well and I enjoyed having her in my home.

When I got up on Saturday morning, I went through to the living room in my dressing gown and, before I could even ask how she was, Nikki said, 'I have been working on something. Come and sit down so I can show you.'

I wasn't sure what it could be and, to be honest, I am horrendous in the morning, I can't function till I have had my morning coffee, so I was a bit shocked when she showed me a website. I was half asleep and the last thing on my mind was escorting, so I said, 'No way, not a chance. I have no intention of going through all that hassle and stress again.'

Nikki quickly replied, 'I promise it'll be different we can download apps on our phones so we can use different numbers; you can deal with your clients' requests, and I can deal with mine and we'd have each other to look out for.'

I stood shaking my head, 'Let me have a coffee, I can't even comprehend this at this time of the morning.'

She waited till I came back through, holding my mug. I sat sipping away on my coffee, still in shock that she was even contemplating doing this again so soon.

I said, 'Right, I've got my coffee. Now, what else did you want to tell me?'

Nikki looked like a child that had just got into trouble. Curled up in the corner of my huge sofa, she sheepishly said, 'Well, I have already arranged two bookings for me this evening and one for you.'

I sat in silence, staring at her from across the room.

'My bookings are both one hour and your booking is for two hours.'

I sat there for a long time, thinking it over and over, and I could not see how it would be any different. After a lengthy discussion, she persuaded me to give it one more try. I said I would talk to her about it after I'd had a shower to wake myself up. I needed to think it through, and I couldn't do that while I was half asleep. When I got out the shower, Nikki had made breakfast and it was delicious. We ate, then went for a long walk to discuss what she had planned for us. When we returned, we had a wee nap before getting ready for our trip into Aberdeen. I have to say it was more entertaining having someone there to get ready with; we had a wee fashion show to sort out what we were both wearing. Nikki was a lot more confident than me, and more experienced at getting ready. She did her hair and make-up in record time, but she was more of a girly girl than me. Driving there was fun; we were able to talk about what we were about to do, not keep it a secret as usual. Nikki had her booking before mine, so I dropped her to where she needed to be, then I headed across town to my booking. Nikki was going to a client's house for an hour and had given herself thirty minutes to get to her second booking in the centre of Aberdeen for her next client. I personally would not even contemplate seeing more than one client in a day, but then I was doing it for fun, and she was doing it for the money. Especially now.

My client was a guy in his forties; he'd been out with friends for lunch and wanted to relax afterwards. I had spoken to him on the phone, and he seemed nice, so I wasn't nervous. I was quite looking forward to it and secretly hoped that he would be good in bed. I really wanted to have some naughty fun.

I got to the hotel and, as I was parking the car, I had a horrid thought about what if I was asked what I was doing at the hotel. I know that the hotels in Aberdeen can be strict on visitors, so I had a little panic then decided that I would pretend I was on the phone. This meant the people on Reception wouldn't try to talk to me. It worked a treat. When I got in the lift, I was the only one in there, so it was the perfect moment to whip my flats off and heels on, then a quick touch up of my make-up; that was the most important part, I had to look my best. I was out of the lift and at the door in seconds. Two knocks and the door opened straightaway. Much to my surprise, there was a very handsome gentleman, clean-shaven, suited and booted, standing in the doorway. He introduced himself as Richard. Richard invited me in and took my coat; there was a bottle of champagne chilling on the table, with roses and chocolates. It was so lovely, and so was he. I could tell he was nervous as he did not know where to look or what to say; I intuitively knew this would be a good booking. I excused myself to check my envelope and there was £480 inside. I didn't know what the right amount was, I completely forgot to ask Nikki, so I quickly texted her to check she was OK, and to ask how much she had said. Nikki replied she was fine, and it was to be £440. I wasn't going to say it was too much; after all, Richard put it in the envelope so he must be happy with what he had given me.

Tartan Temptress

Thirty minutes had passed and not much in the way of conversation had taken place; Richard was so nervous and very apologetic. I reassured him it was fine, and he began to speak. He explained that his wife had left him a few years ago, and that he hadn't been able to have another female in his life, hence why he was doing this. After an hour had passed, he started to relax and then asked if he could take my dress off. I could already see a bulge in his trousers, so I immediately knew this would be quick. He gently pulled my dress up and over my hips, then slowly lifted it over my head. I now stood there in my heels, my lacy black underwear, suspenders, and stockings. He let out a groan and we made our way over to the bed, where he asked me to lie down. He lay down beside me, lightly tickling my skin with his fingertips. I'm not going to lie, it felt amazing. This went on for some time, then he started kissing my neck, slowly moving down my body. Then he asked me to sit up so he could unclip my bra. Cupping my breasts, he started licking my nipples, always asking if it was OK. I always replied with a 'yes, amazing', but this time I wasn't acting, it was...

Richard stood up and undressed. He looked so nervous, I had to try so hard not to laugh. I know this sounds bad, but it really made me giggle that a grown man was intimidated by me. I took out a condom and pulled it over his medium-sized penis, then he moved in between my legs. My pussy had been wet from the moment I walked in the room. He slowly pushed his cock inside me; he was still so nervous and hesitant, so I pushed down onto him so that the whole of his penis was inside of me. He instantly moaned and, at that point, much to my disappointment, I knew this was going to be over in minutes. I would say he managed to get about ten thrusts into me, then it was all over. Immediately he apologised and jumped off the bed, looking rather embarrassed. He quickly disappeared into the bathroom. I got up, composed myself, and, just as I was away to check my phone, he appeared from the bathroom, quickly dashing for his clothes. Richard came over to me, kissed me on the cheek and said, 'I'm exhausted, do you mind if you leave early?'

I was a bit disappointed; he was extremely attractive and, to be honest, I wanted to jump on top of him and have sex again and again, but that wouldn't be very professional, 'No not at all, I'll just gathered my things and head off'. I excused myself to the bathroom. I had a massive grin on my face; I

Tartan Temptress

had just made a week's wages in less than two hours and had had a great time. I gave myself a shake; I could not go out the door grinning like this. We said our goodbyes and off I went.

Walking along that hotel corridor, the feeling I had was amazing. I felt unstoppable, confident, and sexy. I was in charge and the way I dressed made it easy. I had turned into a beautiful, confident female that was able to take charge and was listened to. It was hard to imagine that I used to be a quivering mess that had no control over her daily life, who would be told what to wear, what to do, and when to do it. I waited at the lift for ages. When the door opened all, I could see in the mirrors was my glowing face, a huge grin, and my cute dimples. Heels off, flats on, phone out and at my ear so I could go straight past reception. I wasn't fazed in the slightest; I walked tall, with my head held high.

I went back to the car to wait for Nikki. She wouldn't be that long, but time had ceased to be relevant. I had just done normal things, with a normal guy, for one and a half hours and made £480; I could not believe it. After I composed myself, I started to drive round to where I was to meet Nikki. I didn't have to wait long till I saw Nikki, almost jogging towards the car. She didn't look best pleased; she had a similar expression to when I got back to Emilia's after my round two fiasco. As soon as she sat down, we set off home straight away.

Nikki had not said a word, but, as soon as we got out of Aberdeen, she immediately declared, 'I need the shower first. Please let me go in first.'

I turned to look at her, 'What's wrong?' I asked.

She looked at me, horrified, and said, 'My first client was lovely, but the second one stuck his finger right up my ass, then after started to squeeze my boobs.'

Anal was a touchy subject for us both. I have tried it on several occasions, all of which didn't work out. It was far too painful, and I had to stop. Anal is something that you need to be relaxed for and, well, I have IBS (irritable bowel syndrome) so the words 'being relaxed' and 'ass', don't really go together. I could now understand why she wasn't in a talkative mood. We got home, showered, put our clothes on an awfully long wash and put our feet up. I must admit, as much as I was against this idea at the start, I very much enjoyed myself this evening and hoped to have many more days like this to come.

8. Going Solo

DID YOU KNOW THAT IN Scotland the act of engaging in a sexual service for money is legal? But being a pimp, madam or brothel owner is committing a crime. Now that I am 'going solo', I felt a lot more comfortable than I did when I was working under Nikki and Colin. After some thought, I had decided that I was going to take this more seriously, so I decided to get a phone that was solely for Felicity. Nikki thought it was best that I split my dual life so that when I was just little old plain Jane, I didn't get interrupted and slip away into the fairy tale life of Felicity.

Nikki taught me so much, not only how to be an exceptional call girl, but she also taught me how to love myself again, she could make me laugh so loud it woke the street. What this woman has done to me in these short few months is something that money can't buy; I will forever be in debt to this woman. Applying for that job months ago saved me. I was unhappy in myself throughout my time with Keith and if I'm honest it didn't get much better after the night in question. I started to get hate messages through social media for calling the police on him that night. All those jack-asses that thought butter wouldn't melt in his mouth. It's easy to say, don't listen to them! But it's not so easy to abide by the saying. I thought that things would have gotten easier when Keith changed his plea to guilty, but all that did was fuel people's anger more, it was mostly his friends but the whole town was talking about it for months to come. I was called every name you could think of, and it wore me down. Even when he was convicted of domestic abuse, it didn't stop. I deleted or logged out of my social media accounts then I hid in my house, I didn't want to see people's nasty comments, read their horrid messages, or hear people's whispers, I stopped living and was just existing.

My life now, I couldn't be happier, my life is full of joy, the house is alive with Nikki's infectious laughter, the positive energy that comes of that woman is what makes me able to tell this story today. She taught me to only focus my energy on good things, she reminded me that we get back from life what we put in.

My Monday to Thursday were relatively normal this week, well, as normal as it could be with Nikki living with me. I usually had my boxing class on a Tuesday, but I hadn't been since Nikki moved in. Yoga is a Thursday and Nikki had come along to every session. Emma had got rather serious with her new boyfriend these last few weeks, so she hadn't been coming on walks or going to the gym, which was actually good timing as Nikki had moved in.

I had gotten quite fond of Nikki living with me, so you can imagine the sadness I felt when I got a message from Nikki at lunch on Friday saying,

Hey, little lady. I've got good news. Colin and I are getting back together, and we have an apartment in Aberdeen, so you'll get your house back.

I had no idea why she thought it was good news; I had seen first-hand what Colin was like, and people like that never change. It's not like I was able to say no, I'm not letting you go, but at the same time I was going to try my bloody hardest to get her to change her mind and stay with me.

I replied, *I think we need to talk about this when I am home.*

Felicity Forbes

It would be nice to get my house back to myself. I was never one for having someone living with me, hence the fact I was making my other bedroom into a dressing room and the other one was full of boxes. But I'd rather Nikki was with me and safe than away with Colin and unhappy. I wasn't sure what had sparked the idea, but, in the back of my mind, I felt like Colin had run out of money and needed to pimp her out to make him money to fund his drug addiction.

I returned home and, to my surprise, all of Nikki's things were already packed; she had been in contact with Colin most of the week and clearly not wanted to say. She told me Colin was going to pick her up at 8pm, but I was not comfortable with him coming here and knowing where I lived, so I said I would take her into Aberdeen instead so I could see where she was going to be staying, then if she ever needed anything I knew where to find her.

Once I had dropped her off, I went home. It was strange watching TV all on my own. Just as I was about to go to bed, I received an email regarding a booking in Aberdeen for the following day. The message was professionally written, with a hint of humour, so it immediately got my attention. His name was David and he sounded lovely. We messaged back and forth for a little over an hour before I fell asleep with my phone in my hand.

Saturday was here, and I woke feeling amazing; I had a good feeling about today. It was a beautiful day, so I went out for an early morning run. When I returned home, I had received an email from David to confirm that everything was still on for this evening and to ask if champagne was OK. I sat and had a wee think. Champagne was lovely, my favourite in fact. I had got rather accustomed to it now, but if I drank, I would have to get a hotel in town which cost between fifty to seventy pounds or have to pay around fifty pounds for a taxi home, depending on how busy town was, or not drink at all. Just as I was trying to decide what to do, Lucas popped in as he saw my car in my drive.

'Do you want to go out for a few drinks later tonight?'

'I can't, sorry. I have a booking in Aberdeen.'

It felt strange being able to tell him I was going to a booking. I don't think he approved, but he was my friend, so he supported me.

He replied, 'What if I drive you into town and pick you up, then I know you're safe and you can have a drink. Then, when I come to collect you, we could go out for a while?'

'That would be perfect, thank you.'

We agreed to meet at my house later that day. I messaged David to say that champagne would be lovely and that I would see him later that evening.

With Nikki's help I had finished my dressing room, so I decided to make a Felicity section. I spent the entire day trying things on and deciding whether it was elegant enough to be in the Felicity side. Going through my wardrobe was so much fun. I wasn't one for throwing clothes away, so seeing some of my old dresses was like a trip down memory lane. How I managed to get away with wearing some of them made me laugh. Some of them, well, most of them, were so short I could see my bum, and that was not the look I was going for at all. I mean, you see the girls on other sites that have really short skirts, and photos with their fannies out, advertising a 'fuck for fifty pounds' or, worse, offering Bare Back sex for one hundred and twenty pounds. This was not what I was offering at all; I was going for the classy, elegant look, so I'd decided to dress in a more sophisticated way.

I feel the way you dress projects your mood, personality, and interests. If I look at my normal everyday clothes that I wear, they are minimalistic and mostly dark colours. I have three pairs of my favourite trousers because I love them and they are so comfortable, but they project someone that's not bothered about fashion and probably gives off a free-spirited tomboy or skater vibe. My sister will quite often joke, saying, 'I thought I saw you at the skate park last night, why didn't you wave?'

The clothes I deemed elegant enough for Felicity were my cashmere cardigans and fitted shirts and any of my skirts and dresses that stopped below or just above the knee. I decided to bag up any outfits that were too short or that showed too much skin. I didn't want to be a cheap whore, which is why I priced myself higher. The pricing also removed the undesirable element which I did not want; I wanted the upper-class businessmen who had the money to spend on quality. Now I was by myself, and knew what I wanted, I knew I could fulfil most expectations, so decided to price myself as follows:

1 hour: £260
2 hours: £480

3 hours: £580
4 hours: £680
5 hours: £800
12 hours: £2400 (overnight)

I was not bothered if I had fewer bookings, I wanted quality over quantity. To my surprise, the more I charged, the more business I got. I was shocked! The best part of doing it all myself meant that I was able to personally vet the clients; I could take the time to talk to them directly and was able to ask them questions or call them for a chat if I wanted to. I was my own boss, and it was my decision who I saw and who I didn't. I certainly didn't make a booking with everyone that messaged me.

It was now time to get ready for Lucas to pick me up. My routine for getting ready was getting better, I think having Nikki show me her routine helped a lot. After a shower I would put oil through my hair as it made it go extremely curly without having to do anything else to it, then underwear on whilst I painted my face. I was never one for make-up, but in this job it was essential. I was getting better at it; Nikki had introduced me to eyebrow pencils, and my god that did change things; framing my eyes and giving me a sexy, sultry look rather than the hooker look of smoky eyes and bright-red lipstick...!

Then, time to get into my outfit. I always had it laid out prior to showering, so on it went and that was me ready to go. Just as my dress went on and I was admiring myself in the mirror, in walked Lucas. He stood looking at me for quite some time, saying absolutely nothing.

After a few minutes, I thought it was a bit weird and asked him if he wanted a picture?

To which he replied, 'No, I'm just in shock.'

I laughed. 'Why the shock?'

He laughed too, and said, 'You! I can't believe the change in you!'

I was quite taken back. It was just me. OK, I had make-up on, nice jewellery and a dress, but it was still me. I guess it was because I am normally more of a tomboy type, and his shock was seeing me transformed into Felicity.

Eventually he sat down, and we started talking about our plans for the evening. Once organised we set off, it was funny driving to Aberdeen together. I mean, my best friend was driving me to an appointment with a client. I never could have imagined this would have happened, and nor did he. It was strange in parts; I mean, my best friend knows I am a call girl and is OK with it. We did laugh a lot on the way there. I wasn't nervous; I think I was past the nervous stage now. The main thing on my mind was what David looked like. I mean, two hours with someone you're attracted to can pass so quickly, as I found with Richard. However, two hours with someone you don't seems to go on forever.

Finally, we were almost there. When we turned down the street both Lucas and I were speechless; all the houses looked like hotels and they had very nice cars parked in the driveways. We saw Porsches, Range Rovers, Mercedes-Benz, Audi's, and Jaguars; this must be the posh bit of town. I asked Lucas to stop, and said I'd walk to the house, but he insisted I showed him which house it was. I knew he was looking out for me, but I always promise my clients discretion, and that is very important to me, so we compromised and drove past the house so he knew where I would be, but we stopped a bit further up the street so that David didn't see a car stop right outside his house.

I walked up to the front door; my timer already set. I was now feeling slightly anxious, I was away to spend two hours with a stranger. I rang the doorbell and the door opened straightaway. My first thought was what a beard. It was like Gandalf's.

'Good evening Felicity, let me take your coat and scarf.'

'Hi David, lovely to meet you', I slid my coat off my shoulders and unravelled the scarf from around my neck. 'Thank you, David.' The first interaction was always slightly awkward.

'Please follow me Felicity' as he turned to walk through the marble hall.

My heels were making such a racket while walking on the beautiful tiles I had to slip them off, 'Sorry David but do you mind if I take my shoes off, I don't want to mark your beautiful floor?'.

'Not at all Felicity, they will be coming off soon enough anyway'.

I had a little giggle at that, he had such a deep voice but looked like a huge cuddly bear.

Once in the kitchen he opened the fridge and produced a bottle of Dom Pérignon. Once the champagne was poured, we got the awkward bit out of the way; the envelope was sitting there on the breakfast bar with my name on it. Immediately he asked me to go upstairs, I thought, *oh no, straight to the sex*, but, no, we just lay on his bed talking, he explained how he was not used to this and that his wife was away. They had not been getting on which was why he had decided to call me. After a bottle of champagne and relatively boring chit-chat, he excused himself and reappeared with another bottle of champagne. I normally would have declined as drinking to excess whilst working could be dangerous, however Lucas knew exactally where I was, knew what time to expect me back, and David was clearly a lovely, gentleman. I felt nothing was going to go wrong. He had made the bedroom rather romantic (not that I am the romantic type) with soothing music and candles lit everywhere. We lay there talking some more, and to be honest, I felt like I was a counsellor. It was strange; almost like he wanted friendship, not sex. I wasn't sure what to say to some of the things he was asking my opinion on. David went on to tell me that his wife was away on a weekend with another man and that she had said to him there wasn't enough spice in the relationship, which is why he had organised me to come round to try to find his wild side. An hour passed and he asked if it was OK to take my dress off. Again, I had on some seriously sexy underwear and stockings, and it had the same effect as before; he just lay there with his mouth wide open.

I knew immediately that I was in charge and the next hour was up to me. I went over and lay beside him, he lay looking at me for a few minutes, then asked if it was OK to touch me. I obviously replied yes; after all, he had just paid £480 for the privilege. He lay there, stroking me all over, and this is where the acting side of me kicks in. I'm not much for foreplay, but I guess that's most people's turn-on, so I lay there with a smile on my face telling him how amazing it felt.

To be honest, I felt like I was being petted like I was a baby lamb, but if you smile and say it is amazing, men will believe anything! Before I started doing this, I always thought that men used call girls to get pleasure for themselves, but I had been surprised to learn that they want me to enjoy myself just as much as them, though sometimes it means me pretending just so it gives them the confidence to finish.

After a while he slowly started taking my pants off, by this time I was tipsy and extremely horny. My pants came off and he was slowly running his fingers over my clit. I'm sure his intention was that I was to enjoy it, but I'm not going to lie, it felt pretty rubbish. Still, I smiled and told him it was amazing and how good it felt. He asked if I was OK with receiving oral. I said yes and, within seconds, he was down in between my legs licking my clit like it was an ice lolly! After a few minutes it started being slightly enjoyable, but the main word here is slightly. He continued for some time, which was great for me as time was passing and I didn't have to do a thing. It was starting to feel better and then he slid a finger inside me at the same time. I was getting turned on and I could tell he was thinking the same. Just as we were both getting into it, my alarm went on my phone. David jumped up like he'd had an electric shock, 'Oh, I'm really sorry'.

I wasn't sure why he was apologising, but it was nice all the same. 'David, no need to apologies, you have nothing to worry about', I could tell he was embarrassed. We got dressed and I managed to get him smiling and laughing again in no time at all. He walked me to the door and shook my hand, which I thought was rather strange as ten minutes ago he had his head between my legs! I thanked him for a lovely evening and off I went down the path to where Lucas had dropped me off; we had both agreed that would be where we met after my appointment. Lucas was already there, I was glad to see his car as this was not the sort of neighbourhood that people hung around the street in, it was very upper class, and I would have stuck out like a sore thumb. I got in the car and burst out laughing, I could not help it. It was so easy. Lucas looked at me as if I were mad. I guess I am, to a certain degree, but it was fun, and the adrenaline rush you get is indescribable.

When I finally managed to compose myself enough, I started telling him how my night ended up and he started laughing too. We got home and parked up. I had a quick shower to freshen up and we went to the pub. I still had a huge smile on my face, and I could not wipe it off. Drinks were on me.

Why is it when you're hungover you're far more sensitive to the light? The sun was beating in through my window; obviously shutting my curtains wasn't high on my to-do list last night, which I was now regretting as the sun was so bright, I had to lie with my eyes tightly closed. I hadn't even moved yet; I was dreading it. I could feel a headache starting behind my eyes, the thumbing was so loud that it was like someone was stomping their foot next to me, I was certainly more than slightly hungover. Once up and showered, I went to check Felicity's phone; there were three messages from three different people; one was written in text slang and sounded like he had never been educated, so he was ignored, but the other two sounded great. I had now concluded that if I received a message with poor grammar, then, as a matter of course, I would not reply. I wasn't being a snob (or maybe I was but I still don't care!) about it; I just felt that if they weren't able to form a sentence properly then I wouldn't be able to suffer speaking to them for an hour. I messaged the other two gentlemen back and forth over the course of the day; both wanted to see me this evening. One wanted to see me for one hour, the other for two hours; I decided to go for the two-hour booking. Firstly, it was more time-effective and, secondly, from the way he came across in the messages I felt I would get on better with him.

I messaged the one-hour gentleman to say I could not see him tonight and he immediately replied saying he really wanted to see me; he would happily pay more just to see me tonight. I was now in a dilemma: which client do I see? I sat for a while thinking what to do and also who to see. As I sat pondering my options, the two-hour client asked to move his time to slightly later in the evening. *Fuck it*, I thought, *why not see both? Nikki managed to do it and didn't seem fazed apart from the finger up her ass, so why not give it a go?*

I never thought I would do this, but, I thought, *why not? One of them might last long enough to satisfy me.* My love of sex and orgasms was the initial reason for becoming a call girl, but the thrill of not knowing what to expect and the mystery of clients was somewhat compelling. It was like I was getting my kicks from the intriguing side too. Don't get me wrong; the money was certainly making my life easier. I had really nice things now, had bought lots of expensive shoes and my bank account hadn't been touched in months, but that wasn't the reason I kept being Felicity. I had always known I was a thrill-seeker, but I was starting to realise that the normal everyday life we are expected to lead just wasn't enough for me anymore. I thrived on adventure and stepping into the unknown; becoming Felicity was about more than sex, it was about the adventures.

As it was coming up to late afternoon; it was time to get ready! After two positive reactions from my new lingerie, I'd realised that wearing expensive, classy lingerie was worth it. My absolute favourite was a matching two-piece; a bra and waspie finished off with expensive stockings with a back seem. I loved the old-fashioned, ultra-sexy waspie, lightly boned to sculpt my slim waist, with a lace-up back accentuating my curves. This was what I loved to wear, and what transformed me into Felicity.

When I laced up my body in this lingerie, I knew how amazing my body looked and how easy it made my bookings go. I knew by this point that looking this amazing and sexy would halve the time of my physical contact with my clients, which, if they were not so pleasing on the eye, made what I was doing so much easier.

Don't get me wrong, I was really enjoying this new adventure and I loved dressing up like this. I was really enjoying having this other side to me, the naughty one. I could dress up and wear things that I wouldn't normally, and my make-up had reached a whole new level. Before, I would wear mascara, eyeliner, and a clear lip gloss, now my makeup bag contained five shades of liquid foundation, three shades powder foundation, six blush brushes, five colours of eyeliner and mascara, three shades of eyebrow pencils and twelve different lipsticks. I had watched YouTube a lot to learn how best to apply make-up, so I had come on leaps and bounds from my first few attempts. I was now able to apply make-up to get different looks. Some of the time I was able to do my make-up, so I didn't even look like me!

I guess I was starting to understand things a lot better now; it was certainly getting a lot more interesting. I'd realised that I much rather enjoyed the company of older men, its true what they say, a fine wine tastes delicious. I also found by playing hard to get, by always claiming to be busy, prospective clients would pay more money to see you that night. Also, Nikki was right. Never make the first move; they are paying for your time.

Palms sweaty and my heart racing, I found myself pacing the living room, back and forth, back and forth, *Is it too late to cancel?* I thought completely unaware of the time. I had never thought of seeing two clients in one day before, I'm not sure what changed my opinion, but one was at 18:00 and he was booked for one hour, and the other was at 21:00 and he was booked for two hours. I figured that I would have time to come home, shower and change between bookings, so it would all work out fine. Well, that's what I told myself, over and over again, but it wasn't fine, I felt so nauseas. I couldn't seem to shift the uneasy feeling in my tummy, I was twice as nervous as I felt on my first call.

I set off to see my first client; he'd sounded down to earth and just wanted a normal GFE, so it sounded easy enough. I got to the hotel in the centre of Aberdeen, parked my car and sat for a moment before gathering my things; quick touch up of make-up, a spritz of perfume and a swig of mouthwash, then I was ready to go. Just as I was going into the hotel foyer, I held my phone to my ear. It was so simple, but it made sure I wasn't approached. Into the lift without even having to make eye contact and heels on, this was the last step to transition into Felicity.

I got to the door and did my usual knock, knock, knock and the door opened instantly as if he had been stood behind it.

First impressions; short, not the best-looking man in the world, clean-shaven, smelt nice and was well-dressed, which, in my opinion, is a good sign. I walked into the room, and he introduced himself as Christopher, but I was to call him Chris, then he took my coat. He was incredibly nervous and would not make eye contact; that immediately said to me that he wasn't used to doing this and was way out of his comfort zone. We sat down, and he passed me a can of Coke. He asked how my day had been whilst staring at my shoes.

I could not believe how nervous he was; it was like he was actually scared of me. I tried to break the ice, but it was proving to be rather challenging. Chris then said, 'You have to go to the bathroom.'

I thought this was a rather strange request, but once in there, I realised why. There was my payment in an envelope. I counted it and there was far too much; I could not believe it. I returned to the room and said, 'Why so much? I'm sorry but I'm not able to stay longer than our agreed time.'

He replied while still staring at the floor, 'The extra is for you rearranging your day so that I was able to see you. The money isn't important, the discretion was, and I'm happy to pay.'

I sat down next to him again and managed a quick glimpse at the time; it was already thirty minutes in, and we'd barely had a conversation. I couldn't believe it.

He finally started talking.

'So, how did you get into this, and how long have you been doing it for?'

This was always a bit of an awkward question. I mean, what am I meant to say? I replied, 'I'm new to it. I enjoy company so I thought I'd give it a try.'

I *was* new to it, but I wasn't going to tell him that I love sex but under no circumstance trust men so doing this meant I was able to get sex without having to put up with the male bullshit that goes with it.

After a while he started to relax, he went on to say, 'I've never done this before. It took me two weeks to pluck up the courage to message you.'

I started getting slightly concerned, *was he a nutcase? A stalker?* But he went on to explain: 'My wife is not well, and she said I should have a paid-for sexual experience. Then he kind of muttered under his breath, 'It was my wife who picked you.'

This instantly made me feel weird. I asked, 'Why the urgency to see me tonight?'

'I was meant to have arranged meeting you weeks ago but never did, so when today came, my wife insisted it would happen today.'

I was now mortified. I mean, this guy didn't want to be here at all, and his wife had picked me... We talked until my timer went, and Chris immediately jumped up.

I left the envelope on the table and made my way to the door, but he followed me, putting the envelope into my hand, and insisting I take it. He said that his wife wouldn't believe he had done it if he went home with the money. Before I was able to say anything else, Chris asked, if it wasn't too weird, would I see him again next month? That was swiftly followed by goodbye. Before I even had a chance to respond, he'd shut the door behind me. I left and felt very strange. I could not help feeling sad for Chris and his wife. He clearly was a one-woman man, but, since his wife was so sick, she couldn't have sex, she'd ordered me!

I ended up going to see Nikki as I did not need to go home to freshen up. I thought it would be good to see how she was, and it would be great to talk to someone about what just happened. When I explained the situation to Nikki, she said, 'I get that it's weird, but if his wife wants to do this and she picked you for her husband, it's only right that you go along with her wishes. She's the one paying you.'

'I get what you're saying, but it felt strange. He wants to meet again, should I go?'

'You have to go. Don't let them have to go through the hassle of finding someone else, it's the last thing they need on their plate. And if you know he doesn't want anything to happen physically, take a board game and have a laugh for the hour?'

Nikki was right. I was so glad I came to see her; she always had an answer for everything. 'Thank you, you always seem to make every situation better. Got to go. Miss you. Glad you're doing OK.'

My next booking was at the client's house and was for two hours. Nikki had said I could stay at hers that evening, but I didn't trust Colin – not surprisingly – so I'd said thanks, but no thanks.

I drove into an area of Aberdeen where the houses are as big as hotels and all the cars in the driveways were awfully expensive, similar to David's. I drove past the house I was going to, took a left and parked up. I had decided it was best to park my car out of sight and pointing in the right direction for home in case I had to make a swift exit. I touched up my make-up, put on my new Moda in Pelle shoes and off I went.

I rang the bell; the wait was always the time to think; *who was going to be behind the door? What will they look like: normal or strange; muscular or flabby;*

hairy or clean-shaven, old or young? After a few moments, the door opened.

This time I was surprised but tried my best not to show it. The gentleman was petite, about five three, and was wearing a suit, snakeskin pointed shoes and his look was finished with a bow tie.

'Good evening, Felicity, my name is Florence, I've been expecting you.'

Not only did he look feminine, but he also sounded it too. I would have said that he was in his fifties and had obviously done very well for himself; the house was incredible. Unsure of where to look for trying not to laugh 'Hi Florence, I've been looking forward to meeting you'.

'Please follow me into the living room to begin'.

I followed on behind him, my heels meant that I was taller than him, so I was looking over the back of his head as I followed him into the house.

As I entered the house I rolled my eyes, what's with these fancy houses and the bloody marble floors, every step I took on the marble floor echoed down the large entrance hall. He led me down the hall into a massive sitting room, the ceilings were extremely high, and the cornicing was spectacular.

Florence paused for a moment then moved over to the table and picked up a glass of champagne then turned to pass me the glass. He stood for a moment just looking at me before he picked up a glass for himself. Before we were able to take a sip, he insisted on giving me a tour of his house whilst asking a shit ton of questions. His house was like it was out of a magazine; nothing was out of place, and you could tell everything was extremely expensive. We walked into an elegant bespoke kitchen. Off the large kitchen was a dining room that could easily seat twelve dinner guests. This opened onto another sitting area with a large hallway where there were two doors. This was two bedrooms which were both finished to such a high standard; the fabric was luxurious, and the en-suites were larger than my living room. Both had freestanding baths with the most beautiful tiles. Both bedrooms also had dressing rooms, and they put mine to shame; they were spectacular. We didn't venture upstairs, but I secretly wanted to as I knew it would be so beautiful. I really wanted to ask him what he did as a job to be able to afford somewhere to live like this, but it wouldn't be professional for me to ask the question even though he asked me many.

Florence went on to tell me that he see's girls to have fun and that he had been married several times and been divorced for years; he had always worked away from home which led him to have countless affairs that got him into trouble, so the marriages always ended. He now felt too old to go out to bars to meet girls, so he used call girls to have fun.

So far it was an easy booking as all he did was talk about himself. It was great for me; I'd ask him a question and off he'd go, talking for ages. An hour had passed and a quite easy one at that. As we went through to one of his many sitting rooms, he sat down beside me, still chatting non-stop, and suddenly declared, 'Oh gosh, look at the time.' Then he started undressing, folding his clothes as he took them off and carefully laying them on the coffee table. When he was down to his pants, he turned round, and my heart stopped. The size of the bulge in his pants was by far the largest I had ever seen. I must have had a shocked look on my face as he looked at me and asked if I was OK. He took my hand and asked me to follow him through to the bedroom. Just as we got through the door, he spun me round and slid my dress over my head and then lay me down on the bed. He started kissing my hand, slowly moving up my arm to my neck, then, like a little ninja he was on top of me, moving down the bed still kissing my body all the way down, until he was licking around my clit while letting out what I can only describe as a high-pitched growl! He was obviously enjoying himself. I had to slide a pillow over my face as I wanted to laugh. It was so unprofessional of me, but it was also ridiculously hard to keep a straight face with the noises he was making. I had never experienced noises like this in the bedroom before. He then jumped up and asked if I was ready. I passed him a condom and watched him slide it over his humungous cock. Once on, he climbed into missionary and thrust his huge penis towards me, the first thrust he got the inside of my thigh, the second was somewhat to close to my ass for comfort, the third, well it was certainly in the right direction, it took a few more thrusts before he managed to force his way inside me; it was very painful, but I assumed it would ease the longer it went on.

I was wrong. Each thrust hurt more than the last, I grasped the bed sheets in my hands, holding so tightly that I felt my nails break the skin on my palm. He stopped for a moment; I quickly got my breath back as he wriggled his body on to his knees. As he sat up straight, he put his hands on my hips, I knew what was coming next and it is usually a position that I am very fond of, but old Florence here has a larger-than-life sized penis and, on this occasion, I couldn't have thought of a worst position to of been in. He was thrusting into me, all while pulling me back onto him. I was still in pain and didn't know how long I could go on for. Fortunately, Florence then started letting out even stranger noises, extremely high pitched, then he collapsed on top of me. I managed to wriggle out from underneath him, so his penis came out. My vagina was sore, the kind of sore that I wanted to hold it to make it feel better; like if you cut your finger or knee, you just want to squeeze it tight to make the pain stop. I cupped my hand over my pubic bone to try to stop it from hurting, and it was so wet, too wet for my liking, as I had not enjoyed any part of that at all. I looked at my hand and it was covered in blood; I hadn't put any lube on as we were talking so much, and it all happened so quickly. I quickly went through to the toilet and cleaned myself up, then returned to the bedroom. He asked if I was OK, quickly followed by:

'That always happens.'

'What always happens?' I asked.

'The bleeding. I'm sorry, it's so big it always happens.'

I quickly gathered my things and left.

Within minutes I was in my car heading home. The drive home was always time for me to get back to reality and get any last thoughts of the day out of my head, so I did not take them home. This was something Nikki taught me. This time, however, it did not seem to work. I was terrified. I knew he'd worn a condom, but I was still petrified. I was in the shower for over an hour; I knew it wouldn't make a STD go away, no matter how much I washed. It was more for my piece of mind; each time I rinsed off the bubbles I felt slightly better, but the worry wasn't going to wash off no matter how much I wanted it to.

I was scared, I was angry and a little disappointed that I didn't get myself organised and put lube on. Out of all of Felicity's outings, only two ended with a disappointing situation; both of which happened while working for Nikki. The young man from Glasgow, Andrew. Not only did Andrew try to have sex outside, he also wasn't going to pay me, so

I guess you could say he double fucked me, which is why he was on the Never See Again list.

Then there was the booking with the Middle Eastern businessman. He was on that list too, through no fault of his own; he was a gentleman. I, however, didn't seem to have any attraction towards him. After this evening I would add Florence to my Never See Again list.

9. A Long Week

'A WOMAN IS LIKE A tea bag – you can't tell how strong she is until you put her in hot water.' So said Eleanor Roosevelt. I can tell you right now I feel like I'm a pot of stewed tea; I'm cold, bitter, but also strong. I was not going to let this break me. I was awake at 5am, something that never happens. I felt I should go to the doctor, so I called my work and said I wasn't feeling well. The surgery didn't open until 8:30am, so it was a very long, nerve-wracking wait. I sat in bed with a cup of tea in my hand watching the clock; it seemed to take forever to reach 8:30. As soon as it was time, I called straightaway, the phone rang, and the receptionist answered. Of course, there were no appointments available until Wednesday. I explained that this was too long to wait, so the receptionist told me a doctor would call me back soon. I made another cup of tea and put the TV on. I sat there with a blank mind; it was as if I was in a trance. I seemed to zone out and forgot the situation I was in. Suddenly the phone rang, it was an unknown number, so I knew it was the doctor's surgery. They asked what the matter was, and I explained that I'd had sex last night, protected, but that I had a lot of bleeding afterwards. The doctor said that it was best to come in and be seen by one of the doctors, and I was given appointment at 1300 that afternoon.

One thing I hate are smears; having to lie on a table with your legs open, knees apart whilst you get poked and prodded, never enjoyable nor something I relished, and I knew this appointment would be something similar. I spent the rest of the day feeling sorry myself, moping around in my pyjamas and slippers. I started to get organised just after noon and headed off for the dreaded appointment.

Now for the awkward wait to see if I was lucky enough to get a female doctor like I asked for. 'Jane I'm ready to see you now'. The doctor was male and explained that they would do an internal examination to check everything was OK since I was still bleeding and that it takes a few days to a few weeks for things to show up on tests, but they would do them. They advised repeating the tests in two weeks and once again after three months. The doctor said it was highly unlikely I had contracted anything, and not to worry. I was worried, and also, I was extremely angry. I had to go over to his table and wait whilst he got a nurse. Whilst he was gone, I had to remove my jeans and pants and cover my genitals with blue paper towel. The doctor appeared back with a nurse in tow and explained that they were going to examine the area that has been bleeding then take some swabs, I was instructed to put my knees up with my heels together, then flop my legs open, this is undoubtedly one of the worst, most embarrassing situations there are. After being swabbed, he gave me antibiotics and said to call in three days, three days I nearly choked...!!! I went straight home, got back into my pyjamas, made a cup of tea, and curled up on the sofa.

Wednesday came and I was glued to my phone at work in case the doctor called. I could not wait any longer, I had to know what the results were. I called, no answer. I tried again five minutes later, same again. Just as I had given up hope, my phone rang with no caller ID. I felt like Arthur looked that day I went round to his house, I had sweaty palms, my leg was trembling. Thankfully all was fine. I was so relieved, but I was still in pain down below. I couldn't wait to get home. I was tired from all the worrying and needed an early night.

The following morning, I woke still uncomfortable and grumpy but up and off to work I went. I was fed up wearing my stupid uniform and having to put on a fake smile for customers. I was also fed up with getting up so early in the morning. I had already decided I was having a full week off from seeing clients as I needed the time to heal, so anyone who messaged me got an automatic out-of-office reply.

I was now receiving a vast number of messages from a wide range of gentlemen, and, by now, I had figured out that the best clients were high-end businessmen, or, sorry to say it, married men. They wanted what I wanted, discretion.

Now with a few bookings under my belt, I had decided that there were three types of clients:

- Your Average Joe.
- The shut-your-eyes-and-hope-it's-over-soon type.
- The-very-enjoyable, -I-want-to-rip-your-clothes-off sort.

I was going to meet Nikki for dinner as we hadn't seen each other much due to us both being busy with work. We still spoke daily; I don't think I could go a week without speaking to her. Since she'd moved back in with Colin, I always declined invites to the house. I worried for her, but what could I do? She knew how I felt about him. Nikki said that she had news, so we had to meet up. I spent the day wondering what Nikki was going to tell me – with her it could be anything. We met in town, then headed off to our favourite restaurant. Every so often Nikki would have a few months off meat and this little place had delicious vegetarian things but could also cook a steak to perfection for me. The restaurant was half full, the only downside being that the tables were so close together that people were able to hear your conversation. The staff knew we liked our privacy so they always seated us at the back, next to a wall so that if we did get people next to us it would only be in front or to the side.

As soon as we sat down, Nikki said, 'It's about Emilia. She's offering full sex for fifty quid and her reviews say she is on drugs all the time.'

This didn't surprise me as every time I saw her, she was on some sort of drugs. It upset me slightly that Nikki thought the worst part of it was that she was having sex on the cheap and not the fact that she was high all the time. I asked Nikki, 'Should we go and see her to see if she wants help?'

Nikki shook her head. 'No. I tried before and, to be honest, after the police incident I don't feel I could go back.'

I knew what Nikki meant; it was a night that didn't need to end up like it did. Still, I couldn't let Emilia self-destruct. I tried to call her but got no answer, so I sent a text:

Hey princess, I hope you are well. I will be down your way at the weekend if you are around?

I had to try, I have always been someone who puts other people before myself and I wouldn't be able to just not think about her, not after what Nikki had just said.

I always loved having dinner with Nikki, partly because I was able to talk to her about clients. I hadn't spoken to Emma much let alone seen her since she got serious with her boyfriend. On the occasions she was free, I was off galivanting as Felicity, so it was hard to catch up with her as much. To be honest, it was really nice to be able to talk about things and not have to lie.

Tartan Temptress

By the weekend I had turned down twelve prospective clients, not that I would have seen all twelve in a week! I wanted to be fully recovered before going back to 'work'. I would say that this experience had given me a bit of a scare, but really, I should have been more prepared and gone to slip some lube on. I was fine mentally to go back to being Felicity, I just needed to be fully healed.

I took full advantage of being off for the weekend and spent it with my family on the first day and friends the following day. It was the best weekend, though both family and friends were getting suspicious as to what I had been up to; never able to commit to nights out and changing plans at the last minute.

On Sunday night I got home and switched on my phone. I had over twenty messages, I couldn't believe it.

Monday – one hour, Aberdeen

Wednesday – one hour, Aberdeenshire

Friday – two hours, Edinburgh

Saturday – two hours, Glasgow

It was nice to get a break in between clients; splitting bookings up throughout the week was better for me. I still couldn't get over the fact Nikki preferred to see all her clients in one day. I personally felt sick at the thought of that. She would get a hotel room for a day/night and offer in-calls, so she saw all her clients then, and had the rest of the week off. I couldn't believe it. I'm not sure if I would be physically able to do that. I mean, yes if you are in a relationship, then I could easily have sex five to ten times a day, but not with five or six different guys in twenty-four hours.

Once I had organised my week, it was time to sit down and unwind. It was a beautiful evening, so I decided to sit outside. My garden is like what my life used to be; very private! I loved spending time out there. The last few months it hasn't exactually been warm enough to sit comfortably out in the garden of an evening. However, the seasons were turning, and I couldn't resist watching the sun set. As I opened the double doors leading into my garden, I was welcomed with a cool breeze, it was refreshing but gave me a chill. I turned and pulled the fluffy blanket from the sofa and wrapped it around my shoulders then grabbed my glass of wine and stepped out onto the decking. My garden is very much minimalistic. I made it a haven for me to relax in, wind chimes hung from the trees, fairy lights hung from the covered seating area so that when I was lay on my bean bag sofa it was like looking up at the stars. I have a high fence round the perimeter, but you can't see any of the fence with the beautiful climbing clematis covering it. Infront of the fence on one side I have a three-foot-wide border, mainly roses but also a few other shrubs. The other side I have all the herbs that I can grow, the rest is covered with small gravel with several pots of lavender spotted about everywhere, the smell of it is so relaxing. I sat outside, looking up at the sky and wondering how I ended up doing what I am doing. I am a fully-fledged call girl.

A rush of excitement came over me as soon as I woke. I was immediately bright-eyed and bushy-tailed, even smiling which is very unlike me in the morning. I even started singing on the way to work, I was that excited. All I knew so far was that I had a booking for an hour at 8pm in Aberdeen at their home. I was always slightly worried about going to a house. I mean, there is always a risk when going to meet clients, but I always felt safer in a hotel. After all, if anything did go wrong there would be other people around. In a house though, I could be anywhere, and no one would hear me scream. This was something that bothered me at first, but it was something that I tried not to think about. Nikki had taught me to never attend a booking without telling someone where you were going and for how long. Having the fifteen-minute text window to say all was OK was the most-important thing of all. I think you can tell so much from first impressions; on two occasions I have used the opportunity to say I think the guy is a bit creepy, can we check in again in fifteen? All of my clients are aware prior to booking that I tell a friend the location and length of the booking; I have never had a client question or disapprove of this.

At work I was upbeat. I got on extremely well with my boss, a woman called Milly. We would always discuss what I got up to on my weekends and evenings. She must have thought I was completely bonkers, and I guess what some would call a slut. I obviously did not say it was with different men all the time, just that I had a few guys on the go. I spent the day sneaking peeks at my phone at work; I was really excited now. I only knew that my client was called Jeff. He was in his forties, worked in the oil industry, lived alone, loves animals and the gym. Jeff and I messaged throughout the day; the more we spoke, the more I was beginning to like the sound of him. After lunch Milly asked if I had a date. I asked why she thought that, and she said it was simply down to the number of messages I was receiving hourly. I started to feel a bit paranoid; the thought that she or anyone else would find out what I was really up to freaked me out.

It was soon 15:30 and time to leave work and go home to get ready for tonight. I was excited driving home, singing the whole way. As soon as I got in the door, the shower was switched on, work clothes off and the transformation into Felicity began. I have a fairly rigid routine while showering wet myself all

over, shampoo on, and, whilst that's working, I shave my legs, then rinse the shampoo out and conditioner on. I wouldn't shave my privates the same day I have a client as I've read that shaving the day you have sex can make it easier to contract infections due to the open pores after shaving. I'd tried waxing, but it was far too uncomfortable for me, so I didn't try it again. Now I just used hair removal cream where I can, then shave the rest on my nights off; so just legs and underarms it is, rinse conditioner out, wash my body, then finally wash all over again. I have stuck to this routine for as long as I can remember. When I step out of the shower, I rub baby oil into my skin; once oiled up I lie on my bed and let my skin soak up the oil, it leaves my skin silky smooth, and I love the feeling of running my hands down my silky body. My clients love it too. Lying there, waiting for the oil to soak in, was my time to fantasise about the evening ahead. I always hoped it would be a really handsome guy in his forties with a perfectly sized penis and a body to match and that it would be a full hour of amazing sex. Thinking these thoughts always made me horny. I mean, every woman dreams of a good-looking guy, a decent-sized cock and a great body that makes you tingle just thinking about it, but, seriously, I am still waiting...

I text Jeff to confirm we're still on for the arranged time and asked him what his favourite colour is. I've found asking guys something like that made them think that you care and are making a concerted effort solely for them. It always worked, and I had a reply in seconds... 'blue'...followed by the confirmation that our agreed time was still OK. By now I was horny and hoping that Jeff was going to be able to satisfy my lust.

I had a blue, very sexy corset; just putting on lingerie like this made me feel incredible. And I knew I looked amazing; I was so confident now. I pulled on my sheer seamed stockings, laced my corset up tight, rolled my shoulders back and held my head high! Now the real transformation into Felicity began... Foundation was stage one; I used two colours, carefully blending them, then I apply a bronzer over my cheeks. I never used red; I am always tanned, so bronzer suits me a more. Next, eyebrow time. I would define every line of my eyebrow, the shape really changed my face, then eyeliner over my bottom lid followed by a line over the top lid, finished off with plenty of mascara.

Then I'd put on earrings, watch, and slip into my evening dress. I'd found that once I changed my look to being more sophisticated and showing less skin, I seemed to blend in more when walking into hotels. I looked more like a businesswoman away with work than a call girl. Dress on, bag checked heels in bag and flats on for driving and off I went.

I walked up to the front door of an exceptionally large house, in a very affluent area of Aberdeen; it was amazing with a huge arched doorway. I knocked on the door and waited. The time from me knocking to them answering the door told me a lot about the client. If I knocked and the door opened instantly and they were standing there, they were usually a bit socially awkward. They would normally spend most of the time looking at me and be very hard to talk to. If, however, they answered after a minute or so, they tended to be more relaxed and easier to talk to.

Jeff opened the door after a minute or so, so this was a good sign. When I walked in, I could see the house was split into flats. It was still nice, but a little disappointing if I am being brutally honest. We entered his flat and went into his sitting room; the TV was on, and he was watching football. 'Do you mind if I finish watching the game?' He asked.

Obviously, it was no problem, after all he's paying for my time. 'No Jeff, its completely fine, I'm happy to watch it'. I bloody hate football, but I hate it less if I'm being paid to watch it. I could see an envelope sitting on the coffee table. Jeff kept looking at it anxiously but said nothing. Then he left to make us drinks. He put the envelope in front of me when he returned. The drinks were glasses of water; great, I could not believe it. I excused myself and headed to the bathroom to check my envelope. All was in order, so I made my way back to the sitting room. We sat for a few more minutes until the football finished, then Jeff got up and asked me to follow him through to his bedroom. I followed him and, just as we sat down on the bed, he turned to look at me. He was pleasant to look at; about the same height as me, dark hair (lots of it). He reminded me of a Hobbit. I didn't care, to be honest, as I was so horny. My pussy was tingling and ready to come out to play...!

We lay down together on the bed and he started running his fingers slowly up my leg, sliding my dress up until he reached the stocking straps. Then he asked to take my dress off. I stood up and Jeff knelt on the bed in front of me. He put both hands on my knees, then slid his hand up my legs, lifting my dress up over my hips and finally over my head. By now he was just staring at me with my dress in his hands. After a few awkward moments he declared that I looked amazing and that he was genuinely shocked by how beautiful my body was. Every woman loves compliments, and being told things like that does make you feel amazing whether it's the first time or the hundredth time...

He moved over to me and started to kiss my neck. I am not a huge fan of having my neck touched at all (due to Keith and the way he would hold me) I usually manage to move my clients away from this area, but before I could move him away, he started to push me back onto the bed. Just as we lay down, he started kissing me on my lips, not something I normally did with clients. He then pulled back and started scrambling to get his jeans off. Once off he lay back down beside me rubbing up against me, and, oh, what a cock he had… I was really horny and excited; my pussy was wet, and I didn't need lube, I was ready to go. Jeff took my hand and placed it on his large, throbbing, hard penis and I slowly started teasing him, rubbing it, and squeezing gently. He then slid his boxers off, and I had his big, hard penis in my hand. It was just what I needed as I really longed for some good sex. He was running his fingers over the top of my clit and moaning, I was now fully engaged in tossing him off; his cock was throbbing, and I was ready for sex. Jeff then pushed me onto my back and slid down in between my legs. He started kissing the inside of my thighs, then moved onto licking my pussy and running his tongue over my clit, whilst slowly sliding a finger inside me. I'm going to be honest, at this point I was that horny that I was about ready to flip him over and jump on top of him, but that would not have been very professional. I had to wait until he was ready; fortunately, that didn't take long. Jeff turned over and said he was ready to cum, could I play with him? I started tossing him off, and, within minutes, he had ejaculated. We still had thirty minutes left and I was so horny and, by now, extremely frustrated.

We lay talking and I had to try hard to appear happy but, really, I was frustrated and needed a good sorting out. Jeff then turned round to look at me, perhaps sensing that I did not really want a conversation, never mind a kiss, but to my surprise he was hard again and ready to go. I was amazed and, my smile returned. He asked me to kneel on all fours, then he stood up and slid a condom over his hard penis and started to rub it against me, just putting the tip of his cock into me. It felt amazing. His cock was big, but not too big, it was perfectly sized. Jeff kept just putting the tip of his cock inside me then taking it out, holding it, then pushing it back in, getting deeper and deeper each time, then he put his hands on either side of my hips and started pulling me back, pushing his cock deeper and deeper into me. I was so horny and so needing this; he now started slapping my ass and moving faster. Each thrust he got deeper inside me until he was really fucking me. I had not been fucked like this in a long time and I was loving it; on all fours, my hair being pulled back and held tightly in his hand. I liked that, and I loved the feeling of a big, hard cock deep inside me, pushing deep, hard and fast. He was really going for it now and I did not need to fake it. As he started fucking me harder, he moved his hand round and started lightly tapping his fingers over my clit. I grabbed the sheets in my hand. It felt so good and the next thing I knew, I was climaxing; it felt incredible and long overdue. My body was tingling from my toes to my fingers, and, just as I was finishing my orgasm, Jeff let out a strange woohoo as he started to orgasm as well. After old Florence, I was starting to get used to a wide range of noises – moans and groans – so it did not faze me.

Jeff cleaned himself up and passed me a few wet wipes. I was satisfied, I could not believe it. We lay there for a moment, and he then asked if I would see him again in a month's time. I said yes without any hesitation, then started to get dressed. Once fully clothed Jeff walked me to the door, kissed me on the cheek and off I went. I walked out the door, smiling from ear to ear. I managed to contain myself until I reached my car, then, for some unknown reason, I did a silly jump up and down. I guess it was down to feeling very satisfied!

The whole way home, all I did was sing I was so happy. I was that shocked about how my night turned out that my hands were shaking, and I kept laughing. Once home, clothes off and into the wash, shower on, only this time it really felt like good sex with a normal guy. After a shower is normally when I switch back to being me; PJs on and curled up on my sofa watching TV. Only tonight I could not help but think about the sex I had just had. On reflection, I decided it was most likely only that good as the rest had been so bad.

The following day I woke up in a marvellous humour with a smile on my face. I was up like a shot and away to work, still smiling. I still could not get over the things I was doing or the places I had been to do them. Even at work I was on top form, 'So who is he?', Milly asked.

I blushed and smiled at the same time, 'Just a new man.'

To which she replied, 'I knew you were in too good a mood!' And she laughed.

My day passed quickly and, before I knew it, I was on my way home. Tonight, I have a fitness class followed by yoga. This is one of the nights I am just me, a Felicity- free night. After yoga it's straight to bed, no TV. Just straight to bed to sleep. I loved the way yoga made me feel. How would I describe it? Just a very calm, composed version of myself, I guess.

Reluctantly I woke, dry mouthed and feeling rather groggy, like I could have snoozed my alarm and slept for a week. Unlike yesterday I half-heartedly got up and dressed for work. I drove all the way there like a zombie, sipping coffee the whole way. I was running late due to my reluctance to get up, so finding a space to park in Aberdeen was a nightmare and added another thirty minutes onto however late I already was. As soon as I arrived, I went straight to Milly and apologised. Then I went to get ready to start. Once I had finally caught up with my tasks, Milly came over to see me, 'So, how's your head?'

I was a bit confused and scowled at her then replied, 'Fine?'

She laughed 'So if you're not hungover? Why are you so late?'

I smiled, 'Believe it or not, I was in bed straight after yoga at 9pm.'

Milly burst out laughing, so loud that everyone close-by turned and looked at us. When she finally stopped laughing, she exclaimed, 'Only you are able to be up early for work when you have had an all-nighter, and late when you have had ten hours sleep!'

Absolutely true!

By lunch I still had not heard from my client for tonight, and, just as I was about to message, I got a text through:

Hi Felicity. Sorry to bother you but are you still OK to visit me at home tonight at 8pm, look forward to seeing you. Connor.

I waited for a while, then replied:

Hi Connor, I hope you have had a fabulous morning. I'm really looking forward to meeting you tonight at 8pm. Do you have any preferences to what you would like me to wear? Also, if you don't mind me asking, what's your favourite colour?

I found it was best to ask the client what they would like me to wear as it gave me an idea about them. For example, if they said they would like me to dress up in a sexy outfit then I know they like dress-up role play and they are more on my sexual level. If they say no preference, then it usually means they have a pretty boring sexual side and probably just like missionary sex. I guess this makes it feel like it's a more personal experience and gives them the impression I'm interested in what they think. It's also good to have an idea of what to expect, as much as is possible.

Connor had said that he was into normal stuff, nothing weird, and went on to explain that his normal girl had moved away, and he was looking for a regular girl to visit every two weeks or once a month, depending on his work commitments. I was a little unsure with regard to a regular client arrangement. On the one hand it's good to know what you're dealing with. On the other, they're bound to try to get to know you and I worried that I would get too comfortable around them and then mess up and end up telling them something about my real life, not Felicity's life. Still, I guess I could not overthink it, and, if they seem normal just go for it. It's just like having a friend with benefits or a fuck buddy. After a few messages I now know his favourite colour is black, he's in his thirties, lives alone, works away a lot and has no time or desire for a relationship.

Well Connor isn't sounding too bad at all. I got home in good time after work, with enough time to have an hour power nap. When I went to set the timer for my nap it was already set to an hour; this made me laugh as it was the normal time for a booking. I showered, then got into bed for my nap. I did not wake until my timer went off, so I must have needed it!

I got up and started to get ready. I loved my hair in big, sexy curls, but because of my nap it was more bedhead, so I dried the damp parts and straightened it. I looked in the mirror and was shocked at how long it had gotten. I put on a black lace bra with no pants, just hold-ups, and my thigh-high black boots, a small tartan skirt, little black top, and a long cardigan to hide under.

I was excited and horny and hoped that Connor would be as good as Jeff. I got to the given address, and it was a rundown area of Aberdeen. The block of flats did not look too appealing. I was now feeling slightly nervous. I had to walk up a dingy set of stairs, not all the way to the top but not far off. Once there, I paused for a moment. I closed my eyes and had a deep breath in through my nose then exhaled out my mouth. I was now ready, I moved forward to the doorway, and I rang the bell, the door opened straight away. Hmm, this was not a good sign.

First impressions: Connor was taller than me, chunky build (could easily overpower me), however he was very pleasant and had eyes that made me melt. He invited me in by a hand gesture; he still hadn't spoken. I introduced myself and he did likewise. He wasn't nervous at all; in fact, as soon as the door was shut behind us, he could not stop talking, talking about his circumstances and interest in making this a regular arrangement. We went through to the bedroom, and I sat on the bed. Connor stood there, just looking at me. Then he started stroking my leg. I couldn't believe he was so to the point like that; he seemed more the submissive type. He then demanded that I take my top and skirt off and lie face down on the bed. Before I did anything, I asked if we could get the awkward bit out of the way first; he pointed to the dressing table. I walked over, put the envelope into my bag, and then did as he'd requested. I moved over towards the bed, turned so I was facing him and gently pulled my top up and over my shoulders, then threw it down by his feet! I pulled the condom from beside my boob and placed it on the bedside table. I started to unbuckle my bra, slowly sliding it down to uncover my breast then letting it drop to the floor. I placed my hands over my breasts, lightly squeezing them before I moved my hands down my body. As I got to my waist I paused for a moment and looked right at Connor. 'Come on, hurry up!' he shouted. I moved my hands down, tucking my thumbs in my skirt on the way down. I pushed my skirt over my hips then with a little wiggle my skirt fell to the floor. I turned to the bed then leant forwards and climbed up so that I was on all fours, again a little wiggle of the hips. Connor groaned as I was shaking my hips from side to side. I lay down, unsure what to expect next. I could feel the bed move as he sat down, then he grabbed my ass firmly, and, in a deep voice, said, 'How bad has my little bitch been this time?'

I tried extremely hard not to laugh, burying my face in the pillow. 'Very bad, sir, very bad indeed.'

He reached down and spread my legs wide open, then moved his hands over my ass and slid them in between my legs. By now I was getting slightly excited. Connor pushed his fat fingers inside me, then he pulled them out and started slapping my ass repeatedly, getting harder each time. I was now super horny and ready to be fucked, I was wriggling on the bed in frustration. Without any warning, Connor stuck his head down between my legs. Now this was what eating pussy could be described like; he was sucking my lips, sticking his tongue inside me, touching me with his fingers and sucking my clit, one after the other. He was now as turned on as me; I could hear it in his voice. He was moaning and almost growling, occasionally squeaking too...! Then he stopped and flipped me over, which was easily done given his size and strength. He was immediately back down between my legs; it felt great, he really knew what he was doing. The combination of everything he was doing to me was amazing. He paused and asked me for a condom. Luckily, I had already placed the one I had in my bra a reach away, so it didn't interrupt things. Just as I reached to get it, Connor stood up and took his boxers off.

Unfortunately, Connor wasn't blessed with a cock like Jeff. Poor Connor had one of the top three smallest cocks I have ever seen. I couldn't believe it. I mean, everyone knows there are small cocks, big cocks, thin cocks, thick cocks, bent cocks – no two penises are the same. But this, this was tiny! I could tell that this was not going to be enjoyable for me. I mean, I'm all for 'size doesn't matter, it's how you use it that counts', but no way this time. It was so small I didn't even know what to do with it!

Connor was trying to get it hard, but it was strange to watch. Rather than using his hand, he could only use his thumb, forefinger, and his index finger! I felt sorry for him and realised now why he was so good at oral – and why he did not have a girlfriend. I mean, how could you have a normal, healthy sex life with a penis that small!

I lay there on the bed waiting, Connor now had a condom on; it was as baggy as a chihuahua in a sleeping bag! He bent over me and tried to get his tiny cock in me; it reminded me of being an inexperienced teenager fumbling around. Eventually he managed it.

I felt so sorry for him. He seemed like a genuinely nice guy, and I imagined it must be embarrassing for him. I lay there with him on top of me. He was inside me, but there was no enjoyment or feeling at all. However, Connor was fairly going for it and groaning a lot, so I guessed he was enjoying it. Then he stopped, pulled out of me, and lay back on the bed to pull the condom off.

Connor asked, 'Was everything OK?' He looked worried.

I quickly replied, 'Perfect!'

He turned and looked at me, 'Great. I hope we can meet again sometime?'

'Of course! How could I say no when you can give oral like that?' I replied.

I got myself dressed and Connor walked me to the door. When he opened the door, I moved towards it, and he patted me on the back. Yes, that's right, he patted me on the back. I had to bite my lip otherwise I would have burst out laughing as I was walking down the steps. I glanced at my watch. I had only been there thirty-five minutes.

Driving home, I wasn't my usual hyper self, more zoned out, deep in thought, I guess. I just could not get over the differences in cock sizes.

I mean, take tonight for example. Connor, lovely guy, not the worst-looking – OK, a little chunky but a lot of girls like that – he has a respectable job and owns his own place, granted the area wasn't the best but inside was beautifully decorated. These days a man like that is hard to come by. But the size of his cock would be a no-go for me. I love sex. For me it is particularly important in a relationship to be able to unwind with amazing sex, sex that makes you orgasm again and again, leaving you completely satisfied and totally relaxed, or the kind that gives you jelly legs, and you can't move. Neither of which Connor would be able to achieve. However, he was so good at oral I had decided to think about his proposal for this to become a regular thing.

After my shower I needed food. I never ate at regular times anymore, quite often missing dinner altogether. Just as I started to raid the fridge, I had a dreadful thought. I put down what was in my hand and rushed through to the hall. *How could I be so stupid?* I asked myself. I kept my money in the freezer and when I was in the fridge, I'd remembered that I hadn't counted Connor's envelope. This was the first time, ever, that I hadn't checked the envelope.

I counted it, then counted it again. Surely not. Once more I counted it out; he was £20 short. As much as I was angry with him, I was more disappointed in myself. I guess I had just gotten used to guys always tipping me, so I would never have thought that they would have the cheek to put in less than the agreed amount. I didn't do this for the money, but all the same, I didn't want to be ripped off by people not sticking to the rules! I got my phone out of my bag and texted the following:

> *Hi Connor, I hope you had a lovely time tonight? Apologies for being forward, but you were short 20. I can only assume that this means you don't want to see me again? Shame as I was going to say I was happy being a regular. F. x*

I threw my phone down on my bed, then headed back to the kitchen. I was now less enthusiastic about cooking as Connor had made me mad, so cheese and toast it was.

Still, cheese on toast is one of my favourite things to eat. I put the bread in the toaster, then cover it with thick slices of smoked cheddar cheese, exactly two grinds of my saltshaker on each slice, then, to finish, a splash of Lea & Perrins on top. Under the grill and wait. If I'm really needing to be cheered up, then I put a can of spaghetti and sausages over it at the end. Isn't it funny how it's the simplest things in life that give you the most satisfaction?

I remember a conversation I had while on a walk with an ex-boyfriend of mine. He asked me; 'If you could have anything to eat at all right now, what would it be?'

Without hesitation, I answered, 'Pork pie.'

His head shot round so he was looking at me; it was as if he was looking to see if I was joking. He paused, then laughed. 'No, I mean if you could have any food at all?'

Again, I answered, 'Pork pie. All I want right now is a pork pie.'

We laughed for a long time over that. My diet is something I have always had issues with. I seem to eat healthy, then have a mad blow-out for a few weeks. Thankfully I always seem to keep a small frame; I guess that's down to walking and going to the gym.

I couldn't believe it, Thursday already. Today was a normal boring day and it seemed to drag. Maybe because we were so quiet it made the day seem so much longer. After work I went for a coffee, then straight home. I'd planned on an early dinner then a walk before going to my fitness class, then straight to bed. Once home and out of the shower, Felicity's phone went, I picked it up and threw it in a drawer. I had always given myself two nights to do my own thing, so I didn't get lost in Felicity's world. I liked being little old plain Jane for a few days, so I started cooking dinner.

My favourite morning to wake up on, last shift before a few days off. Unfortunately, it's the worst day to drive into town, there are 38.4 million licensed vehicles on the road in Great Britain and this morning it felt like most of them were driving to Aberdeen. The drive was unusually, unbearably slow. There must have been an accident, or someone broken down. I made it into work with no time to spare.

Milly was there as usual, waiting on me. It's true what they say, you can have the shittiest job in the world, but if you have good people around you to share your day and make you laugh it doesn't matter. I didn't know Milly until I started this job, and we both took our time coming out of our shells. By God, we were shocking to each other now; it was all playful banter, but to others who do not share our sense of humour I guess they may have thought it offensive at times. The day flew by, and that was largely down to the banter Milly, and I had.

At lunch I sent my usual text to tonight's client asking how they were, if the time and address were still the same, and what they would like out of our time together. I had got a tip off Nikki, she said it was best to text either in the morning or early afternoon so that it gives them something to fantasise about during the day. It seemed to work a treat. I got a message straight back asking if we could meet earlier and that his favourite colour was red. I thought this was promising as red is my favourite colour.

I finished work and headed home with a smile on my face. I guess I'm no different to anyone else; I love Fridays. I was also excited about this booking as this was the guy, I should have met on my first booking, but, as I could not make the agreed time, he had gone with someone else; none other than Emilia! When he got in touch, he said that he knew it was me as he recognised my body from the photos on our new website. He must have a good eye for detail! Emilia had already told me about him. John was a part-time model, had an excellent job, an amazing house and, most importantly, was amazing in bed.

I danced around my room as I was getting ready. John had requested a real 'hooker' look; orange face, huge eyebrows, black smoky eyes, lots of mascara, pink cheeks, and red lips.

I put on a red bra, red suspenders and black stockings and a tiny black dress, just long enough to cover the top of my stockings. I double-checked my bag, packed a normal set of clothes and off I went.

As I drove, I was starting to get wet pants. I knew John was hot and Emilia had said he was great in bed, so I was excited. I needed more good sex. Ever since Jeff I had been hoping to find another night of sex like that. I eventually arrived at the hotel – the drive seemed to take forever – but it always does when you're looking forward to going somewhere. I walked into the hotel, straight past reception and up to the fourth floor. There were other people in the lift, so my heels went on once I got out. I got to the door and knocked. John opened the door, standing there in a towel, straight from the shower. Emilia was right; he was tall, dark, and extremely handsome. For the first time, I was so eager to start. As soon as the door shut behind us, John started chatting, 'Hi Felicity, it's great to finally meet you, I'm really sorry but my dinner reservation has moved forward and we don't have much time, payment is the same and I've left it in the bathroom for you.'

'Hi John, sorry to hear that but I completely understand'. I'm not going to lie I was absolutely gutted! Still, I couldn't let John know that, so I put on a fake smile and walked past him to the bathroom. I checked all was in order, I wasn't going to make the same mistake twice. Happy days, all was there and a rather large tip. I placed the envelope in my handbag and returned to find John lying naked on the bed. Bingo. This was the kind of client I needed right now. Normally I would never make the first move, nor would I undress myself, but I was so horny, and I just needed to be fucked. I needed to cum.

As I walked slowly over to the bed, I kicked my shoes off and slid my dress up and over my shoulders. I really wanted to dive on him and start kissing him all over, he was so attractive, but I had to use all my willpower not to do this. So, I calmly walked over to the bed and lay down beside him. Lucky for me, just as my body touched the bed, John grabbed me and moved me beside him. He reached down and slid his hand in between my thighs, moving slowly up until he touched my clit. He grabbed me and started kissing me passionately. Then he moved back and blurted out, 'Can I double F you?' I could not, for the life of me, remember what it meant, but I said yes anyway; I wasn't about to spoil the moment.

John slid two fingers deep inside me and then I remembered. FF; Finger Fucking. Uh-oh. Just then I remembered Emilia saying he was rough and hurt her; she got fucked up the ass by him and his cock isn't small. So, I can understand why he hurt her.

He was really rough, stopping every so often to pull his fingers out and slap my clit; this was not only uncomfortable, but also off-putting. As I have said before, I'm not one for foreplay at the best of times, never mind when it feels like this. I didn't like it at all. Then John stopped, half panting half yelling, and begged me to suck him off. He threw himself onto his back on the bed and lay down with a very cheeky grin. I took his cock in my hand. It was large, exceptionally large. In fact, my thumb couldn't touch my fingers as my hand closed round it. My hand was just up from his pelvic bone and his cock stuck out of my hand by a few inches. I pushed my hand down firm onto his body with my pinkie sticking out just to get my hand down further. I then bent over him and slid his cock into my mouth. I was so horny. I mean, I was in bed with an extremely attractive guy, who wouldn't be?

I started off slowly, but the hornier I got the harder I sucked and the faster I got. His cock was great, if a bit big to play with; it was certainly more than a mouthful. John moved me off him, then fumbled about at the side of the bed until he had a condom on. He then pinned me down on my back. I had my legs wide open, and he was slapping his hard penis on my clit, I wasn't enjoying this very much, but I was completely gagging for it now, and John could tell. John pushed himself inside me, with the first thrust of his hips I was nearly ready to explode; the force took my breath away. I was trying so hard to hold it all together. John wanted me to beg for it, he wanted me to say, 'Please fuck me, sir. Please, I need it!' However, I had completely forgotten my lines as I was lost in my own world with the feeling of me clenching my pussy round the tip of his cock. After a quick reminder I yelled out, 'Fuck me, sir, please, I need it!'. John was instantly going at it like lightning. I had my legs in the air, and he was holding me by the ankles whilst pounding his cock into me. It felt utterly amazing; I was actually trying hard *not* to orgasm. He stopped and flipped me over, then, holy fuck, I experienced a whole new level for doggie style. John really knew what he was doing; it was amazing. He was going so hard and fast no words could describe it; sometimes even I am speechless.

I couldn't hold it anymore. John now had his hands round my hips and was bouncing me on and off his big, hard cock. I was like a wee doll in his hands; he could easily pick me up. I was on all fours with my hands grabbing the bed so I wouldn't get bounced off the edge. His cock was so hard I knew he was nearly finished, and I knew I could not hold this back any longer, just as I started to cum, John let out OHHHHHHAAAA at exactly the same time. We both collapsed on the bed trying to get our breath back. After about five minutes John got up, 'Thank you for coming to see me, I haven't had sex like that in a very long time.'

I just smiled; I didn't know what to say.

'You amaze me, please excuse me I need to go and get ready, sorry this meeting has been cut short, but I hope to see you again soon?'

'Yes of course, I hope you have a lovely meal.'

John headed for the shower, 'I will certainly be seeing you again soon. Do you mind if you could see yourself out, please?'

'That's no bother at all, look forward to hearing from you.' I quickly pulled my clothes on, then headed out to the car. I got there but sat for a moment or two reflecting; I could not believe what had just happened. I mean, I just had sex with a very handsome guy, who was, in my opinion, way out of my league. Not only that, but he was amazing in bed – and I got more than a week's wages for it! It was mad. I mean, this guy had been amazing, and I was the one being paid. Truth be told, I felt like I should have been paying him. Once I managed to get myself together, I started my journey home. By the time I reached home I had a message from John, *Thank you again Felicity, I would love to meet up again very soon.*

Clothes off and shower time for me. I didn't feel dirty; tonight felt like any other night. When I got out of the shower, I had another message from John, *Felicity are you free on Sunday at all?*

I left it and went to get ready for bed, it had been a long day; I had been on the go for seventeen hours.

The noise of birds chirping in the garden woke me; a new day had dawned – earlier than I'd hoped. I lay there wondering what adventures today was going to bring. I was so looking forward to my lie-in. I hated the fact I always woke early, but I was also really excited about tonight, so I messaged my client, Andy. Just the usual chat; *Hi Andy, how are you? Just thought I'd check if the time for tonight was still, OK?*

I went out for a run, had breakfast, a wee nap, shower, then got dressed. I was not seeing my client until later, so I had the entire day to myself. I went to lunch with my friends and, just as we all sat down at the table, my phone started going crazy. There were messages from both Andy and John. I immediately started to blush and turned my phone over, so the screen was face down on the table – I didn't want my friends to be asking questions. Just then, Emma reached over and grabbed my phone. As she sat back in her seat, my heart was beating at an excessive rate, and I was starting to feel a bit paranoid. I guess this is what happens when you sneak about behind people's backs. Emma still hadn't said a word. I was nervous as to what she was thinking but was too afraid to ask. Just then Emma said, 'Is this a new phone? I haven't seen you with this one before. I don't remember you saying you got a new one?'

I didn't know what to say; she had caught me off guard. The only thing I was able to think of was, 'I just got it yesterday. I thought it was time to give Android a go.' All the while terrified that my normal everyday phone was going to go off in my bag. Being caught with two phones would ask a whole lot of questions I didn't have answers too.

Emma scowled at me from across the table; she knew I wouldn't change from an iPhone. I was a creature of habit especially with technology, and I was in love with my iPhone. Emma moved towards me to pass my phone back and I snatched it and put it in my bag. That was too much of a close call and I had a feeling that was just the beginning of Emma's questions. Our lunch was awkward and to be honest I was dying to get away as all I could do was think of tonight.

So about tonight. I know Andy is a professional sportsman and discretion is a must, which suits me perfectly – plus he is paying an exceptionally large sum. Andy wanted the full Porn Star experience; I was to be dressed in purple lingerie, stockings, hair up, and a shit ton of makeup. None of which I felt were unreasonable, nor out of my comfort zone. This was my first time doing a porn star experience, but I had watched porn before. It's basically hardcore sex; me dressed as a slut doing lots of moaning and groaning very loud the whole time. I liked it when I knew there was role play; it seemed to add a bit of spice to things, I guess.

As for John, he wants to have another meet Sunday night, and to name my price. I wasn't sure what to do as I had promised myself to have that day off and to have a bit of a me day. I was looking forward to having lunch with the girls tomorrow as I wasn't able to stay out with them today with seeing Andy later on and I hadn't spent much time with them of late. On the other hand, it was such good sex – it was actually better than good sex, it was bloody amazing – I guess it was still giving me a me day. Still, I didn't want to sound too keen, so I didn't reply. After our lunch I rushed home and lay on the sofa while Andy and I messaged back and forth; he was making me laugh. The whole situation was making me laugh, I was about to meet a professional sportsman, and we were going to be having sex like porn stars; it was surreal. I couldn't believe the things I was doing; I was about to meet a famous person. Once out the shower I started my transition into Felicity. As soon as I had slipped into my sexy lingerie, it was like I became someone else; stunning, confident, calm, and relaxed.

I had to Google porn star make-up, basically heavy make-up, and bright lips. I have beautiful skin, so heavy make-up has never been required before. After twenty minutes of shovelling make-up on, I stopped to look at myself and I was completely different; you could hardly tell it was me! Not a look I liked.

I pulled my dress on, then had another glance in the mirror. I was now ready to go. I was extremely excited to tell the truth; let's be honest, I'm sure many women will have had or want to have sex like porn stars do. The road to Glasgow was starting to be familiar. I knew when I passed the roundabout before Stirling that I was only about thirty minutes away. The traffic was relatively quiet compared to my last few journeys there and I got down the road in record time. I was early, which was nice, so I didn't have to rush about looking for parking. When I parked up, I was just touching up my make-up when my phone went. It was Andy instructing me how to get past Reception and what room to go to, and that he was ready now. Without any hesitation I was out of the car and walking to the front of the hotel.

In the lift like a ninja without being stopped, timer set, six-inch heels on and I was at the door. The door opened quickly, and Andy was standing there. He grabbed me, pinned me to the wall and started kissing me. I was shocked but, just went with it, I am sure I can bend my rules slightly.

Andy was a very good-looking chap in his thirties; he was of muscular build and clean-shaven. So far, so good. When Andy stopped kissing me, he tried to hand me my envelope. I told him I would get it in a minute; one thing I did stick to was that I was never handed money, it was placed somewhere, and I picked it up. Once the awkward bit had passed, it was all go! There was no chit-chat, which was great; it was down to business straight away. We were both lying kissing on the bed, still fully dressed, then Andy started running his fingers up the inside of my thigh. He then slid my dress up and over my head. I struggled to get his jeans off. I was normally good at getting clothes off, but this time was really proving difficult. Eventually his belt was off, and jeans were on the floor. There was a massive physical attraction between us; we could not stop touching each other. Andy lay me down on the bed and, straight away, his head was between my thighs. He certainly knew what he was doing... He picked me up and flipped me round to do a 69. This was the first time his cock was in my face; it was a substantial size, but not too large. I was now squatting over him sucking his cock; we were doing a 69 for a while and I was trying really hard not to cum. He was so good with his tongue; it felt amazing, one of those melt-in-the-moment feelings. Just as I got back into a good rhythm Andy held me up in the air, then almost chucked me onto the bed. It all happened so fast that I wasn't sure what was going on. He was strong, he certainly didn't seem to find it hard to lift me and flip me over, but, then again, I'm only fifty-seven kilos so I guess to a sports professional that's not much at all.

Andy got up and stood at the side of the bed, pulling me towards him by my ankles. My pussy was soaking; I was so turned on. I didn't need to act anymore; I was that into him that it was moaning for real. I thought we would be having foreplay for some time, but that was not the case at all. Andy was trying to slide his penis in me without protection, so I pulled myself back and said that he was missing something. He apologised and stumbled over to the bedside table where he had a packet of condoms out. I don't think I have ever seen one go on so fast, he was ready to go. Andy didn't hold back; he thrust his cock deep inside me on the first go and I gasped in excitement. I was lay on my back at the end of the bed with my ass just over the mattress, Andy was holding me by my ankles and spreading my legs as far as they could go. It was hard and fast sex from word go; I didn't have time to adjust to having a large penis in me, he was forcing it inside me, each time he was pushing harder. It felt amazing. I was screaming, I wasn't even having to act; it was real. Andy kept getting faster and harder. He moved his hands off my ankles and wrapped them round my hips. He was so strong, him pulling me down onto his cock as well as thrusting into me sent me into overdrive. Lucky, he wanted a porn star experience as I think I would have struggled to be quiet. I was dripping in sweat, and I had the sweat from him dripping down on to me.

His fitness was on point; I guess that would have been mandatory with the sport he's involved in. I screamed out that I was about to orgasm, and he pulled his penis out and dropped to his knees, then buried his face in between my legs. With one hand he parted my lips, then he started rubbing two fingers over my clit, lightly tapping his fingers over it while trying to put his tongue inside me, occasionally stopping to tell me to cum on his face. I let go and I could feel the relief that I had built up to for so long just disappear through my legs. Just as I was coming to the end of my orgasm, Andy was starting to lick me like an ice lolly. I never understood why guys do this as I've never found it to be enjoyable, but, nevertheless, it was only for a moment then he got to his feet again and flipped me over, so I was on all fours on the bed. I had just got myself positioned better when he forced his cock back inside me. I shot forward as he seemed to go far too deep too quickly. It wasn't long before he was going at it just like before, harder in fact as he was able to pull me back onto him. I was screaming again within seconds, trying so hard to stay on all fours; I was turning to jelly from the orgasm I had just had. Then Andy grabbed my ponytail and started pulling it back towards him. I moved my head back and it made me arch my tummy down to the bed. It was so hot, I loved it. I was really getting into things now and was screaming out for him to fuck me harder. I could feel his cock throbbing inside me and that was a good indication that things were about to come to an end. I screamed for him to really fuck me and, he did. The thrusts were so hard that I think if he didn't have me by the hair I would have been pushed right off the bed. I screamed out, 'I can't hold it, I'm about to cum!'

'Hold it, I'm not ready yet,' Andy said in a stern voice.

I was trying to push my ass up so that he could go inside me as far as possible when he let out a screeching noise and collapsed. I had just started to orgasm when he collapsed, so I wasn't as satisfied as him, but I was there for his pleasure, I guess, and not mine.

We lay panting on the bed beside each other. I even had sweat on my legs; it felt like it was thirty degrees in the room, but I think it was just that the chemistry between us got the heat up for us both. I lay there, trying to get my breath back and wondering how on the earth all this had happened. Andy got up off the bed 'I'm going to go for a shower to cool down, would you like to join me?'.

Just as he said that the timer went on my phone, and it turned the moment rather awkward. Andy started to turn a rather bright shade of red, I guess the timer reminded him that I was there on professional capacity rather than a personal one.

'Don't worry I understand you've got other plans, thank you for coming down I had a wonderful time Felicity'.

I felt like I should have joined him but instead asked 'Maybe next time I could join you?'

'That sounds perfect, I will be in touch for our next meeting, take your time getting organised no rush for you to leave'.

'Thank you, I very much look forward to hearing from you'.

When Andy went to the bathroom, I got up to get myself organised and glanced at myself in the mirror; my makeup was all down my face from the amount of sweat, so I understood what he meant about taking my time to get organised. There was no way I was walking out the room looking like that! Once I sorted my make up, I pulled my clothes on and had a check round the room for anything I may have dropped. I found my car keys, then got my flat shoes out and stashed my heels away. I held the door and gently closed it. I wasn't one for drawing attention to myself after a booking. The drive home was relatively fast, and I couldn't wait to get in the shower when I got home; I always felt disgusting when I had someone else's sweat on me.

Just as I got in the door, I had a message from John. I threw my phone down and went straight to the utility room to take off my sweaty clothes and stuff them in the washing machine. As soon as I was in the shower, I washed myself over and over. Then I did it again. I felt so mucky; it was very sweaty sex and I needed to get the smell of him off my body. After five washes of my body and three of my hair, I felt I was clean enough to get out of the shower. I wrapped a towel round me, then went to collapse on the sofa. I hadn't even picked up my phone, I was totally exhausted; mentally drained as well as physically. Eventually, I went through to the bedroom and got my PJs on and curled up in bed with a film.

I thought back over the evening. It had been a positive experience, overall. Porn Star Sex was hot, sweaty, full-on, and hard-core fucking, but to be honest, I loved it! We both knew our limits prior to our meet, and we really got involved, I was left soaking wet, and Andy's orgasm was massive, so mission accomplished. Bedtime and no alarm set, so hopefully I could have a lie-in; I was looking forward to it.

Bright light and the noise of birds can only mean one thing, it was morning. I lay still in bed, my body was aching; it felt like I had done heavy weights at the gym, but I guess last night my body did have a fairly demanding work-out. It was only eight-thirty, and I couldn't get back to sleep. I picked up my phone and there were more messages from John pleading to see me today. After some consideration, what harm could it do? I mean, I know who he is, and I know what to expect. We agreed on 7 pm, and he said he would pay double as I had fitted him in. Yes, that's right, getting paid more than a week's wage to go and have sex with a hot guy, life's not bad at all...!

My morning run was fairly pathetic as my body ached, so I decided to have an extremely chilled-out day. I decided to decline the invitation to have lunch with friends, my body was sore, and I needed to relax a while, yesterday took a lot out of me. I sat and watched everything I had recorded on TV, had a bath, and generally did nothing! It was bliss, perfect in fact, and definitely needed. I even managed to sneak in a wee power nap before I had to start getting ready. I think because we got on so well the first time, I thought doing this was really like an extension of my me day. I mean, he is exceptionally good-looking, and he makes me have massive orgasms and I could do with another round of fucking until we can't move.

I got ready and was on the road in no time. I was driving a bit too fast; I couldn't wait, I was so looking forward to it. I now knew my way around the cities I worked in and arrived at the hotel just on time. I was so calm, it felt like I was going on a second date with someone, not that I was about to see a client! Straight past reception, it was just part of the job now, everyday life in fact...!

Into the lift, timer on; my lift regimen becoming second nature. I got to the door and, just as I put my hand up to knock, the door opened. John was standing there, freshly showered and shaved, standing in his towel. He greeted me with a long kiss and took my coat. Then he said, 'I got you a present, can you put it on?'

I love dressing up, but I like classy outfits and I had the feeling John was at the opposite end of the scale. I mean, my makeup was full-on fake, hooker orange – and that was requested by John, of course!

I went into the bathroom slightly nervous as to what to expect when I opened the bag... As soon as I shut the door, I ripped the bag open to see...a bloody nurse's outfit. I had a giggle; I could tell that John had a trashy fetish. It was extra-small; I am a 10 but managed to squeeze into it. The outfit came down far enough to barely cover my ass and came with white stockings and a small nurse's hat. I giggled; it was so trashy, but I did look good in it...! I walked out of the bathroom with a cheeky grin and strutting my stuff. I definitely walk the walk; I can move my hips in such a way that my ass looks amazing... I got as far as the bed before John could not contain himself and rushed over to me. Before I could even ask him how I looked, he had his arms around me and his tongue down my throat. He moved me around and sat me on the bed, and, as I sat down, he dropped his towel. OMG. His cock was huge and throbbing hard. He grabbed me by my hair and pulled me towards him. I started sucking his cock and tickling his balls at the same time. I love giving oral, it gets me so horny and I'm good at it; I have had my fair share of compliments in that department...!

I sat on the end of the bed with my hands on his ass, pulling him forward to fit as much of his cock in my mouth as I could without choking. It was so hot; he loved it dirty, and I was happy to play the role for him. I'd stop, pull out his penis and slap it against my face, spit on it to make it really wet, squeeze it, pull it, and rub my hands all over it until it was soaking wet, then take it back in my mouth with my hand grasping the base of his cock so I was able to toss him off as I sucked him. His penis was big enough to hold in one hand and still have half of it in my mouth.

I was so horny; my pussy was wet, and I was so turned on by John. As I got into a perfect rhythm, John stopped me and pushed me up the bed. He climbed on top, pushing my legs open and literally dove into my pussy. I lay back with my eyes shut, moaning, and groaning as it felt so good. There was no acting or faking, it genuinely felt amazing. He had a long, fat tongue and manged to keep it inside me as I wriggled about the bed in complete ecstasy. Then he slid a finger into me whilst he continued sucking on my clit. I was on the verge of an orgasm; I could feel it building. I didn't want to cum yet; if I did, I would turn to jelly and be useless...! I pushed John off and turned him onto his back and went on top of him. In seconds we were into 69, we were both giving it one hundred per cent, soaked in sweat and moaning so much. It was definitely the highlight of my week to have some hot, sweaty sex. We went like this for some time and my jaw was now getting rather sore as I had been sucking his cock so much. All of a sudden, John screamed STOP. I did and moved off him straightaway. I wasn't sure what was going on, to be honest, we were both totally into the moment, but, as I turned round to look at him, he was fumbling trying to put a condom on. He was taking an eternity, his hands were shaking so much, I asked if he wanted me to help him, but he said no he was fine. Just as it went on, he asked me to bend over the bed. I hopped off the bed, spread my legs and leaned forward, bending myself over the mattress. John was now behind me. He held my head back by pulling my hair, then, with no warning, pushed his penis into me. I was so wet from him licking me and sucking my clit, and it was a good thing considering the size of his cock! As soon as the tip of his penis was inside me, he pushed the rest in slowly. It was that big it made me gasp! I knew John loved to fuck; he didn't like sex, he loved it. He loved it deep and hard, and I was in the mood for just that. He moved back, and I could feel every bit of him even with a condom on. I could not stop wriggling on it, then backing on to him. As I pushed back, John blurted out, 'Well, you bad little nurse, I am about to punish you. How bad have you been?'

Without thinking, I replied, 'You will never be able to punish me.'

And, just as I got the last word out, he grabbed my hips and fucked me, I mean, really fucked me. He was pulling me back onto him as he was thrusting forward, his whole cock was pounding inside me and it was amazing, the feeling was so intense. John slowed the pace and began to slowly slide the entire length of his cock into me, then slowly pull it back out before sliding it back in. I was so ready to cum; he was teasing me so much. Each time he went deep inside me, it was so much that I would take a deep breath and seem to hold onto it until he pulled back out of me. John was really moaning now, and he asked if I was ready. I was more than ready, and instantly replied, 'Yes, yes fuck me.'

Then he started fucking me really hard. I was screaming, he was groaning, and we were both about to cum. John screamed, 'I'm ready, I'm about to blow!'

I let myself go and orgasmed at the same time. We were both screaming as we finished and then we collapsed on the floor, legs like jelly.

We lay on the floor, both out of breath, dripping in sweat and panting. I couldn't even talk, and all John could manage was, 'Thank you, thank you.' I wasn't even sure why he was thanking me, but I couldn't talk to ask...!

I managed to stumble through into the bathroom to try and compose myself. My makeup looked like I had been out in the rain for hours, we had sweated so much. It took a quick five minutes to repair my makeup and get out of the nurse's outfit. I put my underwear on and walked back into the room. John was still laid on the floor but managed to sit up and say, 'Thank you again, I'm totally done, you can leave whenever.'

I was glad; I just wanted to go home, shower and sleep. I thought that if I lay down on the bed here, I would fall asleep. I went back to the bathroom to put my dress on. I was still shaking, and I had a huge smile on my face that I couldn't wipe off if I tried. I walked out the bathroom to find John waiting at the door. He hugged me and asked to see me next Friday. I was obviously delighted and couldn't wait but I couldn't let John see my excitement, so told him I would have to wait and see what my diary was like.

He immediately replied, 'I know you'll come. Name your price; money is no object. There's something about you that I want, and I'll do anything to have you.'

I kissed him on the cheek and smiled, 'I'll see you soon then I guess'. Then walked out the door. As I walked to the lift, my legs were still like jelly; I was struggling to walk in my heels, I had to really concentrate. I got to the lift, and, thankfully, I was the only one in it. As soon as the doors shut, I pulled off my heels to put on my flats. The sex was so good it was in my top three sexual experiences. I was still in disbelief that this was happening, he is ridiculously hot, and got paid for it. My cheeks were aching from smiling so much – either that or from sucking his cock so hard! I felt amazing. I was dreading the drive home; if I closed my eyes for a second, I would fall asleep.

Windows down, music up loud and I still managed to be daydreaming about what had just happened – I even went the wrong way twice! Once out of the city, I managed to get a hold of myself. On the way home the radio station seemed to be playing all my favourite songs, I was singing the whole time. I will admit I am awful at singing, so it was a good thing I was alone. I stopped at some lights and was in full swing sing mode when I happened to look over at the car next to me. They were all laughing at me! Normally that would embarrass me, and I would stop, but I didn't care and carried on. I was on such a high, and I had every right to be feeling like this. I had just had sex with a hot guy, and he wanted to see me again. I was on fire; I had decided I was now a sex goddess! I honestly could not believe it. The whole way home, I had to keep giving myself a shake to see if I was going to wake up, but this dream was my life now.

Walking through my hall, I caught a glimpse of myself in the mirror. I stopped and really looked at myself. Even though I looked like I had been pulled through a bush backwards, I still had a glow about me. I never actually thought I could look like this, never mind as good as this. I was a small size 10, not a bit of fat on me, tanned and had an amazing figure. Don't get me wrong here, I have had to work damn hard to look this good! My routine consisted of a five-mile run, thirty sit-ups, thirty push-ups and thirty squats most days. I have always loved fitness and working out, but, since I started my new venture, this was now mandatory; I couldn't charge what I did if I didn't look this good.

I was ready to just collapse in a heap on the sofa, but I needed to get clean – and I needed a cold shower to wake me up from the dream-like state I was in. Feeling the water run through my hair and over my body was amazing, and I needed it after how sweaty I was earlier. I could have stayed in the shower for hours, but I wanted to sit down. I was exhausted. PJs on, cup of tea and time to relax and chill.

10. It is Getting Serious

I HAD NOW FALLEN COMPLETELY DOWN the rabbit hole. My normal, everyday life had been taken over by Felicity's world. I was finding myself in situations I would never have dreamed of being in before, and, as bizarre as this sounds, it was extremely addictive. Alternating between plain Jane to flirtatious Felicity was just such a surreal experience. I loved transforming into Felicity and the mystery of what I was going to be participating in next was thrilling.

The sheer fright as your heart pounds at the fear of being late for work when you realise you've overslept again. I didn't even have time for a shower; I had to rush out the house and accidently left Felicity's phone at home. Work was quiet; the morning felt like it was never going to end. Even my lunch break was boring, and that was probably because my break was normally Felicity time. That was when I would usually be replying to prospective clients or sending a catch-up text to previous clients that I enjoyed being with to get them to see me again. I guess what I'm trying to say is that this was the first day I realised that I missed Felicity. I know... I couldn't believe it either. I think it was the thrill of being able to morph into this glamorous, sexy, naughty, confident persona, so different to my usual self. It was something that I'd grown used to and now looked forward to. I guess being able to hide behind Felicity's character was giving me the confidence I needed in myself again. I liked the thrill of it the most, but the mysterious side also compelled me. Let's face it, the sort of clients I had met recently – feeling like I was on a normal date with amazing sex and being paid for it – had probably helped.

Foot to the floor, I drove home fast; I was excited to see what was on Felicity's phone. I got home and went straight in the door to the bedside table, where I took out Felicity's phone. Watching the phone load up when I switched it on seemed to take ages.

Emails first. Men who email are normally the best clients in terms of discretion, as they are usually married men who have sent it from the office. They're normally the clients who tip. Tipping can mean one of two things: one that I was amazing, and they want me to see them again, or, two, they're married, and it is hush money. Either way, I don't care. Yes, I know that's bad to say about married men, but the wrongdoing is on their part. There's no emotion; it's more like stress relief. One guy even said he does it so he can last longer for his wife when he gets home. On occasion married men book me because their wives won't or can't meet the man's sexual needs. They love their partner but needs that bit extra. Those guys tend to go for the full hour as they like to lie next to me after. They're normally older, so I assume it's because I'm a very attractive, younger woman. Either way, it works for me.

Hey Felicity, I just found you... I'm coming up from England on Tuesday and am staying in a hotel near the airport, I was wondering if you would do me the delight of coming to visit me on my stay in Aberdeen. I am looking for one hour at around 2000. I'm vanilla, so normal GFE preferred, but open to outfits.
   Look forward to hearing from you.

Martin

That sort of email is perfect. A guy that knows what he wants and he's from England so the chance of me knowing him or seeing him again is minimal. I replied with the following:

> *Good evening, Martin. Firstly, thanks for your email. I hope you're well. Unfortunately, Tuesdays are my day off, but if you tell me a bit about yourself, I could possibly rearrange things since you're only available on that one day.*
> *Look forward to hearing from you, F x.*

It's best to go about things in that manner as you don't want to seem too keen. It's also good to see what they come back with, so you get a sense of what they're like. There's also an email from John. He wants to meet again on Friday. That's obviously a yes, but I'll let him stew for a bit before I reply. The next email was poorly written, so that was deleted straight away. I won't see anyone unless their first message is well written and makes me smile or laugh. On occasion I message back and forth to see if they're going to be fun. If they seem boring, I'd only do it if I was in the mood. A client had asked me to attend a work function with him on Saturday and pretend to be his partner. It was in Edinburgh so the chance of someone being at the event that knows the real me was very unlikely, so I think that would be one to go to. Being wined and dined and with no sexual expectations for the night sounded great.

I couldn't believe that I had already filled my week. After last week I was only planning to work three nights this week as doing more would be too much. I still had several emails to go through and I replied that I only do this on set days on a first-come-first-serve basis so, unfortunately, I was unable to see them this week. Two replied back immediately, happy to book for next week. They both appreciated the fact that I only do it as a hobby; it was something that made them feel special rather than being squeezed into a rota or seen back-to-back like many other girls do. I had three bookings for this week and already two for next. I honestly never thought that there would be such high demand. I mean, if I wanted to, I could easily quit my day job and work one full week a month and I would end up with more than my month's salary! For a moment it crossed my mind, but then I reminded myself that I do it just because I want to do it. The excitement of it comes in part down to the fact that it's a few days a week. I think if I did it all the time it would be too much; it would become an everyday thing, like my normal job, which I feel I'm stuck in.

I didn't make the same mistake as yesterday; I took Felicity's phone with me to work today so I was able to organise my evening with Martin. I was looking forward to seeing him this evening. So far, I had managed to find out that he was in his late forties, worked in oil – but not in the North Sea. He was coming to Aberdeen for a meeting before flying out the following day for work.

My day shift dragged to an end, and I went home. I walked over to my wardrobe. I now had so many Felicity outfits to choose from and kept careful notes of what I wore when, so that I never wore the same thing twice when meeting a client. I had first date clothes for day meetings or evenings and second date clothes for day meetings or evenings. My evening outfits were dresses to just above the knee. I never wore a short dress in the daytime, the last thing I wanted was to attract the attention of reception staff. Regardless of my outfit, I would always wear a brightly coloured scarf so that my clients could easily and quickly recognise me.

Typical daytime meeting clothes were a skirt and top; skirt to the knee to prevent a glimpse of my stockings. After all, although the first layer was on show, it was what went underneath that really mattered.

I'd found that the more effort I put into my underwear and the quality of it really paid off with my clients. Which was a bounce as I love sexy underwear. I always feel so empowered when I put it on; it's as if I drift into a seductive, goddess-like state. I now have something for all occasions. For a vanilla experience I have a vast number of assorted colours of lace lingerie that I use for my everyday underwear look- if the client doesn't specify what I should wear. Everything is expensive and matching, usually a lace set with a garter and stockings if they haven't said a preference but hinted, they like something different. The vintage look is my favourite; it's almost burlesque-like. I tightly pull myself into a corset, then lace it up so my boobs look bigger and my waist tiny. For a dominatrix session it has to be black leather or Latex. I have a few variations of dom outfits though; for a first-time dom session I would wear a long-sleeved, full-body suit, then add thigh-high boots. For a second dom session I'd go for an open cup, crotchless bodysuit, then add in a harness or some kind of restraint. If I am to be submissive then I'd

Felicity Forbes

wear nothing but my harness or whatever the client requested. My kinky lingerie is hard to describe as there is not much material; basically, string in the same area as your underwear. I obviously have all the role play clothes too; police officer, fire fighter, maid, nurse, schoolgirl, cheerleader, the list goes on. I have quite the collection of sexy underwear now; I'd say my stockings alone stretch to around forty pairs. It's not hard when you have such a variety of colour, design, and transparency.

I could tell Martin had money, but he wasn't the arrogant poser type. I selected a pink and black matching set; a bra with French-style pants, thin suspender straps, worn with black stockings with a seam up the centre on the back of my legs. It's sexy, but classy.

Once I'd finished laying all my clothes out, I went to shower. I had plenty of time this evening, so I decided to blow dry and straighten my hair. My hair, well mane, now sits just above my peachy bum; I could almost sit on it. I have always had long hair and have been blessed with thick curly hair, that to be honest, needs truly little maintenance. Normally I could step out of the shower, towel dry and run oil through it and it would be perfect curls all the way down. I was so lucky; all my friends would comment on how amazing my hair was and I wouldn't have done anything to it.

I did my make-up minimal; just enough to transform me into Felicity. After make-up it was jewellery time. I always found it funny how Felicity always wore a watch! I'd changed my approach to the jewellery I wore after losing a beautiful, expensive earing. Now I always wore cheap jewellery in case it got lost. After I'd slipped on my outfit, I had a quick twirl in front of the mirror. Quick check of my bag and off I went into town.

This hotel was one of the harder ones to get into. It was right by the airport, and they always wanted to talk to you; not something I ever want to do. I changed my timer on my phone to my ring tone and set it so that, as soon as I walked in, it would go off and I would answer it just like a call. Bingo, it worked a treat. Off I went into the lift. I was only going up one floor, so I had to be quick to slip heels on and a quick gloss of the lips to give them an extra glow. I changed my timer on my phone to the time slot while walking to the door.

I was just about to knock for the second time when the door swung open; not a good sign. First impressions were that he was tall – very tall – exceptionally well dressed and in his fifties rather than his forties. The bad bit was that he was hairier than a buffalo. As I walked in, Martin greeted me with an extremely large smile on his face and thank the lord, he had nice teeth. They were very white, in fact. Nothing worse than someone with poor oral hygiene.

Fortunately, I couldn't fault his manners. I'd taken two steps into the room, and he asked if he could take my coat and scarf. As soon as he had hung up my belongings, he went to pour me a glass of wine. I wasn't able to have a drink because I was driving, but I humoured him by having a sip or two. Martin pointed, with an extremely awkward look, over to the bedside table where there was an envelope. I picked it up, then excused myself to use the rest room. I quickly counted the money and applied a small amount of lube; Martin seemed to dry me out, so I knew I would need it later; wasn't going to make an *old Florence mistake again*. When I came back out, Martin was laid on the bed in his pants. Yes, pants. I mean, who wears them these days? Just as I started walking over to him, he asked me to stop and take my dress off. I stopped dead, wishing I wasn't driving and that I could have a drink. I slowly slid the straps off my shoulders, then I put both hands on my hips, slowly sliding them up my tummy and over my breasts. Then I tucked my thumbs into my dress, just above my breasts, and started to slip my dress off. I stopped when it got to just below my ribs and twirled round, then slid it down and over my hips. I moved my hands back up my body and shifted my weight from one foot to the next and my dress dropped to the floor. I stepped one foot out and then, with the other, kicked my dress off onto the bed beside him. I was getting good at this. I held my head high with my shoulders back and walked round to the other side of the room. His eyes were locked on me, and I could see his pants starting to bulge.

Martin was still silent with his bottom jaw dropped a little so there was a parting in his lips; I loved seeing someone's face do the look of: holy fuck. On his second attempt he managed to blurt out that I looked amazing and thanked me for coming to see him. He sat looking me up and down several times. I did another twirl this time so I could check the time. I had already done twenty-five minutes and I could see he was fully erect and that was just from looking at me, so I knew it wouldn't last very long. I went to sit on the bottom of the bed, Martin still sat frozen with a shocked look in his eyes. After a few moments, he turned to face me; he was like a schoolboy on a first date, all giggles and smiling from ear to ear.

I moved up the bed to lie beside him, he went to touch me with his finger, then pulled back like you would with a big red button you wanted to touch but knew you shouldn't. I had to bite my lip, watching a grown man turn into a quivering mess was rather amusing. Eventually he started to run his fingers back and forth over my flat tummy, then he moved down the bed so that his head was in line with my stomach. He bent over and softly started to kiss round my belly button, then he moved his hands up to grasp my breasts. Just as he had a hold of them both, he let out a gasp; it was enough to send shivers down my back, not the pleasant kind! He then started to run his index finger along the top of my pants, back and forth. I lay back and closed my eyes. Each time he ran his finger along, he would slowly slide in between my skin and pants. When he got up to the second knuckle, he stopped and almost froze again. He then fumbled, seeming almost unsure of what he wanted to do next. He knelt on the bed and rested his hand on my knee, like he was scared. I reassured him that everything was OK; it was almost like he was awaiting my approval to do anything else. He then slid his hand down the inside of my leg and started to, what I can only describe as, walk his fingers back and forth over my clit. Strange, I know. In this profession, anything can happen. He then pulled his hand away like I had bitten him or something, before asking, in a sheepish voice, if I was able to turn over and lie on my front.

When I lay down, he moved over to be almost squatting on top of me, hovering himself above my thighs, he was rather heavy and if I'm honest this was fucking weird. He started to rub his hands over my back, then ran them down my arms. Martin started to kiss the back of my neck and I got cold shivers right down my back, it wasn't pleasing in the slightest. He fumbled about trying to move down while still straddling me, then started to kiss down my back while still running his hands over my arms. Just as I was about to have a quick, sneaky peek at my watch, he asked me to move to the end of the bed. I struggled not to laugh as Martin nearly fell off the bed. I turned over and started shuffling down the end of the mattress. I wasn't sure what he was wanting to do; he stood in front of me and just stared, it was very awkward. I could see he had a massive bulge in his pants. He asked if I wanted a top up of wine and I said that I couldn't cause I had to drive then he asked if I could play with myself; he moved back and grabbed the chair in the room, pulling it over to the bed so he was directly in front of me. I shifted my bottom to the end of the bed, moved my pants to one side, licked two of my fingers then slowly started to rub my fingers over my vagina. I put my left hand on the bed behind me, so I was able to lean back to be able to show him me touching myself. I was so thankful I put that spot of lubricant on before I started. This is where the acting side comes in; I kept groaning and biting my lip, then wiggling my bum side to side. Bingo, it worked, he was now pulling his penis out of those horrendous pants and tossing himself off. I upped the acting and, just like clockwork, he exploded with cum squirting all over himself, the chair, and the floor. My work here is done.

Out of curtesy I carried on for a moment or two till he said that it was enough. He hobbled through to the bathroom, obviously to clean himself up. I quickly grabbed my bag and gave myself a wipe. When he came out, he thanked me and said that he was done and, as much as he would love to do more, he wasn't able to. I grabbed my clothes and headed to the bathroom and quickly got changed. When I got out of the bathroom, Martin was already standing there with my jacket in his hands. He held it for me to put on, and no sooner than it was on my shoulders, he said goodbye and opened the door. As I walked down the corridor, I wasn't my usual smiling self. Martin wouldn't have been the type of person I would normally have taken home or gone on a date with, but he was a nice enough gentleman. Still, there was no physical attraction there whatsoever.

I got home a lot earlier than I thought I would, but I was straight in the shower when I got through the door and clothes in the wash. I went straight to bed after my shower but kept tossing and turning and having flashbacks of his unattractive body, which is not something that usually happens; I normally manage to keep it all out of my mind after my shower. After about thirty minutes I couldn't take it anymore, so I got up and put the kettle on. One cup of tea was all that was needed and no sooner than I lay down, I fell asleep.

I was groggy when I woke, I knew I had been taking on too much and I needed a rest, so I was glad I limited my clients this week and I took a few days off, I could have had clients, but I chose to have some time to myself, and to be honest, it was great. I didn't wear makeup and I didn't have to constantly pull a thong out of my ass; I wore massive pants because no one could see them. Bliss!

Buzz Buzz Buzz, I woke on my first alarm. Tonight, I was seeing John and I was excited; it was well needed. My day at work seemed to drag; I got to lunch and felt like I had been there all day. I was clock-watching which is always a disaster; I just wanted it to be 1530 so I could go home. Eventually it was home time, I ran out the door and was blasting the tunes and singing the whole way home. I wasn't seeing John till later, so I had time to go to the gym and have a cheeky sunbed. I was racing round even though I knew I had plenty of time; seeing John was definitely like getting ready for a date rather than a client. John had already said that he had got me a present, so I couldn't wait to find out what that was. I was sat with my underarms and legs smothered in hair removal cream so that I was silky smooth for this evening. I was texting John while I was waiting on the cream working on my legs and I was super excited every time the little bubble bit came up to show me he was typing. The timer for my cream went, and I jumped in the shower. I even cracked out the expensive shampoo and conditioner as it made my hair smell amazing. When I got out the shower, I was straight to the living room to get the music channel on. I massaged baby oil into my skin and oil into my hair, so I had perfect ringlets. As I sat down on the end of my bed looking into the mirror, I laughed and couldn't stop. When I had managed to compose myself, I started to look through what I was going to wear, I'd decided to go for a low-riding suspender strap with no pants and a matching push-up bra. Once I had clipped my stockings onto my suspender belt, I jumped off the bed and did a twirl in front of the mirror. I was looking gorgeous, sexy and had the confidence to take on anything and everything.

John was staying in a different hotel this time, one I hadn't been to before, so he messaged me that I had to text when I was parked and that I had to wait on him coming down as reception was a pain in the ass. Even though tonight was more like a date than a job, I wasn't keen on meeting him in the street in case anyone saw me. Granted, it was in Glasgow, so the chances of seeing someone I knew were slim, but it's always a thought that goes through my mind. The hotel was on my side of Glasgow, and I was just getting organised to leave when John messaged me saying he was ready. I texted him back to say I would be a while and he said not to worry; that he had got out of a meeting early and was just chancing his luck.

The roads weren't so bad as it was after teatime, so all the office people had already finished and travelled home. It was a lovely evening, the sun was shining, and I had my music up and was singing away. I was on cloud 9 and couldn't wait to see what John had in store for us.

I drove past the hotel and went to park in a car park off the main street. It was standard precaution that I didn't let clients see my car, in case they would be able to track me through my number plate. I touched up my make-up, slipped on my heels and pulled my stockings up so it looked like I was wearing tights. I messaged John to say I was parked and walking toward the hotel and then I set off. I got in view of the doors of the hotel when out came John. He glanced round for a second before he was able to spot me, but, when he did, I think his grin was even bigger than mine.

'Hi Felicity', he said as he greeted me with a kiss on the cheek, then grabbed my hand. Reception was just as you went in through the doors and you couldn't get to the corridor with the lift unless you had a key card. We got into the lift and John spun me round, then pushed me up against the wall and started to kiss me. Yes, this was totally against my usual protocol, but there are times when rules can be broken!

When we got into the hotel room, John pushed me up against the wall again and we were all over each other. It had to have been the most passionate kiss I'd had in a very long time; we couldn't keep our hands off each other. We were both moaning and groaning; it was hot! John then pulled away. I was trying to keep kissing him and he said no, he had a surprise. He then placed his hand on my back, guided me into the bathroom, and shut the door on me. I was a bit flustered; I admit. I was so horny and, I'll be honest, John hit all the buttons for me. I saw the envelope beside the sink and counted it while I had a quick pee; there was a large amount extra. I felt a bit bad as he was so good in bed that I honestly felt I should be paying him. Just as I looked up, I saw my present hanging on the back of the door.

I quickly finished and gave myself a wet wipe as I was being paid so needed to be perfect. I could not wait to open the Ann Summers bag. I ripped it open. The package was wrapped in their purple tissue paper but was soft to the touch, so I knew it was something to wear. My heart was racing, palms sweating. I tore off the tissue paper to reveal a red wide-mesh body stocking with slits for my breasts to pop out and was obviously crotchless. OMG, I love red. I put on the outfit. Just as I was about to open the door, I saw the bag with a box still in the bottom. I burst out laughing; it was a sex toy kit. Cock ring, vibrator, clit massager and lube. I pulled the door back, gave my head a shake so that my hair was sitting perfect and held my shoulders back, so my breasts were out. I strutted out that door; I felt incredible. I looked like a cheap hooker, but I felt amazing.

John was standing naked at the side of the bed, facing the other way, putting his phone on charge. I cleared my throat, and he turned round. When he did, he was in shock, I think. It was as if his legs had given way and he fell onto the bed with his chin nearly touching the floor. After John's reaction I *knew* I looked a million dollars, so I strutted the whole way into the room, did a spin on my massive heels and then threw the box onto the bed. I was so horny; I could feel myself getting more and more moist below. In my head all I could think was *hurry up and fuck me!* But I had to keep that thought to myself, after all it wasn't very professional, and I had already broken so many rules... I kept walking back and forth, catwalk style, at the bottom of the bed, moving my hips so that my ass shook. John then leaped up of the bed, grabbed my wrists and pulled me towards him. I do not think any words I have would describe the feelings I had; they were intense to say the least.

John pulled me tight into his body and looked at me with eyes that instantly got my full attention. He had one hand round my side, resting on my peachy bum, and the other was resting at the side of my face. He ran his tongue over my lips while lightly brushing my face with his index finger. I was in ecstasy; this was a feeling that I still hold on to, to this day. We started to kiss. It was slow, he kept pulling away and biting my lips, then running his tongue over my top lip. I was now wriggling from side to side and seriously trying hard to contain myself. Well, I was certainly surprised that I managed to find someone who gave me jelly legs this bad while on the job, after all he was basically, a stranger.

It was not long before John started to pick it up a gear and the chemistry between us was electric. I had longed for this, to find someone that had the same sexual desire as me. The high I was feeling was so intense I was almost at the point of being out of control and we hadn't even started yet. We were rolling around on the bed, kissing and taking turns to pin each other down. My heart was beating at a fair rate of knots, our breathing was now quicker and heavier; we were so in the moment. I could feel John's rock-hard penis pushing against my body when he was lying on top of me. I just kept wriggling around underneath him. John was on top and had his hands round my wrists, holding them by my shoulders. I was so caught up in the moment I did not care about the time; I didn't even have an alarm set.

John was kissing my neck, then running his tongue all over my breasts, grinding his body up against mine and kissing me again. He moved down to my belly button and ran his tongue up to my nipples; he was sucking my nipples so hard I was on the verge of having an orgasm right then. I was desperately trying to wriggle out from underneath him so I could go down on him, but, before I was able to free myself, he pushed against me so hard I let out a huge groan. I was so ready for more, I felt like I was going to explode. Just as I closed my eyes to savour the feeling, John pushed his hard cock right the way inside me; it was so big and hard my breath just disappeared. John let go of my wrists and lifted my bum slightly, so he was able to go on his knees. I moved my hands behind my head and pushed them onto the bed so that my body was off the bed, the position we were in meant his penis was going deep inside me. I knew instantly I was not going to be able to contain myself for much longer. It felt amazing; I could feel every part of his penis inside me, even his veins pulsing when he started to go faster. It was at that moment that I realised it felt so good because he had not put a condom on. I was just about to freak out when he thrust his cock so hard into me that I started to feel myself climaxing; at that moment all my worries went out the window. I could feel myself contracting and I was screaming; the pleasure was insane. It was such a huge orgasm and John was still pounding his penis inside me, it lasted forever. I turned to jelly; the sweat was pouring off us, I could feel drips of John's sweat landing on my tummy. He was still going at a rhythm that was perfect, the feeling of complete pleasure lasting for ever. John then slid his hands round onto my hips, and not only was he pounding his penis inside me, but he was also pulling me back onto him as he thrust forward. My eyes rolled into the back of my head; I knew this one was going to top the last. I was feeling it start to happen and I screamed out to John that I was nearly ready to cum again. I was nearly ready to explode, and at that point he moved one of his hands, still keeping the rhythm and pressure of his thrusts into me and started to rub my clit with two fingers. I have no words to give the feeling justice; it was so intensely pleasurable that I was struggling to breathe. I was going into one of the top three orgasms of my life. My arms were trembling still trying to hold me up, my eyes were rolled back into my skull, and my vagina was so wet that his huge penis was no longer too big, but perfect. I struggled to catch a breath and, just as I felt my legs start to spasm, John screamed that he was away to blow. He thrusted faster and on the second thrust I exploded; not only did I have a massive orgasm, but I also started to squirt. In fact, I squirted with such force that it covered John's chest. Just as he noticed, he yelled out, 'Oh fuck, yes!' I could feel every blood vessel pulse and the muscles in his penis contracting. He was still pushing into me, and I was still having an orgasm, I felt the rapid fire of contractions, and I could feel myself fill. It was the most satisfying feeling I had had in a very long time.

We both collapsed into a heap on the bed.

My body was still trembling, my heart racing. I was the happiest I had been in years. I was one hundred and fifty per cent completely satisfied. I could not even lift my arm, I was jelly. We were both exhausted. We lay there motionless, silence for at least ten minutes. I think John felt just as satisfied as me. As my heartbeat returned to normal, I was able to feel my fingers and toes again. I got up and, just as I turned round, John let out a huge snore. I had to put my hand over my mouth, so I did not wake him up laughing. Times like that I wish I did a feedback form; I am sure I would have got 10 out of 10!

Just as I made it into the bathroom, it hit home. I felt his cum drip down my legs... Holy actual fuck, he really did not use a condom. I jumped in the shower. My thoughts were racing round but kept coming back to; FUCK!

I had the fastest shower possible, then repaired my make-up so I was respectable and threw clothes on. I was lucky John was still sleeping, as I was now furious. *Fuck.* He was lying naked on the bed, penis all wrinkled up, so I quietly headed for the door.

I was so annoyed that I let that happen. I broke the most important rule of all; PROTECTION. I could not believe it. I guess I was so caught up in the moment but still that is no excuse. I walked quickly to my car and, as soon as I got in and shut the door, I burst out crying. I was petrified. I mean, I already knew he had been with Emilia, which means he presumably used call girls frequently. I knew he had a girlfriend which made me feel at ease for a second till I thought, what if she has whatever he has and that is why they stay together. My head was going insane, the drive home was erratic, but I was home quickly and, in the shower, straightaway. I sat with my back against the shower wall with the water running over my breasts and down onto my body. I sat staring blankly at the wall. The only thing I could feel was anger and the only thing I could think was that I had better cancel my appointments over the next few weeks so that I could get tested and be sure I was OK. The last thing I wanted was for me to give someone something.

After what seemed like forever in the shower, I finally felt clean enough to come out. I was so angry with myself that I let that happen; I should not have got carried away. After all, John had tried to pull the no-protection stunt before. I did not know where he had been or who he had been with. And I do not have unprotected sex with anyone, never mind a client. The whole thing with John was spoilt now. I was so angry that I knew I could not see him again, as much as the sex was the best I'd had in a long time. He had betrayed my trust and broke my rules, so I blocked his number and deleted him, and John was added to the Never See Again list!

11. Spring Break

WITH ALL THAT HAD BEEN going on these last few months I was well overdue a holiday. And what better time to disappear for two weeks than when you are too depressed to go to your day job and had not been given the all-clear to do your night job. I had been signed off work for two weeks with personal problems as everything had gotten on top of me. I seemed to cry for no reason; I couldn't exactly serve customers while sobbing, so my doctor had recommended that I take some time off and that if I needed more time, it wouldn't be a problem.

I messaged Nikki with the following:

Hi, I was going to call but my head's a mess. I need to go away for a while to get rid of these dark clouds in my head, just thought I should let you know that I was taking time out.

I thought it was best I told her as she had been my rock, especially in these last few days. Nikki was the first person I called when my John disaster happened. After days of her counselling me, she confided in me that she had a situation remarkably similar to mine. I had barely put my phone down when it buzzed.

Great, where are we going?

I was a bit stunned. I had to read what I wrote to her again, just to check that I had not accidentally invited her or given that impression, but, no, it was written as if I was going alone. I put my phone down. I needed a break, to just sit and be alone! Just as I was about to reply with my intention was to go alone, she had beaten me to it:

> *I know you did not ask me, but you'll go away and be alone and just sit dwelling on what's happened and then, by the time two weeks passes, you'll have Googled everything imaginable, and you'll come home worse than you went away. So, I am not taking no for an answer, but I'll let you pick where to go!*

Yes, she was correct. She had me summed up. I guess that is why we're such good friends; she is someone who just gets me! I was straight onto icelolly.com to book a holiday. I love the site as it tells you the temperature of the places you are looking at. My search consisted of ten days or more, any destination, and, finally, beach holiday. Instantly, five destinations popped up that were above 20°C. I did not like long flights, so I looked at Portugal; about three hours and thirty minutes from Glasgow. Faro had nice beaches so that was it, just had to pick our hotel. I called Nikki to see if she wanted to meet so we could choose together.

We met at Costa, got large coffee's and I cracked the laptop open to show Nikki what I was thinking. She seemed less enthusiastic as to my hotel choice and said, 'You picked the place, let me pick the hotel?' She then clicked on one of the most-expensive, indeed, *the* most expensive. Before I could say another word, she said, 'I am paying for the holiday as I have a regular client that has been giving me extra. My tips from them are enough to cover the lot.'

I am not one for taking things from people and I have money, so we had a disagreement about this until we settled on her buying the holiday and me taking our spending money. All set: it was booked, and we had a day to pack and get to Glasgow for our flight. I started to feel a bit more upbeat about things; I think I just needed something to focus on rather than dwell on my current reality.

I decided that I wouldn't tell my work I was going on holiday; they knew I was off for personal reasons. I told my family I was due holidays, and that was it. The joy of not having animals or a boyfriend meant I was all sorted to go away the next day. Nikki suggested she stayed at mine tonight, so we could go to the airport together. So, we went to her place to pack, then headed to my house.

When we got back to my house the feeling of being depressed and anxious came back as soon as I stepped in the door. I was so glad that I was going away, and that Nikki was coming, I was not one for being depressed or letting things get to me, but this was all so over whelming that I think this would have been enough to test anyone's mental health. Nikki gave me a hug and said, 'Go and pack. We are leaving in thirty minutes; we will stay in Glasgow overnight.'

I was a bit like, *What the hell is going on?* At the same time, I was glad that she had taken charge and was taking me away to get a clear head. Friends like her do not come around very often.

Bags packed: bikinis, dresses, shorts and flip-flops. Then just a quick check round the house and we were ready to hit the road. My OCD is a killer when I am going away for more than two nights; I have to switch everything off, then check I did switch it off, then double-check. This is something I always hide from people, but Nikki had stayed with me, and she is well aware of my little quirks.

House locked up, car packed, and we were ready to go. I turned to Nikki, 'So, where are we staying tonight?'

'Well, since our flight isn't till lunch, I've booked us into the Radisson so we can have a nice dinner tonight and get into holiday mode.'

I was starting to wonder if she had secretly won the lottery with all this spending, but, when questioned, she just said again, 'I have got a few really rich, regular clients that kept buying me gifts. I keep the things I like but sell the rest on eBay and Gumtree.'

I burst out laughing as I was not expecting that as an answer. But, then again, it *was* Nikki, so anything could have been the answer. Nikki and I had only met fairly recently, but it was as if we had been very close friends for years; she was definitely my go-to girl nowadays. I had not been away with one person for ten days before; people normally annoy me after three days, but at no point did I feel that way with her. We just got each other; we knew when we could push each other, but we also knew when to stop and take a step back and give one another space. Just as we were about to leave my house, she stopped me at the door and held out her hand. She had one eyebrow raised and her hand on her hip. I could not help but laugh. I said, 'There are no cameras, you don't need to pose.'

We were both laughing, but it stopped when she flicked the back of my head and said in an aggressive tone, 'Work phones are being left at home, this is a holiday for us to have a break.'

I manged to blurt out between laughter, 'My phone is already in the house, in my bedside drawer. You should leave yours there too!'

I needed a break. Not just a holiday; I wanted to get away from everything that had been happening and to find myself again. I believe it is not until you're lost that you begin to find yourself and, at this point in my life, I was well and truly lost.

I could not decide if she was disappointed that I agreed with her or in shock that I was actually leaving mine behind. I understand why Nikki was so reluctant to be leaving her phone; I could tell from the way her pout went to an awkward frown and even a foot stomp, but she went back to my bedroom to leave hers as well, not that she needed to.

That was it. We were now on our way to have a work-free, relaxing break, just the two of us. We got to Glasgow and dumped our bags at the hotel, then went to drop my car off out-of-town with friends. My friend had not met Nikki, so it was rather entertaining when we got there. Nikki was her usual playful self with me, and, as we were leaving, my friend pulled me aside to ask if she was a friend or a special friend. I laughed, winked and closed the door. We got a taxi back into town to the hotel and, to my surprise, when we got in the room there was champagne waiting for us. I turned to Nikki and laughed. 'Thank you so much, I really needed this.'

Nikki poured our first glass and we toasted 'to a well-deserved break and a relaxing time together'. It was lovely; the feeling of sitting in a lush room with a glass of bubbles and no work or driving for a whole ten days.

The first bottle went down a treat. Just as I was about to go for a shower, I heard the cork go on another one. I was giggling my way into the shower as I knew this was just the beginning of a very drunken holiday. Nikki loved wine and champagne and to be honest I enjoyed drinking with her, mostly down to the fact I felt safe around her. When I got out of the shower Nikki was dancing about like she was at a festival; the energy that came off that woman was enough to lift even the darkest of moods. I was so glad that she had told me she was coming. We started to get ready for dinner, I was starving. I had not really had any appetite for the last few days, so I was well overdue for some good grub. A three-course meal and a steady supply of wine and I was well on my way.

Luckily, we had requested an early morning wakeup call from reception; Nikki was worried that we would sleep in. However, with how noisy it was in the city, we were both awake. I lay on the bed with a sore head, but I had a big smile on my face. Nikki was moaning and rolling about the bed; I think by the sound of it she felt worse than me. We lay there for a bit while we properly woke up, then I went for a cold shower to try and shake off my hangover.

I was feeling slightly under the weather; *why is it champagne gives you a bloody sore head?*

At breakfast we were both struggling to eat, but I knew I would feel rubbish all day if I didn't force something down. When we got back to the room, we both felt sick; *maybe it was too soon to eat?* Thankfully, we had time for a wee nap before it was time to go to the airport. We woke to our alarms going off; we had fifteen minutes to get down to reception for our taxi to the airport. It was not a problem because we were packed and ready to go.

Airports freak me out, I always get stressed, I hate how busy they are. Most of all I hate the strange sweaty smelly people that always seem to be bumping into you. Granted the sound of all the tannoid announcements, squabbling siblings and crying babies do not help matters! You would think after having been to the airport so many of time I'd be used to the process. But no each time is just as stressful. It got me wondering, *how do I actually manage to be Felicity?* Once we were checked in and bag free, I did feel a little less anxious. I was not one for having drinks before flying, but Nikki was already at the bar. I had my head in my hands; to be honest, I just wanted to get on the plane so I could go to sleep but I humoured her and tried to take a sip. 'Nope, definitely not, this isn't going to work, it's disgusting.' I had a watery mouth and the full sweats going on; I was certainly not going to be drinking again until I was at the hotel.

I passed out with my head on the table at the bar. I woke to Nikki shaking me. 'Hurry up, get up, it's time to go.' Nikki dragged me up off the seat and started pulling me along behind her. We got to the gate just as the line was getting down to the last few, so straight on the plane for us. No sooner had I sat down than I must have dozed off because, the next thing I knew, we had landed, and it was time to get off! We had landed in Lisbon and, just as we were getting our bags, Nikki looked at me and said, 'I've had a look and we are going to get the train to Faro. It is about three hours.'

My face dropped. Three hours! That is ages. I stomped my foot in protest, just like a small child would when annoyed. Nikki started rolling her eyes and grabbed my arm to pull me along to the train. I really was not in the mood, but I guess it beats being stuck on a bus for longer or sitting in a hot car for ages. Staring out the window in a mesmerising daze was enough to put me to sleep, maybe there is a plus side about being hungover when you travel, as I seem to have slept through the lot.

We arrived at our hotel, and I was a bit anxious about what it was going to be like. I am not one for busy places and nothing infuriates me more than having to wait in a queue to be served, so I was relieved to see that the hotel was huge. There were lots of bars, the pool area was huge, and it was not as busy as I expected it to be. I was so glad that Nikki booked this hotel; it was beautiful. It was certainly weather for a dress, so we checked in, got changed and then headed out for a look around.

After hours of walking around we had worked up an appetite and started to look for somewhere to sit down, drink and eat. Most of the places looked good and, to be honest, I was just so hungry now that I could have eaten anything anywhere. We found this beautiful little local restaurant which looked extremely inviting so decided that we should go and try some of the local wine with tapas. I feel it is best to enjoy the culture of where you are as it's only polite. We got back to the hotel a bit later than expected; one wine ended up with another, and, before we knew it, it ended up in a pub crawl.

Crash, Bang! Instantly I woke to noise. *What the hell is going on?* I thought to myself. Still lay horizontal, feeling pretty shitty I started rubbing my eyes to try to get them to adapt to the sunlight. It was somewhat pleasing waking up to be in the heat. A far cry from Scottish weather anyway! We had left the patio doors wide open last night as it was so hot in the room, so the noise of the hotel staff setting up for breakfast echoed through our room. Nikki was in no fit state to move but I went out to the balcony to have a look. 'Rise and shine beautiful, not a cloud in sight just sunshine beating through the light blue sky.'

Mornings in Faro were something I could get used to; it was such beautiful weather. At home if I was woken that early, I would have probably screamed at the people who woke me as I was hungover and grumpy; but in Faro the weather was too nice to be grumpy! Although we both had extremely sore heads, it was expected, the joys of consuming native beverages. Grumbling tummies meant only one thing; it was time for breakfast. I had more liquid than food the previous day, so straight away we went down for breakfast. I love how breakfast abroad is more about bread, cheese and ham, then finished off with different pastries. Certainly, better than the usual greasy English breakfast we have to offer at home. I had absolutely got my appetite back now and was starting to feel like I had forgotten what was going on in my life. It just goes to show that a change of scenery is enough to change your mindset. We decided on having a lazy morning by the pool, then booking into the spa early afternoon so we had the rest of the day to go on a little adventure.

After breakfast we went to get our bikinis on and headed straight to the pool; it was not roasting hot yet but was warm enough to lie on the loungers in our bikinis and read our books. The pool was huge, there were three different ones, and the spa had a wellness pool, but it was not that busy, so we just went to the normal area and still managed to have spare loungers on either side. I was so glad that Nikki came with me; she always seemed to make me laugh and this holiday was all about me needing to laugh again. It was not long before it was time for lunch; the morning seemed to pass so quickly, but it was nice. I think I must have dozed off at the pool because I only got to chapter two in my book. The hotel lunch consisted of so many different salads, cheese boards and then mostly pasta with some fish and spiced chicken. It was lovely food; I felt spoilt by not having to cook. We both ate far too much, but I guess that is what happens when it's buffet style. I just wanted to try everything; I love trying different cuisines. We ate so much that we needed to have a lie down by the pool. I was glad that I was in a bikini as my tummy had seemed to expand with how much I had eaten. We still had an hour before we were booked into our treatments, so it was perfect timing for a siesta. We had booked in for a body wrap today, then tomorrow massages. We did not book too much in advance as we wanted to see what they were like first before committing to being in the spa all week.

Lay covered in a seaweed paste certainly does not sound appealing but I can vouch that it felt rather bloody incredible. In fact, I was so relaxed that I fell asleep; it was bliss being pampered and feeling human again. The lady woke me up with a glass of water and I could not believe that forty-five minutes had passed. When I got out of the treatment, I was still groggy and rather confused. I met Nikki at the door, and she laughed when she saw me, As I leant against a wall, I said to her, 'I thought a spa was meant to make you feel better.'

She just laughed and said, 'I feel the same, it must be the quantity of food that we have consumed or the weather. Then again, quite possibly it could be the hangover, given the amount of alcohol that we had last night.'

Nine days of the holiday had passed, and it was exactly what I needed; being pampered, relaxing by the pool, lots of lovely food. In that time, I seemed to get back to myself, I no longer felt lost. It was certainly the best thing I could have done, coming away. I do not think I could have got myself feeling like this again staying at home. Today was the day that I could call the doctor for my results and, to be honest, I was not even worried about it anymore. I was feeling great, I did not feel unwell, nor did I have any symptoms of anything. I was ready for the phone call.

I thought it would be better to be by myself in case it was not the news I was hoping for, so I went out of the room to call; I didn't want Nikki there staring at me. After waiting ages, finally the surgery picked up. It was fine; all clear. I was so relieved. I walked back to the room with a bounce in my step and every mirror I saw my reflection in, I was grinning from ear to ear like the Cheshire cat. As soon as I opened the door Nikki could tell straight away from my face. She insisted on us going out to celebrate in town. To be honest, I was happy just relaxing in the resort, but she had been so good to me that I thought it would be rude of me if I said no. After all, we only had tonight left of the holiday, so I guess it was about time we let our hair down. We had a very relaxing day by the pool which was perhaps best as we had not only racked up a massive spa bill but had also exhausted the treatments available – so a day by the pool sounded bliss.

Nikki had our evening planned, she decided that we would eat out to kickstart our celebrations. Once we started getting ready, I got in the mood for partying. I think I just sometimes need encouragement to go out. When we got to the restaurant it was beautiful, everything was spotless. The menu was extensive; it was not a tourist place. It was more a local's place; the majority of the menu was fish, which was just what I was in the mood for. I had eaten too many carbs of late and, to be honest, I had not worked out at all, so I needed to start eating right again and get Felicity's body back. After the second bottle of wine and lots of delicious food it was time to hit the town; after all, Faro has the reputation of being a party town. When we got closer to the main street it was really busy, it was full of young drunk teenagers rolling around and most of them were stumbling and looked like they had been out for days.

We headed straight to the cocktail and wine bar, and I think we were in there for about five minutes before we were approached by a group of six incredibly attractive guys who offered to buy us a drink. I rolled my eyes and smirked at Nikki. Her eyes were the opposite and were nearly popping out of head. We stayed and drank with them for a while; they were on holiday from England so at least we were able to understand them, I guess. Just as I said we were heading to the next pub they all said that they would come with us and show us the best pubs. I was reluctant. You hear too many stories about young women on holiday abroad being spiked and gang raped.

Nikki was the boss tonight and before I knew it, we were six pubs in, and the drink was flowing. I was now on the verge of being extremely drunk. I was at the stage that I did not want to drink anymore. I was not keen on the idea of getting so drunk that I'd wake up in a strange apartment with a strange man; it just wasn't how I wanted the evening to go. I started to slow down my drinking and even accidently spilt a few. Oops! Nikki was the opposite, she was drinking drink after drink and I knew she was probably going to bring one, possibly two of the guys back to our room. That, or she was going to disappear later on in the evening. I was not keen on either scenario, but I wasn't her mother, and she was a grown woman, so it was really up to her what she was going to do.

When we got to the next bar, I pulled Nikki aside, 'What do you want to do?'

'I've not decided which one I want to do, so we have to stay out a little longer!'

I paused for a moment then grabbed her arm, 'That's not what I asked, it's time to go home, come on!'

'No, I'm having fun and they are hot, we can't leave'.

I went into Mother Mode. I started pretending flirting with them so I could find out what complex they were in and what their room arrangement was so that if Nikki went home with one of them, she was not in a room with six men. I even got three of their phone numbers so that, if things did go wrong,

I would be able to track them down the following day. I am not sure why I got so worried about it all as I know Nikki can look after herself. I mean, she has been an escort for a long time and never came to any harm. Nikki and I had a bedroom each, so I was trying to persuade her to pick just one guy and come home, but Nikki being Nikki, she was not able to decide. I was not ready to be naked with anyone yet, so I wasn't at all interested in anyone coming back. That said, I did prefer Nikki bringing them to our place than staying out all night with them or disappearing.

Nikki then stumbled across to me and said, 'Go home. I am happy and you're being boring. I will see you in the morning!'

Well, hell no! I did not want her to be staying out with strangers even if I was struggling to stay awake. Nikki was as stubborn as me, so I knew it was going to be a mission to convince her to come home. Just then one of the guys started bringing more shots over and I was dreading it till, boom! I saw the salt and lemon; it was Tequila. I hated the stuff, but I knew that Nikki hated it more. Now, I know this makes me sound like the worst friend possible, but I knew two of those shots and she would be either sick over everyone or she would be passed out on the floor.

To my surprise, the first one went down far easier than anticipated, and she seemed fine. Me on the other hand; I could already smell the sick in my nose. They were getting another one ready to go, and, just then, Nikki was sick everywhere. I knew now I would be able to get her back to the hotel without any bother. I managed to gather our things together and make our way out of the bar without even having to ask her, so I was glad of that. It took slightly longer than I thought to get us back to our room, but when we were there, it was straight to bed.

Our last day of our vacation and we were both worse for wear; I certainly did not want to do a thing. Breakfast was not an option just now, so we rolled over and went back to sleep. By mid-morning we were both awake and in need of food; hangover food, to be precise. KFC greasy chicken or a McDonald's Quarter pounder would have hit the spot, but neither were within walking distance, so I called down to reception and ordered the biggest feast for us to have as room service. I went out to the balcony to lay out a duvet for us; I certainly was not in a fit state for the public to see me like this so room service it was.

Nikki and I spent the day on the balcony. At first, every mouthful was a struggle, but, after food and a nap we woke up feeling a lot better. So, it was down to the pool to have a sleep in the sun. By evening we felt brand new but agreed to stay in the complex and have dinner as we needed to leave at ten that evening to get the train to the airport. The time had passed so quickly, and I had the best time I'd had in ages; it was good to just be ourselves for a while. No makeup, no having to constantly be on your phone; it was a break we both needed. Being a call girl takes a toll on you, mainly your mental health; it's certainly not a job for the faint-hearted. My most recent encounter had contributed to my need to reset; to focus on myself rather than Felicity all the time.

12. The Masked Man

AFTER WEEKS OF CAJOLING EMAILS and texts from one of my regular clients, Andrew, I agreed to his requests. Andrew is someone I have seen once a month since I first moved my business to Aberdeen. We usually meet at his house near the end of the month as he works offshore; every time he comes home, we meet up. Our appointments have been fairly Vanilla; he has a foot fetish, so our appointments consist of him sucking my toes while he plays with himself and watches me play with myself. I did not think I'd manage at first due to the fact I have super-tickly feet. The first few times I had to try hard not to burst out laughing and I had to really concentrate on something other than the fact that he was sucking my toes otherwise I would have squirmed about and ended up pulling my feet back or, worse, kicking him in the face! Doing this with Andrew was so different to when the middle easter businessman licked my feet, but that's because I have a bit of a crush on Andrew. After about four appointments with him I was OK with it; it was becoming almost a normal feeling, I mean there are so many worse things out there than sucking toes. On our first meeting I wondered why he needed to pay; all in all, he was an appealing package.

Then his pants came off. Unfortunately, like Connor he was not blessed with a penis that was of adequate size. You get small, but his was smaller than small. So perhaps that's why he had a foot fetish; he had to find other ways to get off as the size of his penis would make conventional sex difficult. On the plus side, when he went down on me and was using his tongue the feeling was so intense that I felt like I was floating into a dreamland, so seeing Andrew was always a pleasure.

Andrew had been asking if I would take things to the next level. I was not sure what the next level meant, in this game it could mean anything, so I said we would have to discuss it in detail before our next meeting. Andrew would normally request that I wore no underwear and a dress; he did not like stockings as they got in the way with his foot fetish, my hair was to be curly, and I was to wear minimal makeup. This time, however, Andrew requested that

I wore a black leather playsuit that was crotchless, with an open bust as well as gloves and an eye mask. Andrew also requested that we use toys; he had said he would get them, but I wasn't keen on the thought of him supplying them. I wanted to make sure they were brand new, so I suggested he sent me the links then I would get them after work.

My phone started buzzing every few minutes. So, one minute I would be serving a customer, the next I was getting a picture of a huge dildo or cock rings that would fit on an elephant. Milly was giving me the glare; she could tell I was up to something. I was almost having to bite my cheeks to keep a straight face, so I put my phone away. It got to breaktime and, straight away, I went to check Felicity's phone. He had sent nearly twenty pictures of things he wanted, followed by a text saying for me to get anything from the stuff he had sent, to the value of £400. I should keep the items to bring to our meetings and he would reimburse me. I spent the rest of the day with a cheeky grin on my face; Felicity was back!

When I eventually finished my shift, I ran down to the lockers, got my coat and headed for the door. I only had a few streets to walk before I got to Ann Summers. I was walking round with a basket full of sex toys; even the girl in the store gave my basket a glance, then smiled and giggled. It was not long before I hit the limit, but I still needed a few things on the list, so I decided to just get them. It was a night I was looking forward to just as much as Andrew.

Once home, I laid out all the goodies and took pictures to send to him, I wanted him to be as excited as me. I was also getting curious as to what he had in store for us as I had a feeling, he had everything planned out. It was not long before my phone started to go wild, message after message, so I assumed that Andrew had seen what I sent to him. I was right; he was over the moon. We texted back and forth for the most part of the evening; he was such a lovely guy that I did not mind taking the time to talk to him. Nikki would always moan at me about this, saying that if I was not getting paid then I shouldn't speak to a client, but I was the opposite. I wanted a good relationship with my favourite clients as I enjoy spending time with them and, to be honest, that is why they're regular clients; because I wanted to see them just as much as they wanted to see me.

There were still four days to go before our meeting, which was frustrating, but it is not like we could move the booking forward as he was in the middle of the sea somewhere. We messaged every day, and I would send him naughty pictures with the toys I had bought; I thought it was good to get him excited, and it kept me entertained, too. I had not seen a client since the John disaster, which was months ago now and, to be honest, I had not wanted to. It was so nice having my holiday and then easing myself back into it slowly. Having my first meeting back with Andrew was the right thing to do. I felt at ease around him, so it was nice to be looking forward to seeing someone. I had got my results back from my second lot of tests and all was clear, so I knew I was safe.

It was the night before our meeting, and I was getting everything organised; I think I was looking forward to it even more than Andrew! I put all the toys away in a bag and folded my outfit on top. I was now ready for the booking. I lay in bed thinking about what he wanted to do to me; I was wet just thinking about it. I am not sure what it is about role play and dressing up that I enjoyed the most, but it was my preferred thing by far. I think it is the mystery behind it all and the acting; how you can be anything you want to be. I drifted off to sleep with a smile on my face, that was for sure.

Complete silence, bright light and a dry mouth; it must be morning! This morning was different, I woke refreshed and eager to go. I was glad I had work first otherwise I think I would just have been at home clockwatching. My day at work was easy, it was just Milly and I, so it was a day that we did the bare minimum to get the shift over with; it was Friday after all. I had twenty minutes to go, and Milly could tell I was wanting to go home so she said for me to finish because it was quiet. I was jumping about; I was so excited I could not wait to get home. I didn't need to be asked twice; I raced to my car and went straight home to get ready. I had a huge grin on my face, and I don't think anything was going to wipe it away. I had a couple of hours before I had to be at Andrew's house, but I was straight in the shower and getting ready; I could not sit still. I messaged him to check that the time was still OK, and he replied that he was home so I could go round whenever I was free. I started to get ready faster. I was so looking forward to seeing him; I would say that Andrew was in my top five clients,

I know I probably should not have favourites, but it was impossible not to.

Finally, I was ready to go, I messaged Andrew to say that I was about to leave and that I would see him in twenty minutes. I parked right outside his house; I was not bothered if Andrew saw my car. I quickly got out and rang the buzzer. Andrew always greets me with a kiss and asks to take my coat; he is such a gentleman. We walked through to the living room and, as usual, he said I should go to the bathroom, which is where he left the money. It felt strange taking his money this time; I felt wrong about him paying me, it felt more like a normal date. I mean, who can say they have had sleepless nights because they have been so excited to go to work! For me this was a first!

I went back through to the living room to tell Andrew I was away to start setting things up in the bedroom. Just as I was about to leave the room Andrew looked up at me 'Wait I have something to ask you', followed by a long pause.

I was not worried or scared; if it had been a different client saying this then I think I would have been heading for the door and been worried about what was going to happen, but Andrew made me feel so comfortable I wasn't fazed. I stood looking at Andrew from across the room. *It must be serious,* I thought as Andrew was sheepishly looking at the floor; he had gone all shy, which is somewhat out of character for him.

'Is everything ok? Just ask what you need to ask I'm sure it will be fine.'

Andrew then slowly started to look up at me, 'I've had an idea, but you could say no if you wanted, I don't want you to feel pressured at all.'

My heart rate started accelerating, I was slightly worried now; for a split second all I could think was, *is he about to chop me up in bags or lock me in his closet?* I started laughing, to be honest it was more of a nervous giggle. 'Come on, spit it out, the worst that can happen is I say no? You won't know my answer unless you ask me.'

Andrew glanced at the floor again, 'Maybe you should sit down?'

This was unsettling to say the least. 'Come on tell me I'm intrigued now?'

Andrew looked me straight in the eyes, 'I really want to tie you up and use a Taser on you, I've done it before, I used it on the girl I used to see before she moved away'.

First thought, *no fucking wonder she has moved away*! I must have looked completely shocked, *but seriously how could you put on a poker face when someone wants to Taser you?* 'A Taser, really?'

'Yes, a Taser'. He then pulled out a box from underneath the sofa to show me. As much as this shocked me, I was also intrigued. I do like to experiment, after all, but I can honestly say that never in my life did I think I would be tied up and Tasered for pleasure. Then again, turning into Felicity was also something I never thought I would do and look at me now.

I didn't need to think about it for long. If it was with someone else then I would have had concerns about it, but Andrew was so lovely, and I trusted that he wouldn't let me be harmed in any way, 'Ok yes, let's try it but I have two conditions; firstly, we do it near the end in case I don't like it and secondly, if I say stop, we have to stop?'

'Yes, I completely agree to those conditions, we can have a safe word? Donkey perhaps or Bananas?'

I had a chuckle, how he thought of donkey and banana I have no idea, but we agreed with donkey as our safe word. I went through to the bedroom to sort out the toys. I laid them out on his desk and then started to get into my playsuit. Even with the surprise of the Taser, I was still really looking forward to it. Once I had set up the toys and got in my outfit, I called Andrew through to join me. He walked in and pushed me back onto the bed. He did not waste any time; straight to tethering me. He lay me on my back, spreadeagled on the bed, and finished things off with a blindfold. This alone was making me so horny. I guess the more I had been experimenting with different sexual fantasies, the more I needed to explore new things to get the same satisfaction that I had before.

I had never let a client tie me up; this was the first occasion. It was something Andrew and I had discussed at length, and I was happy about letting him do this to me. Andrew was a subdued well-mannered gentleman, but when he got into role play it seemed to flick a switch and he became confident and demanding. His voice got more dominant, and it was like he got this alter ego. I guess something similar to me when I transform into Felicity. I was wriggling around on the bed, wondering what was going to happen next. The fact that I was blindfolded made every noise I heard exciting and everything I felt was intensified with not being able to see.

I could hear Andrew move closer towards me, then he moved onto the bed beside me. I was trying to see if I was able to move my hand to get a clue as to what he had or what was about to happen next, but he had the rope so short I was stuck, spreadeagled, unable to grab him. I could feel him move closer towards me and then I was able to feel the heat of his breath on my nipples. Andrew would lick my nipples, then lightly blow on them; this alone was getting me so excited. I started to feel what I thought was a feather running across my breasts. Suddenly it stopped. I did not want it to stop; I was just getting started. I was laid there, listening intently to see if I could hear a clue for what was coming next. Just then I heard the top of a bottle of lube close. My pussy was already soaking wet, I knew that he did not need lube on his penis, so I knew that he was coming towards me with a toy. I lay there waiting to see if it was anal beads or if it was a big vibrator; I was driving myself mad wondering what it could be. I felt his hand on the inside of my leg, then he started to lightly rub the tip of the lube-covered vibrator up and down my clit. With each stroke he would push it against me harder, then, after a few moments, he would almost push it inside me, but never enough for it to open me up, just enough to push against me. I was so horny I shouted out, 'Just fuck me with it.'

I could not wait any longer, I longed for him to make me cum. Just then he forced the vibrator into me, switched it on and started to fuck me with it. My moaning turned to screaming, I could not be quiet, it was a bloody big vibrator, and he was a big, strong man so it was pushing into me so hard. I loved it; I was on the verge of a huge orgasm. I screamed out 'Oh my, I am nearly about to cum', and he stopped and pulled it out of me.

'You bastard!' I shouted. I was now very horny and needed to cum; it had built up so much. 'Please fuck me, Andrew just fuck me!', I begged to be fucked, but Andrew wasn't giving in so easy. Everything was quiet, it was almost like he had left the room. Then I felt the bed move. I could feel him untie the rope around my left ankle.

'Be quiet and do as your told, bend your left leg.'

I did what I was told and now my foot was next to my pussy.

He held my ankle in place, 'Keep it there and do not move, if you move, or if you don't listen then I will Taser you early.'

Well, that was enough to make me stay still. I did not even want to talk, having seen the Taser, I knew he was being serious, so I almost froze in the position he held me in. I was now slightly worried about the Taser, possibly because I was actually tied up and blindfolded, I didn't know when it was going to happen. I mean, he could do it any minute now. Andrew then slid one hand between the bed and my ass, lifting me up. He started spreading my cheeks apart, then, without any warning, shoved the anal beads inside me. I had mixed feelings about this which I have already mentioned, but I felt that it was time to try to experiment and they were not huge beads and Andrew was well aware of my anxiety around my bum. Luckily before I was able to put any thought to the anal beads Andrew distracted me by the vibrator. I was wriggling around on the bed; within minutes he was fucking me with it like he was before. All I could do was moan because it felt so damn good. I was so horny, but I did not dare say anything in case it made him stop again. I bite my tongue, so I didn't say the wrong thing. Just as I thought it couldn't feel any better, he started going harder and faster. That was me, my eyes started to roll into the back of my head, and I exploded, so much so that I started to squirt all over Andrew.

I had absolutely no control over my body, I was way past my normal feeling, and it felt like it wasn't going to stop. My body was tingling all over, my eyes were still rolled back into my head, I was panting like I had run a marathon, and sweating so much it was like I had just emerged from a pool. I could not move; I was lay there in complete ecstasy. It was the best feeling I had had in a very long time, and I longed for it to stay. I guess the fact that I was being pleasured in more than one way made my orgasm even bigger. The way it makes you feel like it doesn't matter what is happening around you; I didn't have a care in the world. I lay there trying to wriggle my toes to see if I was able to or if I was still lifeless. I said to Andrew that I needed a minute as he had completely blown me away, and, just as I exhaled a huge sigh, he hit me with the Taser on the top of my thigh.

'Holy fuck!' The pain of the Taser quickly outweighed the shock; it was like the worst electric shock imaginable, then my body started to spasm. I yelled, 'Arghhhh! NEVER do that again.' Andrew waited five minutes till I calmed down before he untied me. I guess I would have done the same as well, considering I was screaming at him. Aside from the Taser, I had had one of the best nights, one that I would remember forever.

13. Three's a crowd

THEY SAY THREE'S A CROWD; but I am yet to find out, I had been seeing Oliver on and off for around six months now. Our meets were dependent on him being home alone; normally his wife went on a girls' weekend once every five weeks or so and, occasionally, she went to stay with her parents. So, sometimes we meet twice a month, other times we might go nearly two months without a meet. Oliver falls under my semi-regular clientele category as we do not have a regular date, but we do see each other when possible. Oliver is a successful businessman who likes company more than sex. Oliver likes me to get a taxi to his street and then sneak round the back of his house to visit him. I am guessing it's so his neighbours don't see me.

Our meetings are normally three hours and Oliver will pay my taxi both ways as it is an expensive fare; he is well off the beaten track. Our usual meetings consist of me making dinner and lounging around in my underwear. I have to say that Oliver is a great client; he is easy-going and a true romantic. Oliver is a large man, as in diameter, he is the same height as me but has an extra ten stone. I am guessing it's because of his love of alcohol; he's definitely one for a dram. The first night we met, Oliver was so nervous that he consumed three bottles of white wine and that was just him as I was not drinking. After several meetings with Oliver, I started to feel safe having a drink around him. So much so that, one night, I even let my hair down so much that I stumbled to the taxi.

Oliver is not like most of my clients; we have the same interests, so conversation flows extremely easily between us. Other than being obese, he was rather handsome, and his humour was great. Our usual meets would be the same every time; it was like he has our time broken down into fifteen-minute slots. We would drink wine together and have basic chit-chat, then, when Oliver was ready to dine, we would head through to the kitchen, which was spectacular. I love cooking and Oliver loves eating, so we made a good team, I would cook him something while I was in my sexy lingerie. I think that alone was enough to keep Oliver happy. Oliver has great taste not only in wine, but also in lingerie. I would always wear the best of the best to Oliver's house as he was a man who liked the finer things in life. After I wined and dined him, we would go and relax next door in his fancy living room; no expense spared. All the seating was high-end velvet, and the paintings would easily exceed the value of my house. Oliver and I had a vast number of meetings, and they were always the same. Until now.

The last time I saw Oliver, he had made the most outlandish request. I honestly nearly fainted with shock. It was not the request so much, more the fact that it was Oliver who was asking. I guess I had gotten used to our meetings and I thought I knew what Oliver was like, but blow me down, I was far from the truth.

I had always wondered why Oliver was more into my company than a sexual experience. Don't get me wrong, I have a lot of clients who want me to dine with them; it's not always about sex. I was rather shocked by the number of men that pay me to socialise with them; I always find it odd that someone would spend so much money just for someone to talk too. The previous visit, we were sat in the living room and both of us were rather drunk. Oliver then asked me to be open-minded about what he was about to say...

When you hear that in this line of work the next sentence could literally be anything... I moved slowly to the end of my seat, eager to find out what he wanted to ask me. Oliver was clearly nervous as he was gulping down his wine while I was impatiently waiting and wondering what the hell it could be. Then he said, in a slow and quiet voice, 'Please don't judge me.'

I was starting to get slightly concerned, but I gave myself a shake and said in a clear and calm voice, 'Do not worry, I won't judge you. Discretion is everything to me. Please say what you want.'

A few moments passed. It felt like forever, but, finally, Oliver started to open up. He was waffling on a bit. I wanted to say, *spit it out, whatever it is,* but I just waited until he felt comfortable enough to open up to me.

After five minutes of Oliver gulping down his wine, he blurted out 'I would like you to organise a meeting in a hotel and for you to bring someone else as well.'

I let out a big sigh. I could not help it; I was so relieved. I was really starting to expect the worst as he was taking so long to tell me. 'That is great! My friend Nikki is so beautiful and the two of us have a special friendship, I am sure you will love her.'

He looked down at the plush carpet in a kind of sheepish, embarrassed way. I felt I had said the wrong thing 'Is everything OK?' I asked.

'I don't think I explained that very well, I'm sorry, I'm finding it hard to tell you, this is something that I haven't shared with anyone, ever...'

I was back to my oh-my-fucking-god face. *What could it be?*

After a few moments of silence Oliver moved over to me on the sofa and rested his hand on my leg. He was so nervous his hand was all hot and sweaty, I reassured him that our time was private and that it was OK for him to tell me what he wanted. Whatever that was. Oliver finally said, 'I would like you to meet me with another guy, and for you to organise it all.'

I was certainly taken back by his request; it was not what I'd expected him to say. I asked what he would like to happen as I needed to know to be able to try to organise it for him. I was slightly worried that he wanted us all to be at it like rabbits all at the same time, and that is definitely not something I have on my bucket list.

Oliver went on to tell me that, since he was at school, he had always been curious about what it was like to be the receiver. I am not going to lie, I wasn't completely surprised; I mean, I've seen Oliver on numerous occasions and at no point have we had sex, so I did wonder what was going on with that. I tried to reassure him and said it was a normal thing and that he would be surprised how many people have the same thought (I don't know if that is true or not, I just felt that he needed to hear it). Oliver was still very unsettled so I said, 'If it's easier for you then email me the details of what you would like to happen if you don't feel comfortable discussing them just now'.

Immediately he said 'Yes, that would be far better, thank you'.

After our uncomfortable chat things went back to normal quickly between us. We drank the rest of the wine and then it was time for me to go. On the taxi ride home, all I could think was: *who am I going to recruit to be my second man?*

Once home and after my shower I sat with the television on for a bit; I was slightly tipsy, but not drunk, and I couldn't sleep. I was trying to figure out in my head how to organise this special night for Oliver. I opened my laptop to put an ad on my website to try to recruit someone suitable for our upcoming evening. I wasn't even sure what to write; so, I decided I'd best wait until I got Oliver's email about what his requests were before I was able to advertise.

Morning arrived sooner than I desired. Before I had even opened my eyes, I could not help but wonder if Oliver had emailed his requirements to me, I jumped up and opened my laptop. I was far more excited about this than I thought I would be. I guess Oliver was too as much to my surprise, he had already emailed me. I sat up in bed looking at the screen, and, before I clicked on it, I decided to get up, make a cuppa. I got back in bed with a strange feeling of excitement. It was not something I had done before, nor thought about, so it was all new to me and new things are exciting.

Felicity,
I am glad that you opted for email as I don't think I'd have had the courage to be able to discuss this face to face, even with you who I feel completely comforta-

ble with. I have never been able to let myself discuss this proposal EVER and the first thought and urge I had was almost forty years ago. I have always had the thought in the back of my mind. I married young and had children early, so that closed the door for my urges until now. My children are now all away from home, and I have met you.

I will start by sharing what I would like to become of our next encounter.

I would like oral and to be penetrated by our plus one, but under your supervision; I do not wish to see or meet the gentleman, that for me is a must! The how, where and when is all up to you to decide.

I shall leave this with you to produce the best outcome for this happening and I hope to hear back from you soon.

Oliver x

I was a little disappointed, I thought it was going to be far more detailed than what he had written, but I guess he must have been nervous and did not want to go into too much detail. I mean, if you have thought about something for forty years, you're going to have thought out everything about it. Everything! I know that if I had thought about something for that long I would have gone through every detail in my head, right down to what the weather was like when it happened. So, I did not for one moment believe that was all Oliver wanted to happen, but I wasn't going to demand he told me. He obviously did not feel comfortable enough just now.

I spent the rest of the day thinking about how to go about getting a guy to help me. After most of the morning had passed, I ended up calling Nikki as she was far more experienced with this sort of stuff. She suggested I place an ad on a couple of sites.

So, I posted the following:

Gentlemen,
I am looking for a clean, well-mannered, well-spoken gentleman who enjoys same-sex company, with a female involved; must enjoy giving oral activities. Meeting to be held in Scotland at a mutually agreed time and location. If interested, please email me a brief description of yourself.

Love FF x

Within moments my laptop was pinging. I was shocked that I had people responding so quickly. I mean, I get that a lot of people have their hidden other side, as do I, but I did not think that people would respond as fast as this. I did not open them. I had a lot to do, so I decided to shut the laptop and get on with my chores then I would spend the evening going through them to pick out the perfect candidate.

After a few hours of trying to get on with my day, I had to stop and open my laptop. I was obviously curious otherwise I would be doing housework instead of reading all the replies. I could not believe it: I had so many people reply to my ad already. Granted, once I opened them, I discarded many straightaway. Most were horrendous. Sleazy and not the right fit for Oliver at all! I went back to four and read them again and again. Finally, I got it down to two that I thought were worth responding to. One guy was called Adam. He was English, in his twenties and attached a link to his website. Adam made the cut because he was professional, experienced and from his pictures, he seemed incredibly attractive. The other to make the cut was Paul: he was in his thirties and new to this but sounded knowledgeable and enthusiastic.

I replied and then closed the laptop and managed to get on with the rest of my day. The thought I kept coming back to was that Oliver had these urges for forty years and never acted on them. He had been so embarrassed by it. I just did not understand why he would spend all those years fantasising about something without acting on it. I guess every person is so different. I mean, I could not go a month without trying something that had been on my mind, but, then again, I have never been shy or bothered about other people's opinions.

My housework was done, and it was time to put my feet up; I was looking forward to getting my laptop open again. I had replies from Adam and Paul as well as another few candidates to go through, so it was to be a busy night. I cosied down on the sofa wrapped myself in a fluffy blanket and had my favourite beer to hand, a bottle of cold Stella Artois. Just as I had gotten comfortable my doorbell went. I ignored it at first. Buzz Buzz. It kept going, then my phone started. It was Emma. I think if it had been anyone else, I would have just ignored it, but Emma doesn't just turn up without texting, so I knew something had to be wrong. I quickly turned off my laptop and went to the door.

Emma stood in tears at my door holding a box of beer. I could not turn her away; she was upset and clearly needed someone to talk to. She had fallen out with her boyfriend (another reason I do not want a boyfriend; they just cause grief). After hearing all the ins and outs of their relationship, my emotions were heightened so much I could not gather my thoughts. I was so relieved that I did not have to deal with all that stuff but still had my sexual needs taken care of. After a Chinese and many beers, Emma went home with a smile on her face. I was not in the right frame of mind to go through the emails at this time, I was ready for bed.

No motivation to get up. Emma had drained me, listening to her rant on for so long about the problems in her relationship. I decided that today I was not going to work. I called in sick, switched my alarms off and rolled over for another sleep. It was well-needed. A few hours later I woke feeling fresh and was glad that I now had the full day to myself. Quick shower, then laptop time. I was intrigued to see the responses from my advert; I was surprisingly excited. In fact, I couldn't get out of the shower quick enough. I switched on the laptop for it to load while I went to get back into my pyjamas, by the time I came through and checked, I had another fourteen replies. I was glad that I had decided to have a day off to go through them.

Two hours passed and I had not moved from my sofa; I was glued to my laptop. I couldn't believe what I was reading, some of the replies I'd had made me speechless, the majority were pictures of a penis with a ruler beside it at a variety of different angles. At first, I thought it was extremely strange, but, after opening the seventh one like that, I guess that must be the average response to something like this. Just as I thought the strangest responses had been opened, I was taken back. It was a video of a guy wanking with a caption attached: easy-to-swallow. It took a moment for it to register what he was meaning, then, six strokes in and there was the cum. It was almost like water, he certainly wasn't lying with the easy-to-swallow bit, but to be honest, it was all a bit too much. Adam was certainly looking like the perfect candidate, after a couple of days of messaging Adam, we decided that the next thing to do was meet for a coffee. He lived in England but comes to Scotland for work in Glasgow every few weeks, so we decided to meet the next time he was up so we could check the chemistry between us.

With butterflies in my tummy, sweaty hands and unusual breathing it can only mean one thing... It was meet Adam day. I mean, come on, this was no average meeting; this was an interview for same-sex sex. It is definitely not something I ever thought I would be doing! Walking into the restaurant my heart was racing as if it was like my first encounter with a client. I walked in and I heard my name being called out. Yes, of course, it was Adam. He was absolutely stunning. It was a yes from me. Adam took my coat and pulled my seat out; what a gentleman. I was onto a winner here. I instantly had an attraction to him; I guess if I was a man, I'd say I was thinking with my dick. We chatted for a while and went over what Oliver wanted to get out of the booking and discussed what Adam would get in return, we settled on a four-figure sum; after all it was his time plus expenses. We agreed that the funds would be transferred by myself on the night, I have to say that Adam was very enthusiastic about it all. I even asked him if he needed time to think about it all before committing, but, before I was able to finish my sentence, he'd said yes to meeting Oliver. It was to be in a fortnight's time when Adam was back up in Scotland.

Obviously, I had to check the date with Oliver, but said that I was fairly certain that would be fine. I got up to leave and Adam went in to shake my hand. Really! A handshake: we were going to be having group sex in two weeks! We said our goodbyes and I told Adam I would confirm the date and time for our encounter when I'd heard back from Oliver. Walking back to my car, deep in thought. This was such a different thing for me to do; I guess I was about to find out if three is a crowd?

With the date confirmed it was time to fine comb the details. Oliver said that he was going to book a three-bedroom apartment so that we would all have privacy. The more Oliver and I discussed things the more I felt like this night could be the start of a momentous change in his life. I could tell that this meeting was well overdue for him, that was apparent, but he was like a different person, he had a spring in his step, and he did not seem nervous at all.

The day had finally arrived, unfortunately I had to go to my normal job during the day as there was already staff off on holiday and I like Milly too much to leave her in the shit. It seemed to take forever for the morning to pass. Serving customers all I could think of was dick. Lunchtime and I was straight on my phone. I had messages from Adam and Oliver, and they were both really looking forward to the evening. My lunch break seemed to be over in minutes, but that was because my head was stuck in my phone texting the guys about tonight. Milly could tell I was up to something as I managed to leave a coffee to go cold; something that is unheard of with me. Eventually my shift was over, and it was home time. I ran out the door and raced home. I was singing and dancing about my house, I was clearly more excited than I thought I was going to be about it. I showered and did my makeup, then packed away my outfit for the evening as well as spare clothes and PJs. I did plan to come home afterwards, but thought I'd better be prepared.

I was to meet Oliver for drinks at seven and Adam was not due to come until nine, so it gave me plenty of time to get ready and for me to go over anything that Oliver was concerned about. I got a taxi into town and was at the hotel suite before Oliver, but that was not a problem as he had put me on the reservation, so I was able to go up and get myself organised.

I knew the suite was going to be fancy, but I was totally blown away. I could not believe it; there were rose petals everywhere and a cooler with a bottle of champagne in every room. I picked the smaller of the rooms as I was planning to go home anyway, so I thought it was only fair. I had just unpacked and opened a bottle of champagne when Oliver arrived. He was nervous and reluctant even to give me a hug, but he said that he needed a shower to freshen up and that he would feel more in the mood afterwards. I went round and lit a few candles, then put some music on, I went for a bit of Jazz as I knew Oliver loved listening to it. I was still in my casual clothes, so thought I would go and slip into something to cheer Oliver up a bit and get him in the mood.

Oliver had requested that I wear a French maid's outfit for the occasion. I loved being a French maid, so I was thrilled that he had picked that for me to wear. I stepped into my outfit and pulled it up over my bare chest; it was one that I could lace up from the front, so, it was not only an amazing-looking outfit, but it was also well designed for getting in and out of quickly. The outfit came with a matching choker and headband and, of course, a feather duster. I loved it! This did not feel like work at all,

Felicity Forbes

I was with one of the nicest gentlemen I had met so far, so, all in all, it was going to be an evening to remember.

Quick glass of bubbly and a wee strut around the room to get my game face on and I was ready. I opened the door to find Oliver sat next to an empty bottle and a very nearly empty glass. As soon as he saw me, he stood up and could not talk for grinning. I went to get him a new bottle and poured him a glass; after all, I was the maid. I had to go and set up next door for our playtime later, so I excused myself to get organised. I lit more candles and laid out the accessories, blindfold, spanking paddle, handcuffs, whip, nipple clamps, baby oil, cock ring, anal beads, balaclava, vibrator and, of course, condoms and lube! Seeing everything laid out on the dressing table was enough to get me overly excited; I could feel my pussy getting wet already.

When I went back into the living area Oliver was not there. For a moment I had the horrid feeling that it was all too much for him and he had run away, but I found a scribble on hotel-headed notepaper saying – *I'm going to go and get ready. I will be in my room when Adam arrives, just knock when it's time.*

It made sense. It was the number one rule of the evening; he did not want Adam to know who he was. There was still twenty minutes until Adam was due to arrive, so I topped up my champagne and went to watch the television. Yes, it was very strange sitting dressed up like a maid drinking champagne by myself in an extremely swanky apartment getting paid an exceptionally large sum, but, hey, every job has its perks! After a flick through the channels and another glass of champagne, I started getting nervous. I think it was more due to the fact that I had done all of the organising. I was well ahead of schedule; it was now just waiting, and I hate waiting.

Knock knock, the door went, it was Adam. It was a shame that he was only into guys, 'cause the things I would do to him... We had a glass of champagne and chatted about the evening's plans. I texted Oliver to see how he was going for time, and he said he would be another thirty minutes. It was great to be able to chat more to Adam. He was such a lovely guy, and, like I said, he was stunning, so it was not as if it was a chore to be looking at him. Adam went to my room to get showered and wait on his cue to join in. Now that Adam was out of the room, it was time to knock on Oliver's door. I gently tapped on his door 'Oliver its time.' Immediately the door opened. Given that his room was massive, he must have been waiting at the door for me to knock. He greeted me with a kiss and then I led him through to the lounge. We had another glass of bubbly then Oliver went to get another bottle from the fridge and more glasses to take through to our playroom.

Oliver came back and grabbed my hand and led me through to the playroom. I could tell he was now getting anxious; I think what gave it away was the fact he was sat at the bottom of the bed taking forever to open the new bottle; he had popped enough corks to do it with his eyes closed. When he eventually opened the bottle, he got up and poured six glasses. I guessed he did not want to waste time pouring glasses later when there would be better things to be doing. Oliver then passed me the baby oil and dropped his towel; this was the first time I had seen him fully naked. His cock was impressive, I was rather disappointed that we hadn't had sex. I went over to the dressing table to get the blindfold and slid it over his eyes, then slowly pushed him back onto the bed. I squirted out the baby oil on my hands to warm it up, then started to massage his chest. I slowly started to move down his body, covering every bit of him in oil. Once I had covered his front, I asked that he turn over, so I was able to do his back and bum too. Just as I had finished covering his whole body in oil, I started to run feathers over him. He was wriggling about on the bed, so I told him it was time to be tied down. Oliver seemed too eager and quickly turned over, so he was lay on his back.

Just as I tied his wrists to the bed, I went to pick up the whip. Then I heard Oliver mumble something under his breath. 'Sorry, what was that?' I asked.

'I think I'm ready for Adam, but please be in the room.'

The plan was that both Oliver and Adam would wear balaclavas, Adam would come in to play with Oliver, starting off with sucking his penis, then slowly progressing to anal beads and onto intercourse.

'Yes Sir, if you're sure, I shall go and get our guest.' Before I even got a chance to move to the door, 'Felicity, please promise you won't leave me though, I feel safe when your around.'

'Oliver do not worry, I promise I am here until you tell me to leave, I can be here all night if you wish so don't worry about anything.'

Oliver lay nodding his head as if to say yes. I opened the door to the living room and blow me down Adam was already patiently waiting sat on the sofa wearing only his balaclava and nothing else. My chin almost fell to the floor, he was stunning. I was quite glad I am female and able to hide my excitement because I can tell you, one hundred per cent, that, if I was a guy, I'd have a boner just looking at him.

Adam was already oiled up and hard, so I was like jelly. I will be honest I was extremely gutted that Adam was there for Oliver, and not me. We went into the playroom, and before I was able to introduce him, Adam was knelt on the bed with a grasp of Oliver's penis in his hand ready to start sucking him off. This was the first time I had ever seen a man suck on a man before. Yeah, I had seen this while watching porn, but things are different in real life. If I am honest; it wasn't for me. I felt left out, and a bit annoyed Adam's head was not between my legs. Still, I quickly reminded myself that this was my job and sometimes at work you have to do things you do not like to do, to be able to please others.

Adam got up off the bed and made his way over to the dressing table. I wasn't sure what he was going for, but I thought it was a bit soon for anal beads, but, just as I thought that he picked them up, followed by the lube. He squirted lube on the palm of his hand, then he slapped the beads, large end first into his open palm, then shut his hand grasping them then pulled them through his closed fist. He was a pro; that was definitely the most efficient way of covering them in lube. Adam then started moving back towards Oliver. I felt awkward just standing there watching them, but Oliver had insisted that I stay, so I thought it was best to join in rather than being a creep in the corner. I picked up my feather duster and started to run it over Oliver's neck. 'Is everything OK so far?' I asked Oliver.

He responded 'uh-huh, all good.'

Adam started to part Oliver's hairy ass and then slid the beads in, a bead at a time. I could see Oliver grip onto the bedding, so I leant over him and whispered 'Stay relaxed and just say NO if anything was too much or if you felt uncomfortable. I am here and not going anywhere'.

Adam seemed gentle and, before we knew it, they were all up inside Oliver; he was growling, but his wriggling had calmed down a considerable amount. I was to stay in the room until Oliver said to leave, so carried on just running the feathers over his neck. To be honest, I felt like a spare prick. Three is definitely a crowd when the other two guys are more interested in each other than wanting to play with me. It felt strange. In this line of work, I was always the important one, I was always the one getting the attention and, more to the point, I was always the one getting pleasured. I felt completely out of place; I did not even know where to put my hands and I'm always someone who knows where they go.

After about ten minutes Oliver said in a very relaxed tone, 'I'm ready for more now.'

I'm guessing Adam was looking forward to more happening as well 'cause as soon as Oliver spoke, the beads were out, and Adam started to put a condom on his penis.

'Felicity, would you untie me please?' Oliver asked.

'Yes, of course.' I replied, just as I had finished the last tie on his wrist Oliver, he turned over and lay on his front. Oliver grabbed my hand and pulled me closer towards him.

'Is it OK if you go into the next room?'

Honestly, I was a little disappointed. But Oliver was the boss, so I had to go. 'Yes of course, I'll stay in the living room so I'm close by and you can shout if you need anything.'

I quickly grabbed my glass and headed out of the room, I was somewhat disappointed that I wasn't needed to do anything else, but also relieved that I didn't have to watch. I was not to leave the apartment until they were finished, I guess Oliver wanted me as his bodyguard. I sat down in the other room, sipping on my champagne watching crap television. I did not want to get changed as I was still working, technically, even though I wasn't needed in person. I could not hear anything next door, but I wasn't worried as I knew that Oliver would shout me if he needed me. Just as I went to go and organise my things, I could hear them chatting, which made me feel a bit more at ease. I packed and moved back into the living room. The boys were now in full swing; I could hear them moaning and groaning. I felt awkward; I could hear everything going on and I felt as if I were a peeping tom just sitting listening to them.

After another few glasses of champagne, Adam appeared out of the room. This time completely naked, no balaclava in sight but with a hot and bothered look about him which made him even hotter than before.

'Is everything OK?' I asked.

'Oh, better than OK. I just need to have a shower and freshen up.'

I was slightly nervous waiting for Oliver to come out, but I was guessing that if Adam was having a good time, then surely Oliver was too?

I waited a few more moments, then I could not take it anymore. I knocked on the door, 'Hi, Oliver, it is just me. Are you OK?'

A moment passed.

'Oliver?'

'Yes, sorry, Felicity, come in.'

I opened the door to find Oliver spread out like a beached whale, also missing his balaclava with the biggest smile I have ever seen on his face.

'Thank you so much, I have had such an amazing night. I would never have organised this myself; I will never be able to repay you for this.'

'It is honestly no bother at all. I have had fun too.' I was so relieved that he was having such a fabulous time, and just as I was about to ask him what he wanted me to do, he blurted out, 'I know the plan was for you to stay too, but do you need to?'

'No, not at all. I am fine getting a taxi home.' I could see that he had a twinkle in his eye. 'Come on, spill the beans?'

He looked down at the floor while turning a brighter shade of pink. 'Mmmmm, well, I asked Adam if he wanted to stay the night.'

I was so happy that I had managed to get someone that Oliver liked so much. I was smiling just as much as him now. I thought it best to double-check, so I asked, 'Are you sure about spending the night with Adam? You were so adamant that he was not to see your face?'

'Yes, I know. We have already broken that rule, I am happy I promise.'

'Phone me if you need me to come back. I don't live too far away.'

Oliver laughed 'Thank you, but I have a feeling we are going to get on fine'.

I smiled and then walked to the door, closing it on my way out. I still had to get changed; I obviously couldn't get a taxi dressed like this. Luckily, I had taken my things out of the other room because

Adam was in it getting ready for round two. I got changed in the kitchen; just as I was packing my things into my bag, Adam came out. To be honest, I was kind of glad I got to talk to him before I left, just to check he was happy staying with Oliver.

'Are you ok if I leave? Oliver said that you were spending the night?'

'Yes, you don't need to stay, we are fine. You were right about him being so lovely, I will call you tomorrow when I'm heading home.'

Adam seemed to be just as happy as Oliver.

My work here was done. I had two happy men, and it was home time for me.

I walked out the hotel and got in a taxi. It was only about twenty minutes to my house. I got home and got straight in the shower. It had been a fun night and more of a turn-on than I had thought it was going to be, but I guess that was because Adam was so damn hot. I could not help but wonder what the guys were up to; probably ball deep in each other by now. I got out the shower and lay on my bed. That was me for the night. I was not going to get up now; it was lights off and bedtime.

14. Choo-Choo Train

AFTER MY LAST ENCOUNTER I was surprised by how much I had enjoyed the thrill of being with more than one person, even if I didn't get down and dirty with them, it got me wondering. I decided to change my website to say that I would accommodate threesomes. I guess it was all new and I was looking to experiment more; after all, you only live once.

To my surprize I had my first request from a couple, a married couple to be exact. Yes, I know, a married couple want to play with me. I wasn't too sure about it. I mean, what happens if they fight, or it gets weird, and I am just sitting there watching them have sex? We talked through email and then had a couple of Skype calls together, just to make sure there was some sort of connection between us. Their names were Dennis and Jane. They were from England and were in their late thirties. They had two little boys and were incredibly open and honest about what they wanted and their previous history. Jane was a lesbian before she met Dennis and, as much as she had tried to be satisfied by Dennis, she still had a side of her that was interested in women. Since having their children, discretion was a must for them, which was why they were willing to travel to Aberdeen for us to meet up. I was far more flexible with dates than they were; Dennis and Jane had to organise babysitters and be able to find the time away from work. I was not one for doing Skype calls, but I had discussed it with Nikki, and she said to do it, so I was able to see them both as there was nothing worse than being with two people you weren't attracted too. After the first Skype call, they wanted to talk every day; I started to think they were just wanting to have Skype calls to get their kicks, but Jane assured me they did want to meet up. I didn't know what to expect meeting a married couple, but I guess I would just have to wait and see.

We were to meet at my favourite hotel in Aberdeen, have drinks at the bar, then head up to the room. I am not one for socialising with clients in full view as I'm always worried that I will be spotted by someone I know, but I thought that as it was a couple, then it's slightly different. I was slightly nervous about the two on one, so I asked Lucas if he was free to drive me and pick me up. Then Lucas knew where I was and who I was with; just in case I was kidnapped. He said yes, for sure, but then said I should not be going if I thought I was going to get kidnapped.

I think if it were just a couple and not a married one, I'd feel a bit more at ease; I didn't really understand why people who had taken their vows to be together forever wanted to have someone else have sex with them. But, I guess, people are all different and it is just sex after all. I was requested to wear an over-the-knee dress with elegant underwear, Felicity's normal clothes. I had plenty of time, so I did my hair in large, bouncy curls and then backcombed the top to give it some height. I put on my expensive jewellery as I was not going to be getting drunk, which meant that I wouldn't lose them. I had just got my new delivery of underwear, so I was excited about wearing my new gear. It was a very seductive lace-up bustier and it did just that; it was great, it laced up at the front, so it really pulled my boobs together. I did not see the point in putting the pants on as they would be coming off and I would be annoyed if I left part of the set somewhere on the first outing, so I skipped the pants and just went for the matching garters. I pulled my dress over my head; it was a bit tight, so I had to do that awkward shake-your-hips thing while you pull it down over your bum. Then I got my make-up on. I went for the classy look; nothing too dark around the eyes, then I brightened it up with red lipstick. A final check of my bag and that was me set. Just as I slid into my shoes, the door went. It was Lucas. He walked in and just stood staring at me. I guess he was still getting used to seeing me like this. I am not going to lie, I was nervous. Lucas could see I was nervous.

'Why don't you make a drink for you to have on the way?' Lucas said.

'That's probably the best idea you've had yet.' I replied, while on the way to the kitchen. The only thing I could find was my protein shaker, so I poured a healthy measure of alcohol into it, with a little bit of mixer and I was ready to go. The car ride to my appointment was a bit awkward; I guess he wasn't sure what to say to take my mind off being nervous. We got to the hotel early, so we parked around the corner till it was time. I quickly drank the rest of my drink, took a few deep breaths and off I went. I opened the door into the bar, and I could spot Dennis and Jane straight away. Jane was wearing a red dress, so I was able to tell it was them. Just as I started walking towards them, my heels started to make a loud clacking noise on the marble floor and everyone in the place turned round to look at me. This is why I try to avoid meeting people in public. My heart was racing, and I was trying to scan the room to check I did not know anyone without looking like a complete weirdo. I was in the clear; no familiar faces or none that I noticed. I glanced over at Dennis and Jane, and they were both gawking at me with grins on their faces from ear to ear. When I got closer to the table, they both got up, 'Felicity, I hope?' Jane asked.

'Yes, how are you both? Lovely to meet you'. I greeted them both with a kiss on the cheek.

No going back now. I sat down at the table. They were just finishing off a bottle of white wine.

'What would you like to drink Felicity?' asked Dennis.

Before I was able to give him an answer, Jane shouted out.

'A celebration like this we all deserve champagne'.

'Champagne it is then,' said Dennis.

Jane turned to me, 'Is that OK with you?'

'Of course, it is!' To be honest, since entering this line of work I seem to drink nothing but champagne – and I never have to buy it, which is even better. We sat in the bar drinking and talking, mainly about their trip to Aberdeen. They were both lovely people and, to be honest, I fancied them both. Jane was stunning; very well kept. Her makeup was flawless, her hair expensively dyed blonde, and her dress was shaped into a V at the front, her boobs were nearly falling out. It was hard not to stare at them; they needed a table of their own. Jane's nails matched her dress, and she was wearing diamonds; no Claire's Accessories for her! She had a vast number of rings on, all of which were diamonds; they were clearly worth a lot of money. Dennis was slightly rugged, with a beard, well dressed and had nice shoes. They were both very tanned, so I assumed they went away a lot. I was not one for asking questions in case they asked me things in return.

I was finding it hard not to giggle. I mean, we were just three people having a drink in an upmarket hotel, surrounded by normal people talking mainly about the weather, and, in approximately thirty minutes, we would be upstairs naked, fucking each other. We looked as normal as everyone else in the bar, so it got me thinking: if this is my secret, what is everyone else's dirty little secret? The bottle of bubbly was finished in record time; I guess we were all a little anxious and drinking like fish to calm the nerves. Jane turned to Dennis, smiled then nodded her head towards the bar, 'Sort another bottle for the room, we will head up now and meet you there'.

On the way to the room Jane kept stroking my arm and thanking me for agreeing to this as it had taken some time to persuade Dennis. I just smiled and laughed as I did not know what to say. We got to the room and Jane went in first, holding the door open for me.

I went in and, my god, did my first impression of them change? I know I like a toy laid out and I am a bit OCD, but they were far more into things than me and they were all laid out perfectly.

Jane handed me a glass, 'You look like you need this'.

I took it and had a sip... Yuk, white wine. It tasted horrid, but it would take the edge off. Just as I thought I had seen everything, I turned around and, blow me down, there was a selection of vibrators in all shapes, sizes and colours. But that was not the only thing; there was also a strap-on. I had not used one or ever thought about using one, it was just something that had never crossed my mind. I am guessing I looked shocked because Jane came over to me, 'Don't worry, we would only do what you were comfortable with.' All while standing rubbing my arm...

I was not so much worried, more curious. I knew that Jane was the instigator in all this, but now I was thinking that Dennis must like it the other way too. I was a bit confused. Jane pointed out the envelope on the bedside table and I picked it up on the way to the loo. A quick touch-up of makeup and a pee while I checked the envelope; it was all there, plus a generous amount more, which was a lot considering it was my going rate for two hours times two as there were two of them. It was already a lot, never mind the extra tip. When I came out, I said to Jane, 'It's too much.'

'No, don't be silly. It is not too much. It is to cover your taxis to and from the hotel as well. After all, it was us that requested that you have a drink with us.'

This was very generous of them, so I added an extra thirty minutes to my timer and texted Lucas to update him with the time I would be out; I did not want a SWAT team coming looking for me! Just as we finished talking, in came Dennis. I think he was slightly drunk, but I was not bothered; it was for them to have a good night. Dennis poured us drinks and we clinked glasses. Jane led the toast by saying, 'To this naughty night and to many more.'

I was less nervous and more excited now; we had previously discussed my terms and conditions, so it was not something to be discussed on the night to dampen the mood. Jane was sat on the bed, then she patted next to her and said, 'Come over and sit next to me.'

I went to sit down beside her, and she was just chatting away. I think it was from all the alcohol she had drunk, but I wasn't bothered; better than sitting in silence. Jane went from telling me how excited she was to asking if she could fuck me with the strap-on. I was relieved; I thought that I was going to be wearing it. I said, 'Of course!' And we all started laughing. She asked if we could do a choo-choo train and I be the driver. I actually understood what she meant (if you'd asked me two months ago, I wouldn't have had a clue). I was relieved that's what they wanted to do. For those of you who don't know, what's meant about me being the driver is it's when I am bent over and being ridden by Jane with the strap-on and Jane is being ridden by Dennis with his cock. It was all rather exciting to say the least; something else to be added and ticked off my list. Jane then stood up, put down her glass and said, 'It's time to begin. The safe word is 'clown', if anyone feels uncomfortable.'

Jane then flicked the straps of her dress off her shoulders, and it fell to the floor. Dennis was still sat in his chair drinking away; it was like he wasn't allowed to join in until Jane said it was OK. Just as I thought that Jane said in a completely different voice, 'Dennis, you just watch till you're told to join us.'

Jane was completely naked in seconds; she was attractive; you could tell that she was one for going to the gym. When I took my dress off, they both just looked at me and then Jane jumped on me, pushing me back on the bed. We started kissing straight away; it wasn't just a kiss; it was full-on passion. I was really enjoying it, far more than I thought I would. I was very attracted to Jane, and I fancied her somewhat, this was just as enjoyable for me as it was for her. My hands were all over her; her body was perfect; her skin was so soft and smooth. Jane was still on top of me and just as I was about to roll her over so I could be on top, she stopped and got off the bed. I was taken back; I was slightly annoyed she had moved away if I'm being honest. She then cleared her throat and in an almost headmaster's voice, said, 'Get up and go and undress him, starting with his shirt.'

I wasn't sure what was happening for a moment; I assumed that she was going into role play mode, which is something we hadn't discussed, but I wasn't against the idea as I loved to act along. I got up and slowly started to move over to Dennis, who was still sat on the chair with a drink in his hands. Just as I was a step away from him, Jane said, 'Unbutton his shirt, then pull him out of the chair.'

'Yes, madam,' I responded.

I bent over to unbutton his shirt, starting at the top. I was stood gazing into his eyes, and I missed a button, so I looked down to check where the next one was. Jane was standing directly behind me, watching me bend over in front of her. I got to the last button, then grabbed Dennis by the wrists and pulled as hard as I could to try and get him up. He wasn't fat, but he was larger than me and needed a bit of a pull.

Just as he was up on his feet, I put both hands on his chest and slowly moved them up to his shoulders. I started to slide his shirt off, then dropped it on the floor behind him. Jane had said to undress him, so I started to undo his belt, then his trousers. Just as I was pulling down his zip the bulge in his trousers almost popped out, like it had been squashed in his trousers all night. I got his trousers down to his ankles and then pushed him back onto the chair so I could pull them over his feet. Just as I was throwing Dennis's trousers over to the side of the room, Jane grabbed my arm and spun me round to be facing her. I instantly started kissing her; I mean, who wouldn't. She was gorgeous. We seemed to get locked in a zone and it wasn't long before we were rolling around on the bed again. Jane then stopped and moved off the bed towards the toy display. She turned round, holding a vibrator and a blindfold, then threw the blindfold at me.

'Put it on and lie down.'

This was really turning me on. I love the mystery of a blindfold, it intensified everything. I felt Jane put her hands on my knees, then slowly started to move them up my legs, just lightly, almost tickling me. I was so horny I was starting to wriggle about the bed. I could feel Jane's warm breath on the inside of my thigh, and it was sending goose bumps down my body. Jane started to kiss my leg, then she would run her tongue over an area and blow on it, it was amazing. I had even forgotten I was working I was having so much fun. I kept grabbing Jane's arms and trying to pull her up towards me, but she pushed me back every time.

Jane then shouted, 'Dennis, fill her mouth to keep her occupied.'

I was looking forward to having his cock in my mouth; blow jobs are something that I have always gotten pleasure from doing. I hadn't seen Dennis naked, but I did see the bulge in his pants, so I was assuming he would be a mouthful. Jane was now licking my clit and lightly rubbing it with her fingers; she was so good at it, far better than anyone who had done it before.

I felt Dennis kneel on the bed beside me and then his hand lightly touched my cheek, guiding my head over to the side. I knew what was coming and couldn't wait. Just as I opened my mouth and felt the tip of his penis on my lips, Jane pushed the vibrator deep inside me; it was big enough for me to let out a large groan which then made my mouth open wide, so Dennis pushed his penis inside it.

Wow, he had a large girth on him. The length, however, wasn't much to be talking about because I was able to feel his body squash against my face when he pushed it fully into my mouth. I was in heaven; I was getting pleasured down below with Jane fucking me with the vibrator and licking and sucking on my clit all while I was sucking Dennis fast and hard.

I was ready to climax, I was so excited and so turned on. I was trying so hard to contain myself, but I couldn't keep it in any longer; I managed to mumble, 'I'm going to cum already.'

Jane pulled the vibrator out and started sucking on me so hard that I just exploded. It was a huge orgasm. I was in a daze for a few moments. Just as I started to come out of my daze, I felt Jane get off the bed. I still had Dennis's cock in my mouth, and I was getting into a good rhythm when Jane told me to get up and turn over onto all fours. I wasn't sure what was going to happen next, but I was enjoying myself far too much to care. I quickly flipped over. I had just got my balance when Dennis grabbed my face, 'Open your mouth little lady, I'm going to fill it.'

I was so horny I was extremely wet and longed for more pleasure. I was now on all fours, well nearly; I had lifted my right arm up so that I was able to grab a hold of Dennis's penis to squeeze it and pull it towards me so I could suck him harder. I was too far in the zone to notice that Jane had got back on to the bed, it wasn't until I heard Jane ask me if I was ready to squeal like a piggy that I realised what was about to happen, I hadn't been spit roasted before, and I'm not sure if it counts if it's with a strap-on and a penis, but I'd say that it's basically the same. I'd paused for a moment to register what Jane had said, but it was only for a second. When Jane pushed the strap-on deep inside me, I went back into full-on sucking mode. I was loving it, it was amazing. I didn't understand till this moment why people did it, but the immense pleasure from both ends at the same time was sending me into overdrive. I was so hot, my pussy was dripping wet, I was enjoying myself far more than I ever anticipated; was this the start of my love for threesomes?

Jane started off slowly, but it wasn't long before she was going faster and harder. I wasn't convinced about the strap-on; I mean, it was good, but it wasn't a penis. It wasn't throbbing like a cock does and

I couldn't feel it pulsing, but she definitely knew how to use it; it was like every time she thrust the strap-on into me it pushed me further forwards to get all of Dennis's penis in my mouth. I could tell from the groaning and moaning that they were enjoying themselves just as much as I was.

Dennis let out a huge groan. 'I'm just about to cum.'

'Hold it longer!' Jane screeched.

I could tell from his penis pulsing that he wasn't going to manage to hold it. Just then he pulled his penis out of my mouth, and I could see the condom fill up with his cum.

Jane was still fucking me and then she let out a yell, 'Oh fuck, it's coming, I'm close!'

I wasn't sure that she was going to orgasm with being the one wearing the strap-on, but, sure enough, she did. We all collapsed on the bed, then Jane burst out laughing. 'I've waited years to do that again.'

Dennis didn't say a word and I couldn't. I was so out of breath. After we got our breath back, Jane got up to get us some drinks and we were all sat on the bed sipping our champagne with huge grins on our faces. It was a bit surreal; I mean, two minutes ago we were all at it and now we were just sat there drinking. After the second glass Dennis stood up to go to the bathroom and when he returned, he had a massive boner again. He must have been on Viagra because no one can get that hard that quick unless they have taken something.

Jane then said, 'We'd better get back to it before the time runs out.'

I saw Jane looking over at the chaise longue and I could see the cogs turning in her brain. She then stood up and turned towards me. Fortunately, I wasn't taking a sip at the time because she still had that bloody strap-on round her waist and I burst out laughing. Jane said, 'I think we should all fuck at once over there (pointing at the chaise longue).'

I started to make my way over to the chaise longue, and, just as I got to it, Jane pushed me forwards, so I was leaning on it. Then, with no hesitation at all, she pushed the strap-on deep inside me. I was still soaking down there so it went all the way in on her first thrust. I don't know if it was the position I was in, but it felt more like a real penis this time rather than just a stick of rubber like before. Jane gave a few hard thrusts, then shouted to Dennis that she was ready. I guess this was my moment of being the driver in the choo-choo train.

Yes, I was being fucked by Jane and Jane was being fucked by her husband Dennis and it was bloody marvellous. Jane was better than most men; she was really hitting the right spots. I didn't have my blindfold on anymore, so I was able to see what was going on, but to be honest, I found myself just looking at the wall. I was trying to get into the zone, but I had a married couple fucking on my back, so it was a little distracting. Last time was different; I had a cock in my mouth, so I had a job to do, and I was involved. This time I felt more awkward; I mean, I guess it was a strange sensation, feeling them shag on me. It was still fun, and I was enjoying myself, it was just a strange enjoyment rather than the fiery passion that makes you drift into a world of ecstasy.

Just as I felt myself get into the rhythm of everything, Jane stopped, then shouted 'Let's swap.'

'Swap?' I asked, looking puzzled. *What the fuck did she mean by that?* I was glad I didn't have that blindfold on now and I was able to see what was coming. I saw Dennis pick up a condom. Phew, I was still going to be at the front, and I was looking forward to a real penis inside me, feeling it warm and pulsing against me; my pussy started twitching just thinking of being fucked properly. Dennis then put his hands on my hips and pushed me forward, so my body was tight against the chaise longue. Then he moved his hands down to my ass and spread my cheeks wide apart, then started to force his penis inside me. It was considerably bigger than the strap-on, so it took a few tries before he was able to be fully inside me and, by golly, was it fat.

I was grabbing onto both sides of the chair, holding tight as he thrust inside me. Then, as he pulled back, I seemed to let go of the chair for a moment until he pushed deep inside me again. I was in dreamland; my legs were jelly. I was completely satisfied now I had his fat cock inside me. I knew that it wasn't going to be long before I orgasmed, I guess the whole evening had me on the verge of it at all times. I wasn't even paying attention anymore to what was going on behind me. Then, just as I opened my eyes, I heard Dennis let out a roar and he thrust forward awfully hard inside me all while he took an extremely firm grip of my hips, it was almost enough to have lifted me off the seat. Then it hit me: when they said swap, they meant the two of them. So not only do I still have a married couple having sex on my back; Jane is doing the fucking and Dennis is doing the receiving from his wife.

I was a bit surprised but was just enjoying being bent over and having a real penis inside me. Dennis must really enjoy being fucked up the ass cause since Jane went inside him his cock had gotten even harder and harder. It was such an intense feeling; I was at the peak of my orgasm; it was huge. He was going harder and harder, I could feel my cum running down the inside of my legs and I was jelly all over, it was like I was on an everlasting orgasm. I could feel Dennis get faster and harder and I moved forward and slightly dipped my back, then squeezed my pussy tight. With the girth of Dennis's penis, it was now really tight, and I could feel every inch of him inside me.

I shouted out, 'I'm about to cum again.'

Dennis was panting and moaning, but managed to yell out, 'Mee too.'

I kept my body tense so that I was able to squeeze his cock as much as I could and about ten thrusts later, I started to cum, but not only that I could feel myself squirt as well. Dennis then started to cum too, and even though he had a condom on I could still feel it pulse out the end of his penis. We all collapsed into a heap on the floor. We lay in silence for a few moments, then, just as I was about to get up, the timer went on my phone. I didn't even know where it was, so it was going off for a while before I was able to get to it. Jane said it was fine for me to use the shower if I wanted and I was so relieved for her to say that because there was no way I was getting out of the room looking like this or every Tom, Dick and Harry would have known what I had been up to.

Just as I got into the bathroom, I texted Lucas to say I was fine, that I'd just be another ten minutes. I tied my hair up and just washed my body; I didn't want to be in there too long, it was just to get the sweat and cum off me, so I looked respectable enough to leave the hotel. When I got out the bathroom Jane passed me a glass of champagne and Dennis excused himself to go to the bathroom. Jane was still naked, but, thankfully, without the strap-on. She was perched on the end of the bed; she looked amazing, even after all the sweat and mess.

This was always an awkward time; the time when you've done what you were there to do and about to leave.

'Thank you, Felicity. Could we do the same in a few months' time, but perhaps for longer next time?' Jane asked.

'Yes, of course.' I replied, after all I had enjoyed myself and they were attractive people, so I was more than happy to work with them again. Jane then gave me a hug and proceeded to open the door for me, even though she was completely naked.

As I left their room and started making my way along the corridor I was stumbling about; I guess I was tipsier than I thought. I got to the lift and when I walked in, I looked like I had been dragged through a hedge backwards; my hair was a mess, my mascara had run from the sweat and the steam from the shower. I looked fucked, but then again that's what I was. Lucas was parked right at the end of the car park and walking towards him felt like an early morning walk of shame. You know, when you've been a dirty stop out and gone back to a house on a night out and you're walking home in the morning in last night's clothes. Well, that was what this walk felt like. As soon as I sat down in the car Lucas passed me my shaker and said it was my favourite. I laughed and said I was already drunk, but after being involved in a choo-choo train I guess another drink wouldn't go amiss.

When we got back to mine, I went for a real shower and, if I'm honest, I could have stayed in there all night, but couldn't. I'd promised Lucas a few drinks to say thank you for driving me, so I was out the shower, hair and makeup on, then I threw on the first dress I could find and off to the pub we went.

15. Airtight

ELEANOR ROOSEVELT WAS RIGHT AGAIN. Well-behaved women rarely make history. After my eventful evening with Jane and Dennis I decided that I was no longer a well-behaved woman and that I was ready to make a few more changes to my website. I added on a few extra services; after all, I had such fun with the married couple I decided to try and get more bookings like that.

Previously, I'd said that I would consider threesomes but now I said I would happily participate in MMF or MFF and, what the heck, even FFF. I felt that I wanted to explore more options out there and that the choo-choo train was just the beginning of my new adventures. After a lot of debating and hours of contemplating, I decided that there was no harm in exploring things further, so I decided to add group sex to my list of activities to see what came of it. Just as I was going to log off and retire for the evening, a message flashed up. I sat and looked at the unopened message, then looked at the time. I knew that if I opened it then I'd end up being in a long back and forth conversation and I was really tired and needed my sleep, so I closed the laptop and went to bed.

I was lay in bed tossing and turning and I couldn't stop thinking what the message was about, so I had to get up and have a look. I was sat waiting for my laptop to load up and it felt like it was taking ages. Finally, it loaded.

Hey, Princess. How are you? I just saw that you now offer group sex, and I was wondering when you're free?

I froze. I wasn't sure what to say, so I shut my laptop and threw it on the chair beside my bed. I needed the night to think of a response. To be honest, I had cold feet, so needed time to think.

Driving to work gave me plenty of time to contemplate it. For the most part I was excited about it now that the initial shock had worn off. So, I was intrigued to find out what he wanted to do, but the other side of me was worried about the group part. I mean, having a threesome is different to group sex.

To be honest, I didn't even know why I added that; I guess I was feeling overly confident after my last encounter. I definitely didn't think it through enough; I wasn't sure if group sex was even something I wanted to do. I mean yes, I really enjoyed myself with Dennis and Jane, but what if it was with creepy strangers? And what if they knew each other and I was the only stranger? I did not respond until my lunchbreak, which gave me plenty of time to work out if I was up for it. I messaged back to find out the details: *no harm in asking, right?* We messaged back and forth most of the day, and, to get to the nitty-gritty, it was a gentleman who was wanting me to attend a swinger's party with him at the weekend. He normally went with his wife, but she wasn't able to go this weekend as she had other commitments, so his wife had said that he should organise someone like me to be his plus one as she felt that it was better than asking one of their normal group to go with him.

Never in a month of Sundays did I think that I would be going to a swinger's party, let alone being paid to attend. Obviously, this was something I needed to think about. I needed time to research what was involved. My day at work seemed to fly by and I was home before I knew it.

I spent the night on the internet doing research and reading other people's accounts. I concluded that my primary concern, first and foremost, was hygiene. I thought this would be a no-brainer, but according to some accounts this was sometimes a problem. The second thing was to 'wrap up' again, I felt that this should be compulsory, as it's rather disgusting to be dipping your dick into everyone. It was widely stated that most places have condoms placed around the venue, but that you should always bring your own so that you're never caught short. What seemed to be third on the list of advice was to expect nothing to avoid disappointment; this was more to make people aware that it won't be full of porn star women or men with magazine bodies; you're more likely come across people described as your aunt and uncle. That's not to say that they aren't beautiful people, but more to show that you need to keep an open mind as to who will attend. The fourth piece of advice was to leave your phone in the cloakroom. Again, a no- brainer, I would have thought. I certainly wouldn't want a picture or video of me with a dick up my pussy and a fanny in my mouth uploaded to social media. The fifth thing I read was No means NO, this was the most important rule. Swingers' parties are full of sexually permissive people, but, regardless of that, consent is always required. Just because you're at a sex party doesn't mean it's a free-for-all; you must ask permission. The next rule was, leave when you're done. Swinger's parties are for likeminded people to go and have anonymous sex so don't hang about after trying to see if you can be Facebook friends. Keep chat to a minimum; after all, you're there to fuck not make friends. The other advice I found while doing my research was to always try and go as a couple. I thought this would have been compulsory, but it seems that it's up to the venue's discretion as to who can attend and if singles can attend as well. Apparently, a man going by himself is mainly deemed creepy and a woman going by themselves attracts far too much attention, so it's best to go as a couple. I also found tips as to how to approach people while at a party; it seems that it's best to send the most attractive of the couple to talk first, but to always give both parties the same amount of attention. Apparently too many men have an idea that it's like going to pick up women at a bar and it's not like that at all.

I was also shocked by the number of swinger's clubs that were around. All in all, it was a lot to take in, but the more I read, the more excited I got. Some of the stories I read made me feel as if a party had begun in my pants without even doing anything at all.

The gentleman was called Kyle and he was a member of this club with his wife. He said that the event was for four to six hours, but that he was happy for me to leave after four hours if I wanted, and that he would pay me for six. It was in Glasgow this coming weekend. I was nervous, but also excited. In fact, I couldn't sleep; I was full of adrenalin and that was from just thinking about it. Imagine what it would be like when I was actually there! Kyle said that he would message me the details in a couple of days, and we left it at that.

The next few days dragged far more than usual. I didn't take on any other clients this week as I felt I needed to be full of energy for my Glasgow adventure.

Finally, the day was here. I booked a hotel close to the venue so that I was able to walk to and from the event, if needed. I had five hours before it was time to leave so I went for a run to clear my head.

When I was out running, I bumped into a friend and we were standing talking for a while, then she asked me, 'What are you doing tonight? Are you going to Lynn's party?'

I burst out laughing and couldn't stop. She obviously thought I was mad, I mean, I hadn't even said two words, just kept laughing. Eventually, I stopped, and, just as I was trying to come up with a decent excuse, my phone went. *Thank God.* So, I apologised and left. That was a close call; I needed to be more careful around my friends.

I wasn't sure what the best outfit to wear was. All Kyle had said to me was that I was to wear something black and sexy. I mean, what sort of details are those to give someone? Most of my Felicity clothing is black and sexy. I picked out my favourite three dresses and packed them first. Then I just threw in lingerie that I loved wearing. I'd decided that I was going to pack my make-up and get ready in the hotel; I was worried about leaving home all made up when I was skipping a friend's party.

I arrived at my hotel in plenty of time to open a bottle of Prosecco and have a bath. Yes, I know I was drinking, but I needed to be just slightly tipsy, so I didn't stand out as the nervous newbie in the corner. As much as I was trying to relax in the bath, it was somewhat hard considering the evening I was going to have. I was so excited that my long soak turned into a quick wash and out.

I started to unpack the clothes I had brought with me and decided on a revealing lace dress that would show enough for people to be intrigued but would conceal my lingerie. For lingerie I went for a black, floral satin lotita corset with suspender straps and thin, sheer stockings. I loved this corset so much; it's lace-up-the-front style, so it made my boobs look amazing and kept my tummy super flat. Now that I had my outfits laid out ready, I started my routine of getting ready. Just as I'd smothered myself in baby oil, my phone went. It was Kyle. Again. It was lovely that he was messaging me so much, but he kept asking if I was nervous or saying it was OK to be nervous. And to be honest, I wasn't until he kept asking so much. I wanted to reply telling him to shut up about being nervous, but I couldn't do that to a paying customer. I started to do my hair; I thought I would go for a wild look of big, bouncy curls with the top backcombed to give heaps of volume. Just as I was putting my curlers down on the table, I started to giggle. I wasn't sure if it was the three glasses of prosecco or the fact that I'd started to think about what I was about to do.

I went for smoky eyes with extra-long eyelashes and very bright-red lipstick to finish it off. As I began to lace up my corset, Kyle texted asking how long I'd be as we were to meet for a drink to get the awkward bit out of the way. I was doing OK for time; I just needed to slip into my outfit but told him I'd be thirty minutes or so. I didn't want to meet him too early as it would be a bit awkward. Truth be told, I was more looking forward to the party than drinks with him. As I was walking out of the room, I passed a mirror in the hall and thought I looked a little prostitute-like. I think it was the make-up and minimal clothing.

I had booked a taxi to take me to Kyle's hotel. I didn't fancy walking down the street alone dressed up like this. I texted Kyle to say I was on my way, and he messaged straight back saying he hadn't been this excited in about ten years. When the taxi pulled up at the hotel Kyle was waiting outside and, wow, he was so handsome and very fit; he clearly visited the gym a lot. I was in for a treat tonight. He came over and opened my door and, of course, paid the fare. Not only handsome, but a gentleman as well.

Kyle took my hand, his eyes locked into mine, 'Hi Felicity, I'm looking forward to this so much, thanks for coming.'

Instantly I blushed, 'It's lovely to meet you.'

Kyle smiled, 'Shall we go get a drink?'

'Definitely.'

The first exchange of words was always the hardest. Kyle led me into the bar and ordered drinks; it was certainly needed!

After the first one Kyle seemed less nervous and told me how he and his wife met at one of these parties many years ago. After about thirty minutes of listening to him tell me about his encounters I was not only extremely horny, but also petrified. I mean, this was going so far out of my comfort zone. But, then again, having a threesome with a married couple was out of my comfort zone so I decided I was going to take the night in my stride and be open minded. It was time for us to head off to the party. I felt a little strange having so much money on me at one of these events, but Kyle said there were lockers for me to leave my things. Walking round to the venue, I wasn't as nervous. In fact, I was relaxed and really looking forward to it.

We arrived at an exceptionally large house and walked up the steps to the front door. Kyle took my hand, which was probably a good thing as I started to get overwhelmed by fear. I shook it off and kept going. As soon we rang the bell, the door opened. We were greeted by a woman in a red dress. She introduced herself as the hostess for the evening and walked us through a marble hall. I hate marble floors; heels are so loud on them, and it always makes me try to tip-toe, which, in heels, is impossible and looks dreadful. We were guided into a room on the right and Kyle sat down on the sofa, then patted the seat for me to join him. Everyone knew Kyle so I felt a bit like a spare prick as I wasn't getting spoken to, just stared at. There were three other couples in the room with us and I'd say that most of them were physically attractive, one guy was far too old for me to be attracted to him. Just as Kyle said he would take my coat; a lady came over with a tray of canapés and champagne; it was all very surreal. I mean, for a moment, it felt as if Kyle had taken me to a fancy restaurant for dinner. Just as I got my glass of champagne, I was handed a clipboard. When I looked down, I saw that it had a consent form attached to the front. 'Please fill this out as you are a new guest.'

I froze. I wasn't sure what to do. Do I fill it out as Felicity, or do I fill it out as me? After a few moments I decided to go for Felicity. I mean, I didn't know who Kyle was, so thought it best to keep my true identity concealed, but as the emergency contact, I put Lucas. I didn't know of anyone else to put and I just secretly hoped they didn't have to call him! I hadn't told Lucas I was doing this. The form was unsettling for me as they needed personal information, but it was also reassuring that they had things like this in place. I was more nervous now, I was fucking petrified in fact, but in a safe way I think. I didn't feel unsafe or that I was going to come to any harm, it was just such a new experience, and I hadn't even started yet.

The form had things similar to what I had read doing my research:

If you are told NO, the answer is NO.
If you are told NO, then do not try again.
Always wear a condom.
No drugs.
Shower between sessions.

If a door is closed, don't open it.
No sex for money.
No water sports or hard sports.
Safe word is Penguin.

I signed it and handed it back, then took a gulp of my champagne and a deep breath. Kyle passed me another drink, 'Take this and I will give you a tour.'

'Thank you, I'm excited to see round'. I didn't know what else to say.

The best way to describe the venue was that it was like a rich person's house; it was large and tastefully decorated. There was a lot of marble and hardwood flooring and fine art on the walls. The chairs and sofas were incredibly old fashioned but were well cared for. After leaving the first lounge area we went through double doors to a kind of bar area with three large sofas in it. I'm guessing this was more of a meeting room as there were four doors to this room. We opened the second door, and I gave a sigh of relief; it was a corridor with bathrooms and showering areas. I knew that if it all got too much for me, I could come down here and get my shit together. The third door was at the other side of the room, and it was double doors. When we got closer to them Kyle whispered into my ear, 'This is the area we would be in.'

I nodded and smiled, he opened both doors wide and they creaked open. This door was down to a corridor to which there were four more doors, this was where the majority of the party was held. Each room had a sign on the doors saying if it was for two, three or four people. I felt far more relaxed now that I knew everything was laid out like this. I mean, if I was freaking out and I couldn't do it then I could just stay in the room for two or the room for three and be in my comfort zone. When Kyle started walking towards the door at the end, he turned to me and said, 'This is the room for group sex; sometimes there can be twelve to eighteen people in here at once.'

My face obviously dropped because Kyle said quickly, 'Don't worry, I do not expect you to participate in that.'

I was so relieved; I gave him a nervous grin back. 'Oh Good, I think that would be too much.'

He opened the door just so I could see where the group sessions took place, and it was like a massive living room with different sofas and chairs. In the corner of the room there was what I can only describe as a dentist chair then across from that a swing in the other corner, it was held in place by large ropes coming down from the ceiling. I was so relieved that he did not expect me to go in there. I was not up for that. After the tour was finished, we went back to the first lounge area.

'Should we go and pack our things in lockers, then have a bottle of wine in the room for two?'

I liked this idea. 'Yes, that sounds like a good plan indeed.'

I went to the changing rooms and slid out of my dress. My heart was racing this actually happening. I was so relieved that we were going to a private room together first. I got to the room before Kyle, so I had time to make myself comfortable. It was nicely laid out and everything was spotless so that made me feel a bit better. There was even a telly in the corner that had porn on, I'm guessing that was to get everyone going. When the door went, I freaked out for a moment as I was worried it wasn't Kyle, but, sure enough, it was. Just as he closed the door he turned round and nearly dropped the wine. He looked shocked, then, after an exceedingly long pause, said, 'You look incredible, I'm completely blown away.'

Kyle came over to me and pulled me towards him. I could feel his fingers run up my back and his penis push on my side; it was in that moment that my fears melted away. I wasn't thinking about being at a swinger's party anymore, I was thinking about what his dick would feel like inside me. Kyle moved away to pour me a glass of wine, 'Felicity, I think we should just relax for a bit. Is it OK if I change what is on the telly? I'm missing my favourite show.'

'Yes, of course, you're the boss I'm happy to do whatever you wish.' I was dying to find out what this show was that was so important, so we both lay on the bed and Kyle changed channel. It was *Grand Designs*! Yes, that's right, *Grand Designs*. Saying that, it was a good icebreaker; it certainly made me giggle anyway. By the first break it was starting to get noisy outside; I could hear hellos and doors banging. Thankfully, no sex noises yet, but I was sure they would soon start.

I turned to Kyle, 'Should we be going through, it's getting noisy?'

Kyle giggled, 'We are better waiting till people have started so that they don't all want to bother the newbie.'

Gosh, I hadn't even thought of that. By the second break on the telly, I was getting bored and starting to feel tired; I wasn't really in the mood for this anymore. I wasn't really watching the telly and I wasn't keen on drinking anymore; I didn't want to be too drunk and do something I later regretted, so I didn't fill my glass up again. When the telly got to the third break, Kyle jumped up off the bed then downed his wine. 'Let's go, it's show time.'

It was all a bit sudden, but I was glad to be getting out of the room before I fell asleep. Kyle was in just a tight pair of boxer shorts, and I was in my black lace corset and seamed stockings with my matching briefs on. Yes, I got to wear the pants that coordinated my set; for the first time, may I add.

Kyle got to the door, then stopped and turned around. He took a firm grip of my hand, pulled me in towards him. 'Follow me, but please say if you aren't comfortable. I want you to have fun.'

It was nice that he was thinking of my feelings too. Kyle started to open the door and, I got an instant burst of anxiety; the kind that gives you clammy hands and a sweaty back. We stepped into the corridor and all I could hear was lots of people having sex. The first couple I saw were on a sofa naked, just kissing and touching each other. Then I turned towards the bar area and there was a man sat on a single chair with a lady bouncing so hard on his cock I was surprised the legs of the chair were holding it together. Suddenly the only thing that was now wet was my pants; I was very aroused and ready to join in. Kyle walked me over to the bar area and got me a glass of wine. We went over to the large sofa and sat down. I had a few sips, then went to put my glass down. I turned back to Kyle, and he had a woman sat next to him, fondling his leg. I wasn't sure what to do or where to look! I gazed round the room and when my eyes returned to Kyle, they were now snogging each other and the woman had just started to wrap her hand round his penis. I didn't know what to do, so I gulped down the rest of my glass in two larger mouthfuls. Just as I leaned over to put my glass back down, I felt a small hand grab my breast, I knew it wasn't Kyle's, it was far too small, so I turned round to find it was the women's hand. I was shocked, but I guess I was at a swinger's party so it's not like I wasn't prepared for this. The lady then got up and squeezed in between us. I was just going to go with the flow; it was fun after all. The lady started to suck Kyle's cock but was also rubbing my breasts. Then the lady started to run her hand down my side and took hold of my hip. I was getting turned on by this. I also felt like I had finally met people with an even larger sexual appetite than mine. It was not long before her hand had slid down onto my thigh, I could feel her squeeze her fingertips on the inside of my leg, then she gently pulled her hand so that I opened my legs. As I opened my legs, she pulled my pants to the side and started to slowly rub her fingers over my clit; it felt really good, there is a massive difference to a woman doing it to most men. I mean a woman at least knows what it feels like, so I am assuming that's why they are far better at it than most men. Just as I felt myself melt back onto the sofa a gentleman started walking over towards me. I wasn't sure what was going to happen next, but I was intrigued to find out.

I was sat on the sofa with the lady tickling my clit as she has Kyle's penis in her mouth, then the other man stood in front of me. He pulled out a condom out and slid it on. As he pulled it over his penis he leant forward towards my mouth; it was small and thin so I was glad that it was in my mouth rather than anywhere else as it wouldn't be enough to satisfy me. I was on my fifth suck, and he pulled away and I saw all the cum gathering in the end of the condom. *Well, that's over with*, I thought, trying not to laugh. The lady had stopped playing with me and was in full swing with Kyle on the sofa, so I excused myself to go to the bathroom. As the door shut behind me, I let out a huge sigh of relief. I have never had two cocks so close to me before; I didn't think I was up for a spit roast situation with two guys. I had a few minutes to myself, then decided I was ready to go back through. I didn't want to disappoint Kyle, after all.

When I went back in, Kyle was on the sofa with a man's penis in his mouth (I certainly wasn't expecting that), the lady was straddled over him bouncing on his penis and there was a guy who was knelt on the ground trying to get his cock up the lady's bum. It was not my scene; three men and one woman was not for me and never will be my thing. I made my way to the bar so I could get a drink to try and relax, but it was going to take more than wine.

Just as I was considering doing a runner, I got a tap on my shoulder and a soft voice whispered in my ear, 'Can we go to a room by ourselves, please.'

I wasn't really up for that until I turned round. He was stunning, more my age, and very well kept. I didn't think twice about it. I was looking forward to a bit of normal pleasure. The penis to pussy ratio was all wrong for my liking, he took my hand and started walking towards a new room, one I hadn't been in before there was a double bed, a chair and table; the table was covered in condoms, lube, wet wipes. It was all rather professional. We went in and closed the door behind us, and he asked if it was OK for people to watch. I wasn't sure what he meant, but I said yes anyway. Just then he flicked a switch and one of the walls went like glass and you could see everyone at it in the room next door. It was a bit strange, but it wasn't something that bothered me. He leant over towards me and ran his tongue from my earlobe to my breasts. I pulled him towards me and started to slide his boxers down and there it was, a tiny penis. I knew someone that good-looking couldn't have it all.

To say I was disappointed would be an understatement; of all the men in the place I had to be picked by the most inadequate. I got his boxers off and was praying that it would be a grower. I had my doubts but managed to keep my disappointment hidden. I lay back on the bed and he slowly started to run his hands up and down my legs. When he got to my toes he stopped. I knew what was coming next, so I took a deep breath and closed my eyes. Sure enough, I felt his tongue tickle my little toe. I'm not sure what it is about men with small penises having a foot fetish, but I knew of a few now and it seemed to be a pattern. I was glad that I spent all that time with my client Connor, otherwise I wouldn't have been able to let him touch my feet at all. I was somewhat used to it now; I just find it a bit creepy that so many men like to suck my toes.

Fortunately for me, it didn't go on for very long. I picked up a condom and flicked it down the bed to land beside him. He picked it up and started to put it on straight away. Just as I thought it couldn't get worse it did; he wasn't a grower; it actually hadn't grown at all. It was still ridiculously small. I went along with it purely because he was so gorgeous and some of me thought that I'd enjoy it because I fancied him, but that was not the case. It was like he was a virgin; he didn't have a clue what was going on, it was more like the motion of the ocean – just back and forth. I was a bit taken back by how little experience he had. I mean, we were at a swinger's party; I thought that everyone who came to these events would be pros at it, but clearly, I was wrong. I was shocked; surely someone couldn't think this was enjoyable? Just as I thought this, he let out a very high-pitched yelp and that was it; he had ejaculated. Game over!

We lay on the bed for a bit, then, just as I started to get up, I noticed a few more people were starting to gather in the room on the other side of the glass. We both sat up and watched the people through the glass wall. I asked what room it was, and he told me that it was the group room. I remembered then that Kyle had said there can be up to eighteen people in there at once. The thing that had caught my attention was the woman in the swing; she appeared to be watching everyone as she played with herself as she swung back and forth. Then a very muscular man walked in the room. We watched as he stood and scanned the room, obviously looking for the woman or man of his choice. He saw the lady on the swing and walked over to her. He took both her hands and lifted her to her feet. They stood face to face for a moment, then he moved his right arm round her side and whisked her upside down, so her legs were up in the air and his head was between her legs. It was a seamless move and she seemed to instantly wrap her mouth around his cock. The next thing that got my attention was two women on a bed; they were knelt on the mattress facing each other kissing, then the next minute one of the women pinned the other down and flipped her over so they were doing 69. My new friend and I looked at each other and laughed. It was a live sex show.

So far, I had seen a lot of women on women and only Kyle with a cock in his mouth, so I was interested to see how things were going to unfold. The room seemed to get fuller. Three guys were now standing wanking, watching the two ladies. Just then in walks a man, I'd say in his late 40's with pale skin, not well kept in the slightest, a rather large overhang but that wasn't the worst part, he was in leather shorts that had braces holding them up, I couldn't believe it. Then another man walked in. His shorts had a massive bulge to them, a bulge far too big to be a penis. Well, I have never seen anything like it in my life. He walked over to the three wanking men and opened a flap on his shorts. He was wearing crotchless shorts with a Velcro leather patch so he could hide his manhood as needed. He had a penis the size of a horse that just seemed to fall out from being so tightly squeezed in there. His huge dick instantly became hard, and he then walked up to the bed to where the ladies were doing 69. He headed to the back of the lady who was on top; he just seemed to go over and force his penis inside her, all while she was still doing 69 with the lady below her. She didn't even lift her head to see who it was that was sliding inside her. After the third thrust she seemed to be unable to hold herself together, she lifted her head up for a moment, almost like she needed breather. Then one of the other guys stormed over and put his cock in her mouth. I felt a bit sorry for the lady on the bottom; after all, she was essentially just a bench that the lady above was being fucked on. I could see her try to wriggle out from underneath the other lady, but it seemed like she was slightly stuck.

I think that would have completely freaked me out; definitely a nightmare position to be in and I was grateful it was not me. The two guys that had just been standing watching the whole time went to help. They walked over, one at either side of the guy getting a blow job and lifted the lady up by resting one hand under her shoulder and the other at her hip, all while she still had a dick in her mouth and one up her pussy. It was like a strange, synchronised swimming move; the lady underneath managed to wriggle out, but she didn't get too far away. Just as she got to her feet she turned and bent over the bed and one of the guys walked over, slid a condom on and was inside her before I was able to blink. The other guy just seemed to be standing in the room watching everyone while still playing with himself.

This was the first time I have watched other people have sex and, to be honest, I didn't think I would be into it. I wouldn't say I was getting off on watching them, but I did seem to keep watching. I think it was more the fact that I was watching from through the glass; I don't think I would have enjoyed actually being in there with them watching. I certainly wasn't thinking of going in there now or ever. All the guys had to have been on Viagra as when they ejaculated, they seemed to just go over to the corner, take off their condom, use a wet wipe and put another one on. I guess they didn't want to miss out on any fun that they could be having so they needed it to be able to stay hard.

After watching the eight people swap partners for a while, I was getting a little bored so decided to head through to the bar area to get another drink.

My new friend said he'd rather stay in the room but told me to leave the door open when I left so that people were aware that they were able to go in. Just as I got to the main area, I got anxious again; it was far busier than before. All the rooms had their doors closed, so I was assuming they were all full. I glanced round the room; every chair was full, and people were gathered at the bar area. The chair that looked like it was going to break before was managing to last with another couple on it. At the back of the room, I saw a younger couple on the sofa that seemed to just be chatting, then I saw Kyle. He hadn't moved far, he was sat with another woman on top of him, but no cock in his mouth this time. I walked over to get another glass of wine. I tried not to draw attention to myself as it was nearly time to head home; I had decided that this wasn't my sort of thing. Don't get me wrong, I love sex and orgasms, but the novelty of being here had worn off.

Just as I wrapped my fingers round the stem of the glass, I could feel someone move awfully close behind me. I froze, then got a shiver all the way down my back. I was reluctant to turn around. Just as I was trying to figure out what to do or say, I heard them whisper Felicity in my ear. Only Kyle knew my name. When I saw it was Kyle, I put my arms round him.

Kyle whispered, 'I can't believe that you are still here, I thought you left ages ago.'

I looked up at the clock. It was five hours in, and I hadn't even noticed. 'Felicity, do you want to go to a private room to play?'

After seeing him have another man's penis in his mouth I wasn't as keen as I was before to entertain him, so I said, 'I'm so sorry but it's late and I was just going to have this drink and head off home, if it's OK with you?' I was so overwhelmed with how the night had gone that I needed to unwind.

'Of course. That's not a problem, Felicity. I would love for you to come to another party with me next month?'

I smiled, 'I would love to, just message me.' That was clearly a lie, I was going to go home and take the group part off my website as soon as possible. Kyle walked me through to the door of the changing room as there were far more guests there now and I think he knew that I was feeling uncomfortable. I thought I was ready for this after my Jane and Dennis night, but, after tonight, I think I rushed into things a bit. It's one thing having a threesome. Attending a swinger's party is a whole different thing. I'm not ruling it out forever, but I feel I need to have a few more threesomes before I'd feel comfortable being at another party like this. Kyle went to give me a goodbye kiss, so I quickly moved my head and kissed his cheek instead.

'Thank you for coming Felicity, I'm so glad to have met you and I hope to see you soon?'

'I'm glad too Kyle, I hope you enjoy the rest of your evening.'

As I walked into the changing room, I felt instantly relieved that it was the end of the evening, I stood over the sink staring at myself in the mirror. I wasn't happy, but I wasn't exactly sad either. I didn't really know what I was. All I knew was that I was glad that I went, but I was also glad that it was time to go home. I called a taxi to get me while I was still in the changing rooms. I did not want to be hanging about outside waiting all alone, so I sat for a few moments. When it was time to go, I gathered my things and made my way for the exit. The taxi ride back to my hotel was slow, it wasn't far away but I was very deep in thought, and it seemed to take forever especially since all I wanted to do was shower.

Felicity Forbes

Bang. The door to my room was closed. I stood with my back pressed hard against the door, took a few deep breaths. Finally, I was alone. I stripped off my clothes while walking across the room. I needed to get clean. On the way to the bathroom, I grabbed a bottle of red wine out of my bag. I'd brought it down as an emergency drown your sorrows drink if I needed it, not that I was feeling like a total disaster this evening, but I was feeling somewhat overwhelmed and knew I'd be in the shower a while.

Each time I washed myself I seemed to feel cleaner, but I still wasn't happy, nor smiling, but perhaps that's to be expected. After the fourth wash I slid down the tiled wall and sat in the bottom of the shower with my back against the tiles and the water running down over my breasts. I sat for the time it took to drink half a bottle of wine. I think I could have stayed in there all night, but by now the bathroom looked like a steam room and it was late. I got out, put my robe on and went through to the bedroom. I didn't feel like watching telly, nor did I feel like going to sleep so I sat on my bed and drank more wine before finally drifting off.

In my younger years I would never of I woke with my head thumbing like it did now, I spent the morning drifting in and out of disturbed dreams. It was late afternoon before I decided to get up and get organised. The drive home this time felt like my drive to my day job; boring and I just wanted it over with. I guess I needed to have a big think about why I got into this. I did it for excitement and sex, not to be driving home feeling the way I do now. Perhaps I needed another break from Felicity. Did I still want to lead my double life or was it time to hang up the stockings?

www.ingramcontent.com/pod-product-compliance
Lightning Source LLC
Chambersburg PA
CBHW021051080526
44587CB00010B/206